Performing Englishness

New
Ethnographies

Series editor
Alexander Thomas T. Smith

Already published

The British in rural France:
Lifestyle migration and the ongoing quest for a better way of life Michaela Benson

Ageing selves and everyday life in the North of England:
Years in the making Catherine Degnen

Chagos islanders in Mauritius and the UK:
Forced displacement and onward migration Laura Jeffery

Integration, locality and everyday life:
After asylum Mark Maguire and Fiona Murphy

An ethnography of English football fans:
Cans, cops and carnivals Geoff Pearson

Literature and agency in English fiction reading:
A study of the Henry Williamson Society... Adam Reed

International seafarers and the possibilities for transnationalism in
the twenty-first century Helen Sampson

Devolution and the Scottish Conservatives:
Banal activism, electioneering and the politics of irrelevance Alexander Smith

Performing Englishness

Identity and politics in a contemporary folk resurgence

Trish Winter and Simon Keegan-Phipps

Manchester University Press

Published by Manchester University Press
Altrincham Street, Manchester M1 7JA, UK
www.manchesteruniversitypress.co.uk

British Library Cataloguing-in-Publication Data is available

Library of Congress Cataloging-in-Publication Data is available

ISBN 978 0 7190 9730 0 *paperback*

First published by Manchester University Press in hardback 2013

This paperback edition first published 2015

The publisher has no responsibility for the persistence or accuracy of URLs for any external or third-party internet websites referred to in this book, and does not guarantee that any content on such websites is, or will remain, accurate or appropriate.

Printed by Lightning Source

Contents

List of figures

Preface – using this book

As for all authors compiling an ethnography of such a populous and complex cultural field, connecting the many intersections of factual detail and ideas within this book has posed a significant challenge for us. Signposting backwards and forwards through the book to related points of discussion is essential, but this can at times be detrimental to the readability of the text. For this reason, we have opted to apply a numerical system for the identification of sections and subsections within chapters. Thus, a reference to a specific section can be quickly signalled with a number (e.g. 'see 3.7.3'). This, we hope, is the least obtrusive way of locating related material elsewhere in the book.

Whilst some of the primary research presented in this book involves analysis of visual images, we have taken the difficult decision not to include plates here. This is for several reasons – some related to the practical parameters of publication, and others to the difficulties experienced in obtaining permissions from record companies and some other copyright holders approached. Where images are referred to in this book, we provide descriptions in prose, but we have also supplied information (e.g. web links) to ensure that the images in question can be quickly and easily located online. We encourage the reader to examine such images in this way; they will undoubtedly find online versions of the pictures that are of higher resolution and colour quality than would have been possible through reproduction here. To assist in this process, the web links we have included are in form of mini-URLs.

Acknowledgements

This project would not have been completed without the support of a number of people and institutions. We would first like to thank all of those folk artists and activists who took part in our research, particularly those who generously gave their time to participate in interviews. Many thanks to those artists who gave us permission to reproduce song lyrics in this book: Maggie Holland, for her lyrics taken from the song 'A Place Called England'; Chris Wood, for his lyrics taken from the song 'On English Ground'; and Steve Knightley of Show of Hands, for lyrics taken from the song 'Roots'. We are grateful to the artist Faye Claridge for allowing us to reproduce her work on the book's cover. Particular mention should be given to Steve Heap for his interest in and support of our research, and for helping us to gain access to many individuals and events. We thank the staff at Manchester University Press for their help and patience. We have presented our research findings in numerous seminars and conferences over the last five years, and we are grateful to everyone there who commented and gave feedback on our ideas. In particular we would like to thank our colleagues in Film, Media and Cultural Studies at the University of Sunderland, and the Department of Music, University of Sheffield, who have been a constant source of support and inspiration. Special thanks go to those colleagues who read and commented on drafts of this book, Professors John Storey and Rachel Woodward. We would like to acknowledge the support of the Arts and Humanities Research Council for funding the research on which this book is based, a project entitled 'Performing Englishness in New English Folk Music and Dance' (Ref. AH/E009867/1). Many thanks also to the Centre for Research in Media and Cultural Studies, University of Sunderland, for research leave support towards our writing. Some of the material in this book has been developed through publication elsewhere. Some of Chapter 2 was originally published in *The Oxford Handbook of Music Revivals*, edited by Caroline Bithell and Juniper Hill, and is reproduced by permission of Oxford University Press. Some of the ideas for Chapter 3 were developed in an article for *Radical Musicology* (Keegan-Phipps, 2009). Finally, we would like to thank our respective families and friends for their love and support during the time we have spent researching and writing this book. Trish would like to thank Bob, Marjorie and Hazel Winter, and Peter Robertson (who also read and

Acknowledgements

commented on drafts from the perspective of the general reader). Her thanks also go to Frank Lee, for teaching her so many excellent English tunes. Simon would like to thank Ann Keegan, Fred Phipps and Rachel Brennan for their continued encouragement with this – and every other – endeavour. Matthew Keegan-Phipps and Miriam Ayling each deserve special thanks for taking the unenviable role of informant-/discussant-on-call. Our thanks also go to Matthew for last-minute assistance in the creation of figures. Simon would finally like to thank his many friends within the English folk scene who have guided him through the field since he first jumped the gate as a teenager: in particular, Simon Bannister, and the Iron Men and Severn Gilders.

Series editor's foreword

At its best, ethnography has provided a valuable tool for apprehending a world in flux. A couple of years after the Second World War, Max Gluckman founded the Department of Social Anthropology at the University of Manchester. In the years that followed, he and his colleagues built a programme of ethnographic research that drew eclectically on the work of leading anthropologists, economists and sociologists to explore issues of conflict, reconciliation and social justice 'at home' and abroad. Often placing emphasis on detailed analysis of case studies drawn from small-scale societies and organisations, the famous 'Manchester School' in social anthropology built an enviable reputation for methodological innovation in its attempts to explore the pressing political questions of the second half of the twentieth century. Looking back, that era is often thought to constitute a 'gold standard' for how ethnographers might grapple with new challenges and issues in the contemporary world.

The *New Ethnographies* series aims to build on that ethnographic legacy at Manchester. It will publish the best new ethnographic monographs that promote interdisciplinary debate and methodological innovation in the qualitative social sciences. This includes the growing number of books that seek to apprehend the 'new' ethnographic objects of a seemingly brave new world, some recent examples of which have included auditing, democracy and elections, documents, financial markets, human rights, assisted reproductive technologies and political activism. Analysing such objects has often demanded new skills and techniques from the ethnographer. As a result, this series will give voice to those using ethnographic methods across disciplines to innovate, such as through the application of multi-sited fieldwork and the extended comparative case study method. Such innovations have often challenged more traditional ethnographic approaches. *New Ethnographies* therefore seeks to provide a platform for emerging scholars and their more established counterparts engaging with ethnographic methods in new and imaginative ways.

Alexander Thomas T. Smith

1

Introduction

When Lord Coe, chair of the Organising Committee for the London 2012 Olympic Games, quipped that the opening ceremony would match the spectacular opening of the Beijing Olympics by featuring five thousand morris dancers, his remark was meant as a joke. For this comment to be interpreted as amusing relies, of course, on the maligned status of England's most iconic folk dance style as something of a national joke: to poke fun at the English folk arts has indeed long been a national pastime within British culture and media. Lord Coe's innocently disparaging remark provoked some debate about the cultural status of English folk dancing, which had actually been enjoying an increase in popularity in many quarters. The remark acted, for example, as the catalyst for a large-scale publicly funded event in London entitled '5000 Morris Dancers', an event intended to showcase the new popularity of morris dancing and to show, in the words of the artist David Owen, that morris dancing 'can look cool' (*Arts Council England*, 2010). Evidence of a shift in profile and popularity can be seen not just in relation to folk dancing but to the folk arts in general, particularly music. Folk festivals in England have become increasingly popular, and the demography of folk music audiences has been getting younger – folk is enjoying considerable and growing popularity with people in their teens, twenties and thirties. Folk music has moved further beyond the boundaries of the folk scene and towards popular cultural contexts like Mercury Music Award nominations, mainstream music festivals and events. The media profile of folk has experienced a shift, exemplified by folk's greater media visibility within national television programming. Whilst it is possible to point towards the consolidation of an increasingly professionalised 'folk industry' (which will be examined in Chapter 2), this surge of interest is not limited to the mediated or professional spheres but has reverberated across the spectrum of English folk's culture of participation. As musician Jon Boden points out, 'there's folk music as a professionalised industry, and there's folk music as … a social activity. And I think they probably are … both enjoying growth at the moment' (Jon Boden, interview, 2008). Within this new wave of interest in the folk arts an increasing number of folk acts and participants are foregrounding their Englishness, explicitly and often emphatically declaring themselves to be exploring *English* folk traditions. We argue that the early twenty-first century can be seen as a period of resurgence in the English folk arts, and it is this resurgence that we set out to examine in this book.

This is not to suggest that the English folk arts disappeared in the years that followed the previous period of folk revival in the 1950s to the 1970s. Musicians from that period, such as Martin Carthy, Richard Thompson and John Kirkpatrick, had continued to perform and produce albums; folk festivals were still taking place; traditional dance sides and folk clubs were still in existence, albeit with an ageing demographic in some quarters (see MacKinnon, 1993; Brocken, 2003). A number of significant shifts have, however, taken place since the early 2000s. The beginnings of this recent resurgence are difficult to date precisely, although perhaps the release of Eliza Carthy's album *Anglicana* (2002) may be seen as a marker of the explicit engagement of a new generation of folk artists with ideas about Englishness: Carthy's description of her album as 'an expression of Englishness as I feel it' featured in many reviews.[1] During the period of research for this book (2007–9) there was a widespread perception within the folk scene of this resurgence in English folk. When asked whether they agreed with this premise, almost all of our research participants did so emphatically, albeit with different levels of agreement about the nature and meaning of that resurgence. We should note here that this wave of interest in English-identified folk is entwined with a wider blossoming of interest in folk more generally, and we will be examining this further in this introduction, along with questions of definition (see 1.2).

The folk resurgence has taken place in a cultural moment in which there has been an intensified public and political debate around Englishness and Britishness and a wave of popular expressions of Englishness, as well as the coming to prominence of nationalist groups such as the English Defence League. There is evidence from polls and surveys to suggest that there has been, amongst some English people, a growing sense of identification with Englishness over and above, or in combination with, Britishness (Kenny and Lodge, 2009: 225). This wave is usually dated as having begun in the 1990s. Aughey, for example, notes that according to many accounts 'something happened to English national identity' in 1996, citing the popular flying of the flag of St George that accompanied the Euro96 Football Championship (Aughey, 2007: 1). A popular concern with Englishness has often been manifest in attempts to discover, recover or celebrate England or Englishness, as in the publication of numerous books whose authors embark on journeys into, for example, English identity, the English landscape, English history, English culture and traditions or English food (see, for example, Wood, 1999; Lewis, 2005; Slater, 2007; Titchmarsh, 2007; Irwin, 2005; Paxman; 1998, Bragg, 2006). Another example of this developing fascination was the government-commissioned website 'Icons: a portrait of England', which was launched by the Culture Minister in January 2006. The site, which closed in 2011, described itself as 'a rich resource of material about our lives and cultural heritage comprised of the top 100 icons that best represent England, as voted for by you' (Icons: a portrait of England, 2009).[2] We will be examining the folk resurgence in the light of this social and political context.

1.1 Englishness, folk and scholarship

In recent years Englishness has been a growing scholarly, as well as political and cultural, concern. A body of academic work has been built since the 1980s on the notion that Englishness, once taken for granted as the dominant hegemonic component of Britishness, needs to be investigated, questioned, problematised and historicised (see, for example: Hobsbawm and Ranger, 1983; Dodd and Colls, 1987; Morley and Robins, 2001; Colls, 2002; Rapport, 2002; Kumar, 2003; Perryman, 2008). A detailed consideration of the cultures of English folk music and dance is, however, largely absent from academic examinations of contemporary debates about Englishness.

The relationship between music, place and identity has been addressed in a number of disciplinary fields including ethnomusicology, popular music studies and cultural geography (Stokes, 1994; Connell and Gibson, 2003; Whiteley *et al.*, 2004; Biddle and Knights, 2007, and the 2000 issue of *Popular Music*, devoted to the subject of place). These studies offer many insights in their examination of the ways that place and national identity are constructed or imagined through music, and the politics of those constructions. None of these bodies of work, however, address themselves to cultures of English folk, tending to follow the conventional ethnomusicological focus on non-Western cultures or to focus on popular rather than folk music. British folk music has generally been the domain of historical and sociological research (see, for example, Harker, 1985; Boyes, 1993; MacKinnon, 1993; Brocken, 2003; Sweers, 2005). Historiography predominates, and has tended to centre on the two British periods of folk revival of the twentieth century, generally stopping short of contemporary issues since the turn of the twenty-first century. With the exception of Boyes' landmark study of the first folk revival and Sweers' study of the electric folk of the second revival, this research has commonly spoken in terms of British – rather than specifically English – folk. It has also tended to comment mainly on the poetic content, collection or significance of folk song, without giving much attention to instrumental music. While ethnomusicologists have conventionally concentrated on non-Western musical cultures, there has been a movement in this discipline towards the interrogation of British musical cultures, as demonstrated in the 2004 special issue of *The World of Music* on 'Contemporary British Music Traditions' (see, for example, Stock, 2004). Despite such recognition of the discipline's neglect of contemporary British folk music traditions, however, work in this area remains piecemeal and there is very little attention to contemporary artistic and cultural practices defining themselves, or being framed by others, as 'English folk'.[3] There is some evidence that this is beginning to change as doctoral research undertaken in the 2000s moves towards publication (see Keegan-Phipps, 2008; Hield, 2010; Burns, 2012. See also, for detailed local ethnographies: Keegan-Phipps, 2003; Russell, 2004; Stock, 2004).

The contemporary English folk arts are, however, a significant site for the construction of English identities. In an examination of the performance of national identity (a concept which will be discussed in 1.4), Edensor (2002) distinguishes four key cultural fields within which national identity is performed.

He makes only brief references to the place of folk arts in the performance of national identity, but we can see that the English folk arts occupy all four of these fields. Firstly there are formal rituals and national ceremonies, 'the grand, often stately occasions when the nation and its symbolic attributes are elevated in public display' (2002: 72). English traditional music or dance has not historically been central to the grand public ceremony or pageantry of the nation, which has been orientated around Britishness. There are signs, however, that in the wake of a renewed public and political interest in Englishness it may begin to be incorporated into some of the nation's grand occasions. For example, we have already spoken of the debate concerning the idea of the inclusion of morris dancing in the opening ceremony for the 2012 London Olympic Games, a grand spectacle that conventionally offers a performance celebrating the national identity of the host nation. This idea had previously been seriously debated in 2005 when the Liberal Democrat peer Lord Redesdale had called for its inclusion in the ceremony, sparking some media discussion of the issue (Parkinson, 2005). Morris dancing did in fact make a brief appearance in the closing ceremony of the 2012 Games, albeit as a figure of fun within a celebration of British humour, rather than as representing traditional culture *per se*.[4] However, in the opening ceremony, another brand of English folk dance – maypole dancing – appeared as a serious performance of tradition as part of the bucolic opening scenes depicting a historical rural England. We might also suggest an expansion of Edensor's 'elevated' category by pointing to the number of the higher-profile English folk musicians who have in the early years of the twenty-first century received honorary doctorates and degrees, conferrals of institutional approval made with ceremonial trappings.[5] In addition, the folk artists Martin Carthy and Norma Waterson are both recipients of the MBE.

Edensor's second category of national identity performance is 'popular rituals' (2002: 78). His examples are taken from the worlds of sport and carnival, but he could well have cited those many folk arts and customs that take the form of popular rituals. An extensive documentation of these can be seen in Doc Rowe's archive (Doc Rowe Archive and Collection, 2010), and Irwin (2005) gives an account of a journey through England in search of them. Similar journeying narratives are common in relation to the resurgence, and will be discussed in 6.3 and 6.4.

Thirdly, there are stagings of the nation that are made by the tourist industry. Compared, for example, with the Scottish and Irish tourist industries, which make traditional music and dance an important part of their commodification of national identity, the English folk arts have not thus far featured so centrally in the discourses of English tourism. They are, however, present. The website of the English Tourist Board, for example, features a page on 'traditional entertainment' with references to morris dancing, framed as one of England's 'weird, wonderful and downright freaky traditions' along with traditions such as seaside Punch and Judy shows or the Whittlesea village straw bear tradition. The traditional Abbots Bromley Horn Dance finds itself at number ten in a list of '10 unusual events' including the World Toe Wrestling Championship, Gloucestershire cheese rolling and the 'famous flaming tar barrels' of the Ottery St Mary Carnival (Enjoy England, 2010).

The final category of performance concerns the performances of everyday life, the everyday practices through which people live and embody their identities. Here we would point towards the close integration of practice of the folk arts with the fabric of everyday life. This is music and dance making and performing that takes place in and around pubs, public spaces and homes, for example. For some folk participants there is often little or no distinction made between their practice of music or dance and their everyday life. In other cases, the naturalisation of such practices within everyday activity is actively sought and celebrated. Extending across all of these cultural fields, and enjoying increased interest and exposure, the English folk arts are a highly, and increasingly, significant site for the making and remaking of Englishness within contemporary culture. An understanding of contemporary English folk music and dance has much to offer to the investigation of contemporary constructions of Englishness, and to debates about the current repositioning of British and English identities.

1.2 Folk

Given the centrality of the term to our field of study, and the complexity and range of meanings evoked by it within both contemporary culture and contemporary scholarship, it is important that we devote some space to explaining what we mean by the word 'folk'. It is beyond the scope of this book to give a full account of the term's complex etymology. (For more on this subject, see Pegg, 2001; Williams, 1983; Nercessian, 2007.) It is, however, worth highlighting the central role that *English* culture has played in the concept's development. Whilst a relative latecomer to the collection and revival of traditional culture that was so fervently taken up across the nations of Europe throughout the nineteenth century, Cecil Sharp's work in the field of English traditional music, song and dance has been often cited as an important turning point in folk scholarship. We begin, then, by tracing some of the historically shifting definitions and uses of the term 'folk'.

Williams suggests that, subsequent to Herder's coining of the term *Volkslieder* in 1778–79, folk song was used throughout Europe for most of the nineteenth century as a synonym of 'national song' (Williams, 1983: 136). The concept of folk song and folk music (although the former was the more commonly employed term) is now understood to have been something of a constructed vehicle of European romanticists during this period: a 'pure' or 'authentic' musical expression of a nation's people that could be harnessed to bolster nationalist sentiment in the face of growing cosmopolitanism and crises of national identity. Such was the context in which England's first period of folk revivalism (herein referred to – as is colloquially accepted – as the 'first folk revival') took place between the 1880s and the 1920s. One of Cecil Sharp's central contributions to the development of the concept was to make incisive attempts to identify 'the folk': a specific social class with whom (and only with whom) unadulterated folk song would certainly reside. Sharp's theories, set out in his seminal work *Folk Song: Some Conclusions*

(1907), were designed to focus more clearly the efforts of his fellow folk song collectors and were quite specific. The 'folk' were 'the unlettered, whose faculties ha[d] undergone no formal training, and who ha[d] never been brought into close enough contact with educated persons to be influenced by them' (*Ibid:* 4). The idea chimed with the thoughts of many contemporaries, but the level of unwavering specificity has been widely considered as momentous. Sharp's insistence on these criteria for the denoting of the authentic source came under some criticism at the time (see Francmanis, 2002), but his political influence and published rhetoric ensured strong support from the majority of active musicians, academics and antiquarians.

It is now accepted that Sharp's definition of the folk portrayed a group of people unlikely to have existed during his time: by the end of the nineteenth century, literacy in rural England was steadily increasing, the church impacted upon the lives (including the musical lives) of the vast majority, and the music hall was a ubiquitous phenomenon. Sharp's 'folk' were, rather, a whimsical ideal that was both symptomatic and a perpetuating construct of the essentialising nationalism to which he and his numerous followers subscribed. Critical deconstruction of this myth has been the main focus of much late-twentieth-century sociohistorical scholarship concerned with this period (Harker, 1985; Boyes, 1993) but its impact has been considerable in establishing the ongoing veneration of 'source singers' (as they would continue to be named).

Sharp's second important contribution lies in his attempts to theorise the musical material that constitutes folk song. This too, was aimed at avoiding the unintended contamination of the 'pure' crop of folk songs by songs of lesser worth, although his need to do this rather undermined the certainty of his definition of the folk – if such a class truly existed, then anything they sang would surely have met the collector's brief. Sharp identified three processes essential to the development of any folk song: 'continuity' with the past (that is, tradition); 'variation' over time by individual singers; and 'selection' (i.e. internalisation) of such modifications by the folk community (Sharp 1907: 16). The significance of this model is demonstrated by its use as the basis of the working definition adopted by the International Folk Music Council (IFMC) some fifty years later:

> Folk Music is the product of a musical tradition that has been evolved through the process of oral transmission. The factors that shape the traditions are: (i) continuity which links the present with the past; (ii) variation which springs from the creative impulse of the individual or the group; and (iii) selection by the community, which determines the form or forms in which the music survives.
>
> The term can be applied to music that has been evolved from rudimentary beginnings by a community uninfluenced by popular and art music and it can likewise be applied to music which has originated with an individual composer and has subsequently been absorbed into the unwritten living tradition of a community.
>
> The term does not cover composed popular music that has been taken over ready-made by a community and remains unchanged, for it is the refashioning and re-creation of the music that gives it its folk character. (IFMC, in Lloyd, 1967: 15)

The second period of folk revivalism in England (which we will refer to as the 'second folk revival') took place between around 1950 and 1970. This revival developed in the context of the socialist movement of post-war Britain, and was aimed at providing a communal musical space for the celebration of the industrial proletariat, whilst also taking inspiration, methods and personnel from the American folk and blues movement that had taken hold in the previous decades. Clearly, to meet this objective, modifications to Sharp's definitions were required. Most significantly, it was no longer considered reasonable to define the folk as only rural labourers – it became necessary to include the industrial working classes under this label (Lloyd, 1967: 14). With the revival's interest in folk songs composed on narratives reflecting the contemporary injustices of capitalist modernity, emphasis was shifted away from models of communal evolution and towards communal relevance. Emphasis was also placed on the authenticity of an egalitarian performance context. This led to the development of the folk club, a space in a suitably working-class setting (usually the back room of a pub) which encouraged participation from all attendees, provided performance opportunities for a new generation of solo artists, and was run by committee. The popularity of these clubs declined during the 1980s and 1990s (see MacKinnon, 1992), but they are still acknowledged by professional performers of all ages as an important performance context, a noble concept and a revered institution within the English folk community. As shall be discussed in 2.3, renewed interest in the folk club concept amongst younger English folk performers and activists has been a small but important feature of the contemporary resurgence.

In the late 1980s and 1990s the term was subjected to vigorous critique. In particular, the concept of 'folk song' has been revealed by the histories of Dave Harker (1985) and Georgina Boyes (1993) to be riddled with assumptions and inconsistencies. Harker's polemic goes so far as to call for the abandonment of the term, which he labels 'intellectual rubble which needs to be shifted so that building can begin again' (1985: x). Since its publication, Harker's account of the folk revival periods has been criticised as inflexible and selective (e.g. Bearman, 2002). Nonetheless, his important deconstruction of 'folk song' and 'the folk' as necessarily subject to invention, reinvention and mediation, has endured in most quarters of folk scholarship, and it is now impossible to talk or write about folk song in absolute terms. This destabilisation of the concept has not gone unnoticed by those who perform and otherwise identify with folk music and dance. Since the second revival period, a large proportion of 'the folk' (those involved in playing, singing and dancing to folk music) have been, in fact, members of the educated middle classes, with a considerable proportion coming from backgrounds such as teaching or university lecturing. Many in the folk music and dance communities are aware, therefore, that most definitions of those labels are wide open to challenge, and that the term 'folk' is problematised yet further by the conditions of modernity within which their own contemporary experiences of tradition are set. This broader awareness can be illustrated, to some extent at least, by the multicultural English folk project the Imagined Village (discussed in detail in 7.3), whose name directly references the title of Georgina Boyes' seminal book.

A number of specific features have become commonplace among twentieth-century definitions of folk music, including oral transmission, communal recreation and the significance of the concept of tradition.[6] All are, however, found wanting as definitive, not only due to their relative absence in some folk music cultures but also through their presence in other non-vernacular musical genres throughout the world. In the folk music cultures considered in this book, for instance, the process of oral transmission is present but by no means the only method of repertorical transmission. A conceptual opposition to commercially manufactured and distributed pop music remains fairly central to contemporary conceptions of the folk arts by those within and outside of English folk culture; however, recent events in the resurgence (discussed in Chapters 2 and 3) demonstrate the ambiguity and permeability of the boundaries between these two idioms, and this ambiguity has now become the subject of explicit celebration by contemporary English folk musicians and dancers.

Rather than attempting to offer a new definition for the modern age, this book takes as its foundation Bohlman's premise that folk music 'belies the stasis of definition' (Bohlman, 1988: xviii). At the heart of Bohlman's statement is the anthropologically grounded assumption that folk music is a cultural construct undergoing constant discursive renegotiation by the participants of that culture. This book is based on an understanding that folk is whatever those who identify most closely with it (folk musicians, dancers, audiences, etc) proclaim it to be. Like Harker (1985) and Boyes (1993), we acknowledge that folk – like all other labelled forms of cultural activity – is a culturally and socially constructed category. The ossificatory activities of earlier movements are only some of a number of factors influencing the continuous redrawing of its boundaries.

It is particularly important to examine our use of the term in the light of a recent schism in its vernacular usage in contemporary England. In recent years, in parallel to the resurgence that we investigate in this book, another folk music has emerged. This other folk, sometimes referred to in the media as 'nu-folk' and typified by professional acts such as Mumford and Sons, Noah and the Whale or Laura Marling, is one whose musical heritage is more directly locatable in the British and American folk movements of the mid-twentieth century than the folk on which this book focuses. Nu-folk has been even more commercially successful and visible within mainstream music media than the folk with which we are concerned (Mumford and Sons, for instance, have enjoyed considerable success in America). Artists in this nu-folk genre are generally singer-songwriters whose music foregrounds those acoustic instruments that have arrived in Britain via American folk culture (e.g. acoustic guitar, double bass, and banjo), while free-reed instruments (common to the English folk culture discussed in this book) are relatively absent. Typically, the lyrics and music are newly composed by the artists, with no 'traditional' material involved. Song texts include relatively enigmatic, poetic and introverted lyrical content. Crucially, it has not been closely associated with any significant discourse on English identity; occasional comments in the press emerge regarding a general sense of authenticity that is deemed to surround nu-folk, but it is not commonly accompanied by a clearly specified sense of place or group identification. Finally, nu-folk is a musical genre only, whilst the folk that is investigated in this book is a culture in which there are strong connections between engagement in music, dance, and other traditions and customs.

For these reasons, the nu-folk phenomenon must be considered as to some extent distanced from the English folk culture with which this book is concerned. That is not to say that these different folks are unrelated – far from it. For two disparate versions of folk to have found popularity simultaneously but independently seems an unlikely coincidence. Rather, both are manifestations of a wider cultural interest in immediacy and authenticity of expression, each engaging with discourses and narratives of tradition, history, nature and locality to very different extents. What we are terming English folk culture tends to engage with or reference older and more specific traditions, particularly those that predate the steel-string guitar, but the most significant line of separation falls where English folk explicitly expounds such discourses through emphasis on the embodiment of *England* in the music, dance or other materials involved.[7]

Finally, it is important to clarify our uses of the words 'folk' and 'traditional', terms that are generally used interchangeably with regard to the English folk arts in the contemporary context. The English context differs markedly from the Irish in this respect. In Ireland, 'traditional music' is generally regarded as more 'traditional' (that is, ancient, authentic, valuable) than the separate genre of folk music, which is generally more closely associated with acoustic guitar-led, singer-songwriting. Similar – although yet more complex – classifications are examined in Hughes' account of Japanese *min'yō, fōku songu, enka*, etc. (2008). In England, the boundaries separating these terms are ambiguous and inconsistent, but for many working within the English folk arts they have become synonymous. Overall, the word more commonly used to describe the activities discussed in this book (itemised in 1.6) is 'folk'. This is made manifest in – and is reinforced by – its appearance in the titles of related institutions such as FolkArts England, the English Folk Dance and Song Society (EFDSS), and Folkworks. That said, in recent years, the label 'traditional' has come to be used a little more regularly (e.g. 'English traditional music/dance'). This is likely to be the result of a number of factors, but it may have much to do with an implicit rebranding of English folk by some who feel less comfortable with the historical connotations with which the 'f' word has been associated. In particular, use of the term 'traditional' directs attention towards the 'authentic' qualities of the materials being performed, and away from those stereotyped images of geeky, bearded, middle-aged folk enthusiasts that were so vigorously mocked in the media and wider public discourse over the last two decades of the twentieth century. However, the term folk continues to loom largest in this area, also being taken up within popular culture in the form of the nu-folk discussed above. Witness, for example, the reassessment of beards, pipes and dated fashion (including Arran sweaters) as the new 'cool' (or one of a number of new 'cools'). This was demonstrated most clearly by a piece with seven double-page spreads in the UK edition of *Vogue* magazine (July, 2011), which depicted various folk-related costumes, including morris dancing outfits, in a manner and context normally reserved for *haute-couture* fashion.

In this book we will use the term in line with its common usage by the musicians, dancers and audiences with which we are concerned. Generally, we will use the term 'folk' as a label for the specific genre of music or dance discussed, the artists that perform within it and its culture of participation. Those who closely associate with or regularly participate in folk-based activities will sometimes be referred to in this book as 'folkies', in line with the common self-identification of that group. Occasionally, terms like 'traditional music' are used as a general label for similar musics across Britain and the West more widely (folk music in England can reasonably be referred to as traditional music, but the synonymity of 'folk' and 'traditional' is not universal, as illustrated in the case of Irish traditional music above). More broadly, 'traditional' is used as an adjective denoting those practices, repertories, etc., that are considered ancient, as opposed to innovative or recent features.

1.3 Resurgence

Our use of the term 'resurgence' to refer to this most recent wave of interest in English folk deserves some explanation. Previous periods of growth and popularity of the English folk arts are usually referred to as folk revivals – often the 'first' and 'second folk revivals', as discussed above. Our choice of the word 'resurgence' reflects a need to distinguish the present developments from those of these preceding revival periods, as well as from the established concept of revival as outlined by Livingston (1999). There are a number of reasons for this differentiation. Firstly, there is no clear discourse of a tradition in need of 'rescue' (to borrow the term from Livingston 1999: 70). None of our research informants showed any concern that the material performed by folk musicians was in danger of falling into disuse. Rather, this resurgence is most clearly understood as a growth of popularity and profile of pre-existing practices. It is also unlike previous revivals (and those in other cultures) in the extent of its engagements with aspects of mainstream culture. As will be discussed in Chapter 3, many musicians, for example, go to great lengths to emphasise folk music's status as one kind of popular music, or to engage in a deconstruction of the folk/art/pop boundaries. Also, the collection of traditional material – cited by Livingston as a 'basic ingredient' of any revival (*Ibid.*: 69) – plays little discernible role in the resurgence, although consultation (and celebration) of existing collections made during the previous revivals is common, and there have been increasing moves towards publication, in print and online, of such materials.

Furthermore, there is no unified (or even predominating) methodology for a reinvention of traditional material or performance. In fact, the resurgence has foregrounded and celebrated a considerable diversification of stylistic approaches. These will be examined in detail in Chapter 3. Although some acts have developed new and unusual ways of presenting traditional material, many are performing in much the same way as would have been expected before the resurgence began, but all are enjoying increased popularity and media profile. Musicians, for example, tend to consider the resurgence as a newly positive, receptive attitude towards folk music by those coming to the genre from outside, assisted by a new generation of performers who have made the music more appealing to younger audiences. While other labels are occasionally employed by various commentators for the contemporary movement, use of the term 'revival' is fairly rare, with participants perhaps seeking to distance themselves from what are perceived to have been the more heavily politicised objectives of the second revival, in particular. Thus, interviewees in our research have generally responded positively to the term 'resurgence', even taking it up in future public discussion.

Related to the above points, the current resurgence also differs from the preceding folk revivals in that the majority of its practitioners do not tend to express any explicitly political motivations. Any political statements locatable in the resurgence are generally subtle, ambiguous, multifaceted and often downplayed (see Chapter 7). Nonetheless, this does not mean that the resurgence does not have political meanings or implications, nor that it can be divorced from its political context, and we contend that the current resurgence of English folk music and dance is closely related to a rise of interest in and concern for English national and cultural identity.

1.4 Performing Englishness

Here we will explain why we have used the phrase 'performing Englishness' in the title of this book, and what it signals about the way that we are conceptualising national identity. Since the 1990s the concepts of performance and performativity have come to be widely and variously used across multiple academic disciplines such as ethnomusicology, cultural studies, anthropology, gender studies, per-formance studies, dance studies, cultural geography and sociology. Some scholars have referred to this as a 'performative turn' in cultural studies, social sciences and the humanities (Gade and Jerslev, 2005: 8). The idea of performance does not, however, have a unified meaning across disciplines. Gade identifies two main tracks within the performative turn, the use of the concept of performance in fields like anthropology, ethnology, sociology and theatre studies, and the use of the notion of performativity within (language) philosophy, literary studies, gender studies and theatre studies. She notes that while these concepts have both gained ground, 'there is little agreement on what they stand for separately' (2005: 21), citing Parker and Sedgwick, who write: 'while philosophy and theatre now share 'performative' as a common lexical item, the term has hardly come to mean "the same thing" for each' (Parker and Sedgwick, in *Ibid*: 21. See also Hellier-Tinoco, 2011:36). We will not offer a full discussion of these different uses of the ideas of performance and performativity, but will focus here on selected issues that are pertinent to, and clarify our own use of, the concept in relation to Englishness and the folk arts.[8]

The theoretical concept that has informed our understanding of national identity is that of performativity. This concept relates to the processes of identity formation. Judith Butler, who has been its most influential theorist, uses it to characterise the way that gender identity categories are produced through the repeated citation of regulatory norms. Butler's theories of performativity have been highly influential within and beyond the field of gender studies as an approach that offers a non-essentialist way of thinking about gendered (and, by implication, other) identities as produced, rather than being naturally given (see, for example, Butler, 1993). Butler's focus is on gendered identities, but the concept of performativity can be extended to other facets of identity too, and a number of scholars have used it to understand the construction of national identity (see Balzano *et al.*, 2007; Brady and Walsh, 2009; Edensor, 2002; Hellier-Tinoco, 2011; Negra, 2006; Storey, 2010; Wulff, 2005).

The key point to make about this approach, for the purpose of our book, is that national identity is understood not as something that is naturally given or pre-existing, but as something that is made. This resonates with Benedict Anderson's influential idea that the nation can be understood as an 'imagined community' (2006). Englishness is produced through, as Butler says, 'a stylized repetition of acts' (1990: 140), and this makes it appear as if it were natural. As Storey puts it, in relation to Britishness:

> There is not anything natural about nationality. One is not born British, one becomes British … The performance of nationality creates the illusion of a prior substantiality – a core national self – and suggests that the performative ritual of nation-ness is merely an expression of an already existing nationality. However, our nationality is not the expression of the location in which we are born, it is performatively constructed in processes of repetition and citation, which gradually produce and reinforce our sense of national belonging'. (2010: 19)

It is particularly important to bear this in mind in relation to the folk arts, which have historically been treated as if they were a natural manifestation of national belonging. To perform Englishness through doing English folk music and dance is, then, to produce and circulate particular images and concepts of nation and national identity. Performing Englishness in this way is not restricted to activities culturally framed as performance (although it does involve many of those), but includes a wide range of activities from the spectacular to the everyday, public to private, amateur to professional and presentational to participatory (see 1.6), in a variety of contexts. It encompasses not only music and dance making but also the making and circulation of ancillary images, websites, albums and other related products. It includes talking and writing about the folk arts. It includes the activities of different kinds of participants – audiences, promoters or festival organisers, for example – as well as those who are seen, or see themselves, as practitioners of music and dance. Finally, it includes performances that range from highly reflexive and intentional projections of Englishness to more subtle or implicit ones. The English folk music and dance phenomena that we are writing about here involve many different degrees of reflexivity in their constructions of Englishness. Some of those performances are explicitly reflexive – sometimes reinforcing, sometimes strategically subversive of particular ideas about Englishness. Others are less reflexive, and there are many that blur the boundaries.

In identifying the ways that England and Englishness are constructed in and around the folk arts, particularly in Part II of the book, we will place a focus on discourse, and on identifying discursive constructions of England and of Englishness. 'Discourse' is another of those terms that means different things across disciplines, including the two disciplines represented by the authors of this book. Our deployment of it to understand constructions of Englishness broadly draws on its use by the French theorist Michel Foucault. We take the idea of discourse to refer to systems of ideas through which things are given meaning.[9] When 'England' or 'Englishness' is invoked by folk artists or audiences or journalists writing about the folk arts, for example, they draw on and circulate particular sets of ideas, particular discourses, and it is these that we have set out to identify. We are interested in the frameworks with which people think about England and Englishness, by looking at how it is talked about, pictured, imagined, defined, and conjured up in music, song and dance, in this particular cultural field at this moment in English history. We often use the term 'discourse' to refer specifically to talking or writing around particular topics (as, for example, in looking at 'media discourse' on Englishness), but we see discourse as embedded in musical and image-based sources as well as linguistic ones.

1.5 The project

The research that led to this book has been a meeting between the two disciplines inhabited by its authors, ethnomusicology and British cultural studies. Despite the widely different historical and institutional backgrounds represented by these two fields, we found a great deal of theoretical and methodological common ground. Both disciplinary approaches are invested in the study of culture, in the widest sense of the term. Both have concerns with issues of identity and of power, and both have strong ethnographic traditions. There are also many differences in approach and language, and it may be that certain parts of this book will involve analytical processes that may be more or less accessible to readers within different specialist fields. For instance, examination of musical practices and features requires the use of technical terminology with which ethnomusicologists (and musicians generally) may be more comfortable. This is particularly the case in Chapters 3 and 4.

The book is the product of a body of ethnographic research that took place between 2007 and 2009, with some updating between 2009 and 2011. This included participant observation at a range of events, activities and performances, including seven festivals in England: Loughborough Folk Festival, Chippenham Folk Festival, Wychwood Festival, Cambridge Folk Festival, Towersey Village Festival, Shrewsbury Folk Festival and Whitby Folk Week. Whilst this fieldwork took in many informal conversations, a series of in-depth interviews were also conducted with a range of folk participants including professional musicians, dancers, festival organisers, spokespeople, and animateurs: a list of interviewees is included in the book's References section.

Both authors have been active as amateur and semi-professional folk musicians within the folk and traditional music cultures in England for some years prior to consideration of the area as a research interest. Whilst our background as grassroots folk participants has inevitably informed our approach, much (although not all) of the research on which we draw here has been with individuals whose respective roles in the contemporary English folk scene go beyond participation (in Turino's sense of the term; 2008: 26) to include: the giving of presentational performances; the provision of solicited learning opportunities such as workshops; the production of tangible and widely circulated outputs such as recordings, visual materials or choreographies; and the active facilitation of some or all of these things. In short, most of our informants can be considered to be of relatively high profile in the context of English folk music and dance culture as a whole. Given the inherently vernacular and participatory implications of the concept of folk within contemporary Western society, our choice to concentrate on these relatively high-profile artists and activists deserves explanation.

We have already noted the general lack of scrutiny afforded to contemporary English folk music and dance practice by the academy in general. Whilst historical investigations abound, research on the English folk arts as it has existed in the last twenty or so years has been less than commonplace. But, as mentioned earlier in this introduction, smaller-scale contemporary research has been conducted by British ethnomusicologists – either as a secondary research area (Finnegan, 1989; Stock, 2004; Russell, 2004) or, more recently, as a primary specialism outside the conventions of the discipline (Keegan-Phipps, 2008; Hield, 2010). Significantly, these studies are emblematic of a wider trend to accept England as a field for ethnographic research of all kinds, as the various subdisciplines of cultural anthropology contemplate 'home' in a bid to shrug off the last vestiges of orientalist othering (e.g. Rapport, 2002). Beyond that significance, such investigations have provided invaluable insights into the activities of small, grassroots, amateur communities. These studies have shed much light on the musical behaviours of folk musicians in contemporary England and pave the way for what we hope will be a good deal more research in this rich vein. However, a desire to observe English folk culture in micromusical terms (to borrow from Slobin, 2003), as in a session, a club, or a festival, is necessarily limited, and problematic if it ignores English folk's development as a 'macromusic'. English folk musicians are currently learning tunes from the latest release by Spiers and Boden and ordering instruments online; dancers are critiquing or even noting down a morris figure captured in a YouTube video; festival-goers are Googling unfamiliar artists before deciding on next year's itinerary; and enthusiasts are comparing their own positions on national identity with that expressed by Eliza Carthy in her latest interview with the *Guardian* newspaper. The resurgence in English folk has operated on a grand, heavily and widely mediated scale that draws together the individuals, the sessions, clubs and festivals with a shared

– albeit dynamic – lexicon of artists, soundscapes, experiences, and discourses. Whilst close scrutiny of small-scale activities and interactions is equally essential to the ethnographic record of the field, it is this 'bigger picture' that we aim to address in this book.

It is also important to note that the relatively high-profile individuals whose activities we have concentrated on in this book are not removed from the 'normal' or 'everyday' experiences of the majority of participants in English folk culture. Within the small world of the English folk scene, numerous artists and activists occupy a dual role of both folk celebrity and grassroots participant: many musicians or dancers who are (in terms of profile) at the very height of the English folk resurgence can still be seen performing with a local morris side at a weekend dance out, playing a ceilidh for a wedding, or participating in a pub session. We have not, as is common in ethnographic work, presented our interviewees' words in anonymous form, but, with their agreement, we have named them. This is primarily because of their high profile: not only is the identity of the speaker often relevant in this context, but it could be easily surmised in any case. Many of them have also spoken publicly about Englishness and the English folk arts in press interviews, for example, and we have also drawn on these public statements.

There are some key figures in the English folk scene whom we would have liked to interview but who were not contactable or available to participate in our research. In part, this is a function of the mainstreaming of English folk: once an artist is signed by a major record label or engages the services of an agent or manager, they become less easy to contact. Where individuals have spoken publicly – through press interviews, for example – we have examined these discourses, which are interesting to us precisely because of their public and mediated circulation. Our approach therefore has been a multifaceted and multilayered one that draws together the analysis of a range of materials – musical, choreographic, linguistic, visual – including those expressed both publicly and privately.

As a general comment, we do not wish to suggest that the constructs of Englishness identified in this book – through the methods outlined above – are the only ones in circulation: different methods (such as a concentration on purely amateur informant groups) may well have identified alternative ways of thinking about and discussing the current resurgence, or may have placed different emphases. Through our interviews and participant observation, in connection with the examination of a wide range of texts, from musical works and programme notes to websites and CD liner notes, we have aimed to identify the constructions of Englishness that are the most visible, the most widely circulated and therefore, arguably, the most important for an understanding of the resurgence. We make no attempt to generalise a unified concept of Englishness in the English folk arts: a central finding of our research is the striking plurality of approaches currently being developed, and a primary aim of this book is to demonstrate what such a plurality can tell us about contemporary English identity and about the folk arts as a contemporary vehicle for cultural expression.

1.6 English folk music and dance

It is not the role of this book to provide an exhaustive taxonomy of the various activities that are currently included within the category of English folk music and dance, as it is practised in contemporary England. Such a text is lacking in the modern ethnomusicological record: a catalogue of the English folk arts would be fascinating and helpful to future scholarship on the topic, even if fraught with problems and anomalies – exceptions to the rule would be queuing up to thwart almost every attempt to accurately characterise subgenres, types of activities or repertories. Much of the research necessary for that kind of perilous task has been conducted ahead of writing this book but has not been included in its pages – this work has privileged analysis of meaning and context over the description of stylistic and structural features for its own sake. Nonetheless, it is essential that some basic descriptive introduction is offered to the more significant elements of the English folk arts for the reader who is unfamiliar with them.

The music and dance of the contemporary English folk culture can reasonably be understood in relation to a classification of activities between, on the one hand, those designed for reception by an audience and, on the other, those for which the presence of an audience is incidental. This binary classification was suggested by Blaukopf in the form of 'participatory music' and 'performance music' (1992: 193) but has recently been revisited by Turino as 'participatory music' and 'presentational music' (2008: 26). It is important to recognise that this categorisation raises a central problem, in that the inherent qualities of *both* concepts must be, to some extent, appreciable in all musical activities. Nonetheless, it can assist us in observing and understanding the orientation of music and dance activities towards either end of a single spectrum.

1.6.1 Music

As we will demonstrate and discuss through the chapters that follow, a particular emphasis is placed upon participatory music and dance contexts within contemporary English folk culture. It is the substantial range of activities towards this end of the participation–presentation spectrum that is commonly thought to distinguish the folk arts most clearly from mainstream pop and high-art cultures. Within this category, musical activities include the song-based folk clubs, mentioned earlier in this introduction as a (relatively) public performance opportunity for amateur singers of any standard.[10] Whilst club-based activities and 'singarounds' tend to encourage round-the-room turn-taking, the 'singing session' is a less explicitly organised version of the scenario. The ratio of solo singing to collective chorus singing varies from one instance to another. Instrumental versions of this activity are called sessions, and are relatively similar to the sessions of Irish and Scottish traditional music cultures (see Stock, 2004; and Keegan-Phipps, 2003 for more on this). In an instrumental session, the group is expected to join in with the person whose turn it is to lead the proceedings. The music generally played at English folk sessions takes the form of 'tunes' (as with other British traditional musics) – units of melodic material normally made of two or three repeated phrases, each of eight bars' length, with the full tune repeated upwards of three times in a rendition. The specific content of these tunes will be discussed in 4.2. Clubs and sessions often take place in a backroom of a public house (pub), usually on the same night of every week, every other week, or every month. They also take place, usually in local pubs, as part of festival programmes.

Presentational forms within English folk music performance most commonly take the form of stage-based concerts. As will be discussed in Chapters 2 and 3, these performances tend to occur either on stages at folk festivals or in generic arts venues. There is no standard format for ensembles performing English folk music in these contexts, with acts ranging from solo artists to sizeable bands: at the time of writing, the largest is eleven members (Bellowhead). The range of instruments and vocal combinations deployed in such acts is also fairly wide, although certain combinations have become particularly common, as is discussed in more detail in Chapter 4.

1.6.2 Dance

Dance forms in English folk culture can also be understood in terms of a continuum ranging from the participatory to the presentational. The main form of participatory dance activity is the ceilidh. [11] Despite the apparently Gaelic spelling of the name (shared with the equivalent Scottish traditional dance event), the ceilidh is a central and integral element of English folk dance culture. To distinguish it from Scottish and Irish (ceili) counterparts, the term 'English Ceilidh' is sometimes used. At these events, a 'caller' instructs the attendees in the figures and steps of the impending dance; the participants then dance these figures while accompanied by a band. As will be discussed further in 3.4, English ceilidh bands come in a variety of forms, but they very often utilise some form of pop-based rhythm section (usually drum kit, bass and guitars), indicating roots in the folk-rock idiom of the 1970s (Sweers, 2005). The dancers tend to be couple-based, and begin in formations known as sets. A common set would be a group of four couples, arranged in two lines of men and women respectively, facing each other. The dances usually consist of figures (units of interactive movement) that might take eight or sixteen bars of the music to complete: some are common to a variety of dances, whilst other figures are rare or particular to a specific dance. Most ceilidhs will include a mixed dance repertory: some dances will be traditional and well known to regular ceilidh-goers (e.g. the Nottingham Swing) whilst others may be original choreographies, usually written by a caller, who will often work hard to develop new figures for new dances. However, English ceilidh callers will very rarely assume any prior knowledge of any dances or figures on the part of the participants, and will give clear instructions for a 'walk-through' – without music – before each dance is begun.

Ceilidhs are one of the central components of all folk festivals – at many festivals, the on-site evening entertainment will consist of a concert and a ceilidh happening simultaneously in separate venues, with audience members moving between the two over the course of the evening. However, ceilidhs are by no means restricted to that context. In fact, ceilidhs are likely to occur at a number of public functions throughout the year, including school or community fundraising events, and large-scale family or community celebrations or parties. Most importantly, ceilidhs have seen a marked increase in popularity as a form of wedding entertainment across England since the turn of the twenty-first century, with weddings now making up a large proportion of the bookings taken by any caller or ceilidh band. The popularity of the ceilidh for weddings has mainly to do with the accessibility of the dancing to people with no prior knowledge of the form. Due to the fact that the simple figures are fully explained before each dance by the caller, and normally danced to a basic hop-step, ceilidh dancing is available to even the most inexperienced of dancers, requiring minimal creative input from the individual (as opposed to a disco – the alternative wedding entertainment – which is by its nature undirected, and therefore requires maximum creative input from each dancer). Given this particular context for ceilidh dancing, the significance of ceilidhs for increasing the profile and popularity of English folk music and dance generally is considerable, since they constitute an element of the English folk arts that is likely to take place outside of the self-identifying folk culture's nominated performance spaces, and garner participation from those within British society who have little or no identification with folk more generally.

Presentational dance contexts within English folk culture are numerous and quite varied, but the most common and widely recognised is morris dancing. A pervasive stereotype of morris dancing as the preserve of ageing, bearded eccentric men has, as noted at the opening of this chapter, circulated within British media and culture since the second revival period. This has, however, been challenged by a growth in the activity's popularity among men and women in their teens, twenties and thirties. Of the various forms of morris, that with the highest profile – nationally and internationally – is named Cotswold morris after the region with which it is most closely associated. This variety is characterised by predominantly white costumes with bells, the regular use of handkerchiefs held in the hands and waved, and a very particular variety of steps and leaps. When morris dancing writ-large is referenced outside of English folk circles, it is Cotswold morris that has most often been used to represent the whole dance culture. It is this form that has been the most visible within the developments of the current resurgence: it has featured, for example, in stage shows (see 3.5 and 3.7.3), as well as being the subject of a comedy film (*Morris: A Life With Bells On*, 2009) and a serious documentary (*Way of the Morris*, 2011). Perhaps the next best known form of morris is known as border morris, and is thought to have originated in areas of England around the Welsh border, although this – like Cotswold morris – is now danced by groups (usually known as sides) throughout the country. A significant characteristic of border morris dancing is the practice of blackening the face (although coloured face paint is now also common amongst dancers), and steps tend to be of the simple step-hop variety.[12] Other presentational dance forms include: sword dancing, including longsword and rapper dancing, a variety of sword dancing that originates from the North East of England; molly, a form of dancing specific to East Anglia with a distinctive step; and North West clog morris, a processional form.[13] Except for a small portion of the Cotswold repertory, the forms of presentational dancing mentioned above mainly involve multiple dancers dancing in formation.

A growth of interest in what is usually referred to as 'clog dancing' has also taken place. Traditions of percussive step-dancing in wooden-soled clogs can be located in numerous parts of England, and are usually identified in terms of their local associations, rather than as a single 'English clog' tradition or repertory (although see 3.5 for an exception to this). Often traced back to the Industrial Revolution of the nineteenth century, where it took place on the music hall stage and in competitions (Radcliffe, 2001), clog dancing is still associated with competitions, such as the Northern Counties Clog Dancing Championships. Unlike forms of morris dancing that are also performed in clogs, the creative element in this kind of dancing primarily resides in the movements of the individual dancer rather than in group formations.

There also exist some unique dances that are specific to particular places and local customs. These include the Britannia Coco-nut Dancers of Bacup, Lancashire, and the Abbots Bromley Horn Dance, Staffordshire.[14]

Rapper and clog dancing can often take place inside a pub, since only a small amount of floor space is required for these. The other presentational forms of dancing discussed above have traditionally been performed in outside spaces, usually for a transient audience of onlookers. This kind of 'dance out' remains the most common context in which members of the public are likely to encounter such English folk dance performances, but festivals and other organised events offer alternative scenarios. Morris dancing, for instance, can regularly be seen performed – indoors – as a spot (intermission) within an evening ceilidh. Crucially for the purposes of this study, the resurgence has seen an upsurge in the likelihood of witnessing morris dancing on the concert stage (see 3.5 and 3.7.3). Clog dancing has also received some national media attention, featuring in 2011 as the subject of two BBC television programmes. *Come Clog Dancing: Treasures of English Folk Dance,* presented by conductor Charles Hazelwood (BBC4, 2011) and *Still Folk Dancing … After All These Years,* presented by folk artists Rachel and Becky Unthank (BBC4, 2011).

English folk tunes are generally closely linked with dance contexts, and the majority of the instrumental repertory can be heard both in sessions and as accompaniment to dance – there is little segregation of the repertory between these contexts. That said, certain tunes are more strongly associated with specific kinds of dance than others. For instance, some tunes are particularly identifiable as morris tunes due to anomalous time changes designed to accompany specific figures within Cotswold morris.

1.6.3 Festivals

As a category of cultural and social event, the folk festival constitutes a significant performance arena for the resurgence in English folk music. Earlier studies of folk music in England have focused their attentions on the folk club, but that legacy of the second revival period weakened steadily in significance through the 1980s and 1990s (a decline documented and discussed by MacKinnon, 1993). Barring one or two notable exceptions symptomatic of the current resurgence, club audiences are far from representative of the younger generation (under forty years old) that apparently resides at the heart of the contemporary movement. Younger participants often associate folk clubs with unappealing residual features of the second revival period from which the establishments were born, such as an older personnel, anachronistic cultural capital, unacknowledged formalities and heavily (if not always explicitly) politicised ethos. Festivals, however, have seen a considerable increase in attendance by younger audiences. They are also sites of concentrated activity across the full range of the folk arts – music and dance, from the fully presentational (e.g. formal concerts) to the fully participatory (such as open workshops and ceilidh dancing). In recent years, many key innovations in the contemporary English folk arts have been premiered at, or instigated by, festivals rather than other performance venues (as with the first performance of the ground-breaking morris dance group Morris Offspring at Sidmouth International Festival in 2003, which went on to develop into the show *On English Ground* that played the South Bank Centre, London (2005) and toured arts venues nationally in 2007; see 3.7.3 for a full discussion).

Estimates for the number of annual folk festivals throughout the UK were set in 2003 at around 350 (Association of Festival Organisers, 2003: 3). Such estimates can only be approximate for a number of reasons. Firstly, festivals can range from week-long, high-profile events attracting upwards of ten thousand attendees to something more akin to a series of workshops over one or two days, perhaps attracting less than a hundred people. Most significantly, the identification of folk festivals is complicated by the fact that generic boundaries and labels are ambiguous. Even among those festivals that include the term 'folk' in their title the nature of the content programmed varies immensely. Different festivals choose to include to greater or lesser extents music that is – or can be – described as 'world music', early music, singer-songwriter, American old-timey, blues, acoustic pop, and jazz, alongside that which is unambiguously traditional music of the British Isles.[15] Meanwhile, symptomatic of the current resurgence is a new found willingness by music festivals widely regarded as 'mainstream festivals' to programme folk music. However, those festivals that identify themselves as 'folk festivals' (and are thought of as folk festivals by participants) are distinct from other kinds of festivals not merely by way of programming, but also because greater emphasis is placed on active artistic participation by attendees.

As festivals vary in size and content, so too do they vary in their location and immediate physical setting: for the vast majority of folk festivals, most attendees stay on a campsite, and this is often a focal space for festival activities. In the cases of larger festivals, a sizeable field plays host to almost all of the programmed activities, with space portioned out for camping, vendors' stalls, catering vans and temporary performance venues (commonly marquees of varying sizes). For many, at least some of the performances are housed in a nearby building, such as a school or leisure centre, while others make greater use of local public buildings for performances (town halls, churches, theatres, large pubs). A smaller number of folk festivals basically amount to a concert series, hosted by an arts venue, with attendees expected to organise their own accommodation.

1.7 Synopsis

This book falls into two parts. Part I examines the salient characteristics of the twenty-first-century English folk resurgence. Chapter 2 looks at the development of a 'folk industry', beginning with a broad analysis of the historical context of the first two folk revivals. Taking the emergence of folk industry conferences as a case study, it traces the folk industry's web of intersecting institutions and discourses. Its second case study of the new folk club the Magpie's Nest examines further the coming together of commercialisation and professionalisation with the folk ethos.

Chapter 3 offers a detailed discussion of the actual music and dance being performed within the English folk arts, and considers the various ways in which these texts are engaging with both popular and high-art cultural products and processes. It demonstrates the extreme diversity of stylistic approaches to the performance of English folk music and dance, examining a variety of case studies and genres, and considering how they connect with mainstream cultural forms. We will begin to consider how these versions of English folk might be related to concepts of authenticity and vernacularity, and how they might therefore speak to broader constructions of English identity. Chapter 4 continues in this vein of analysis, but focuses instead on emergent trends and patterns within the music and musical discourses of the resurgence. It details specific approaches to the performance of English folk music, questioning the possibility of an 'English style' and the possible musical and cultural factors contributing to aesthetic developments in the music of the resurgence.

Part II of the book broadens out the analysis with a focus on questions of place and identity. Chapter 5 gives a brief contextualisation of the wider cultural interest in Englishness within which the folk resurgence is situated. Chapter 6 examines the various ways in which 'England' is being imagined within and around the English folk resurgence. Following on from this exploration of England, Chapter 7 analyses the versions of Englishness that can be found within the work of contemporary English folk artists. This chapter codifies a range of English identities under construction in the resurgence, and examines their politics. The book concludes with a consideration of some broader theoretical issues raised by our findings.

Notes

1 See, for example, a feature in the *Guardian* (Sweeting, 2002).

2 'Icons online' was commissioned by Culture Online, which was part of the Department for Culture, Media and Sport until 2007.

3 This relative paucity of scholarly work could be contrasted, for example, with the amount of research into contemporary Irish traditional music and dance culture or non-Western diaspora in Western contexts (e.g. Hast and Scott, 2004; Slobin, 1993).

4 It could reasonably be argued that the appearance of morris dancing in the closing ceremony of the 2012 Olympic Games did much to reaffirm its status as deserving of ridicule: here it featured for a few seconds as an accompaniment to an anarchic rendition of the Monty Python song 'Always Look On the Bright Side of Life', performed by Eric Idle (posing as a failed human cannonball), and including absurd amusements like ice-skating nuns and can-canning Roman legionnaires.

5 Bob Copper (MA), University of Sussex, 2000; Martin Carthy, University of Sheffield 2002; Norma Waterson, University of Hull, 2005; Richard Thompson, University of Aberdeen, 2011.

6 See for instance Pegg (2001); Nettl (1965: 85–111); Nettl (1986: 315).

7 That is not to say that expressions of Englishness are completely absent from nu-folk or other popular music. A notable example is the rock singer P. J. Harvey's album *Let England Shake* (2011).

8 For surveys of the multiple uses of the ideas of performance and performativity, see Campbell (1996); Hellier-Tinoco (2011); Parker and Sedgewick (1996); Schechner (2002).

9 See Macdonald (2003) for a detailed discussion of the concept of discourse, its use within media studies and its relationship to other concepts such as representation and ideology.

10 For a detailed account of the folk club and amateur folk singing in contemporary England, see Hield (2010).

11 Pronounced *kay-lee*.

12 The practice of 'blacking up' will be discussed further in Chapter 7.

13 On molly, see Bradtke (2001). On English sword dancing, see Corrsin (2001).

14 On the Bacup Britannia Coco-nut Dancers, see Buckland (2009; 2001a; 2001b.) On the Abbots Bromley Horn Dance, see Buckland (2001a).

15 Whilst we recognise that the term 'World Music' is by no means stable or absolute, discussion of the world music genre is beyond our scope here. For readability we will hereafter present this term without scare quotes. For discussions of it, see Born and Hesmondhalgh (2000).

I

Contemporary English folk

2

The folk industry

In the opening decade of the twenty-first century, the term 'folk industry' began to circulate, particularly amongst folk promoters. It came to prominence in 2007 when the folk development organisation FolkArts England offered two 'Folk Industry Focus Days' as part of a four-day conference. In their promotional material for the event, the organisation triumphantly proclaimed that the conference represented 'what may well be the biggest gathering of folk activists, promoters and media folk since, well, who knows?!' (FolkArts England, 2007). Taking place in a business conference centre, its professional surroundings, in combination with the use of the term 'folk industry', spoke of a growing sense of the folk arts in England as becoming increasingly professionalised and engaged with commercial processes and markets. A further consolidation of the folk industry concept was achieved over the following two years with a shift in the title of the longstanding Association of Festival Organisers (AFO) Conference to become the 'Folk Industry and AFO Conference' (FolkArts England, 2008; FolkArts England, 2009). The 2008 conference brochure promised that attendance would be a 'fantastic opportunity to be part of Folk's cultural renaissance and to share and connect with the people who are shaping its future' (FolkArts England, 2008). There is an assumption here, then, not only that there is indeed a 'renaissance' in the folk arts in England, but that a burgeoning folk industry forms an integral part of it.

This embracing of the idea of a folk industry is interesting, not least because it appears to contradict the established ethos of English folk which has traditionally spoken of itself in terms that draw on discourses ranging from the resolutely amateur to the philanthropic to the explicitly anti-commercial, all feeding into the sense of authenticity that is so fundamental to the idea of folk. This chapter will trace the various strands of the contemporary folk industry and will examine the coexistence of folk ethos with folk industry. It will do this through a consideration of two main case studies: firstly the folk industry conferences (drawing on examination of the 2007, 2008 and 2009 conferences), and secondly the new folk club the Magpie's Nest. A further development of some of the ideas explored in this chapter and an account of the folk festival as a significant site for the operation of the folk industry can be found elsewhere (Keegan-Phipps and Winter, forthcoming).

2.1 Historical contexts

Whilst the notion of a folk industry has become crystallised and explicitly mobilised within the recent resurgence, it would be wrong to suggest that the folk arts have previously existed as genres unaffected by – or totally separate from – commerce, or economic considerations. Its relations with capital-driven processes and structures have been numerous throughout the twentieth century, albeit often uneasy and complex. We therefore begin this chapter with a brief discussion of English folk as both resistant to and complicit in economic activity during the two revival periods of the last two centuries, in order to more clearly evaluate and understand the development of a folk industry in more recent times.[1]

A central mission of the first folk revival was the discovery and recovery of the cultural expressions of an idealised rural underclass. The movement can be seen as an attempt by the educated elite to counter two developments within their society. On the one hand, concerns were strongly held by revivalists that the orchestral and chamber music of other European nations (in particular, German Romanticism) were disproportionately influential in instructing the works of British art music composers. On the other, they sought to oppose the apparently pervasive presence of music hall, described by Storey as the 'supposedly degraded culture of the urban working class' (Storey, 2003: 11) . Most significant for our understanding of folk's relationship to economy is the latter of these two things: the idea of degradation referred to by Storey was indexical of a mass-consumer market. It was believed that mass production and commercial motivations necessarily precluded artistic quality. This point was made clearest by C. Hubert H. Parry in his inaugural address of 1899 in the *Journal of the Folk Song Society*, which characterised 'modern popular music as 'made with commercial intention out of snippets of musical slang' (Parry, quoted in *Ibid.*).

This is not to say that an opposition to commercialism within the arts was the – or even one – central objective for the revival. For the most part, disdain for capitalist motivation was implied – embedded within a discourse centred more explicitly on a socially conscientious philanthropy:

> The revival of our national folk music is … part of a great national revival, a going back from the town to the country, a reaction against all that is demoralising in city life. It is a re-awakening of that part of our national consciousness which makes for wholeness, saneness and healthy merriment. (Mary Neal, quoted in Gammon, 1980: 81)

The reuniting of the English with their lost musical inheritance was a strategy designed to result in cultural enrichment and, ultimately, patriotic sentiment.

> Please allow us to teach the children to know and to love what we believe to be the natural and spontaneous music of our ancestors. Then we may hope (with Mr. Cecil Sharp) to have in the future Griegs and Glinkas of our own to do for English music what these patriotic musicians did for the music of their own countries. (J. Heywood, quoted in Francmanis, 2002: 13)

Heywood's statement is a useful summary of the two main operational objectives of the first revival movement: firstly, the embedding of folk song, music and
dance in schools, as promoted by Cecil Sharp; and secondly, the incorporation
of folk music material within a self-consciously English body of art music, as
undertaken by composers such as Ralph Vaughan-Williams, C. Hubert H.
Parry and George Butterworth. In the case of both practices, justification was
expressed in terms of a discourse which consciously distanced the movement's
protagonists from economic motivations and emphasised instead the ultimate
aim of a national identity and patriotic pride. Whilst the over-riding strategic
aims of the movement sought to benefit the nation at large by enabling its self-
discovery, these practical endeavours involved unavoidable financial considerations. The materials produced through the revivalist's activities (e.g. song
books, commissioned compositions, performances, etc.) were saleable items
enabling income generation for the cause, whilst Sharp's civil list pension was
an indication that his service to society had an economically expressible value.

The politics and ideology of the second revival period differed considerably
from those of the first. The predominating socialist agenda of the new movement
reconstructed the folk arts as the expressions of 'the people' in a proletarian sense
– workers, both agricultural and industrial, rural and urban. The Marxist politics
underpinning much of the movement was openly expressed by exponents such as
A. L. Lloyd and Ewan MacColl, and this approach positioned folk as an alternative
to the capitalism of the steadily developing popular music industry. This ethos
was embodied in the immediacy of presentation and the social narratives of the
songs themselves, but also in new circuits of distribution – the folk clubs – which
celebrated amateur participation (see MacKinnon, 1993: 33–41). Despite this
anti-commercial ethos, however, folk music was engaged in various ways with
the marketplace during this period. For example, the folk clubs, whilst imbued
with an ethos that took an oppositional stance towards the professionalisation
and commercialisation of music, developed at the same time as a circuit for
the professional performance of folk music, as paid guest artists were booked
to perform alongside the clubs' amateur floor singers.[2] In the realm of recorded
music, the independent label Topic Records rose from the 1950s onwards to
become a significant producer of recorded folk music and inevitably had to
reckon with its position within the music marketplace. Brocken, describing
Topic as 'realistic, albeit reluctant capitalists' (2003: 43), captures something of
its ambiguity in this respect. In this period, English folk music also entered the
popular music marketplace through its hybridisation with popular music. The
folk-rock and electric folk of this period achieved some commercial success that
reached a peak, argues Sweers, between 1972 and 1975 with Steeleye Span's chart
successes.[3]

Throughout the first and second revival periods, then, the ethos of English
folk largely construed it as an alternative to commercialised popular musics. As
such, it was characterised as more authentic, either in terms of Englishness or as
an authentic expression of the people. At the same time, English folk music did

engage with commerce throughout these periods and become, in some ways and to various extents, professionalised. (We should note, however, that, at this stage, English folk dance resolutely maintained its amateurism.) These tendencies can be traced into the contemporary folk industry.

2.2 The web of the folk industry

A more detailed consideration of the folk industry conferences mentioned above can help us to map the web of discourses and infrastructures that collide in the contemporary concept of a folk industry. The 2007 conference, for example, offered a number of thematic strands that illuminate the many dimensions of the burgeoning folk industry. These included 'Fundraising for Folk', 'Folk in Education' and 'Publicity, Marketing, Media and Promotion' (FolkArts England, 2007: 4).

2.2.1 Fundraising for folk: philanthropy

Led by professional fundraising experts, the Fundraising for Folk workshops offered a guide to funding opportunities such as sponsorship, trusts and foundations, and public-sector and individual donations. The presence of this strand within the folk industry conference recognises that many folk arts activities are reliant on public or charitable backing. By taking part in this training, conference participants were invited to adopt a professional approach to fundraising, comparable to that of other arts organisations (Arts Council England, Southwark Council, and Birds Eye View Film Festival, for example, are all named as clients of the trainers). This aligns folk with other art forms deemed worthy of public or charitable subsidy and highlights the philanthropic motivations and discourses that underpin such activities. Folk is thus characterised here as a worthwhile part of the national culture and deserving of philanthropic support.

Commonly circulated discourses within the culture of English folk during the period of our research fieldwork often highlighted a perceived lack of government support for folk arts designating themselves as English, especially in comparison with that claimed to be afforded to other cultural groups within multicultural Britain (see 6.2.4 for further discussions of this discourse). It is noteworthy, however, that in 2009, following a period of research and consultation and seemingly in response to the burgeoning folk resurgence, the major public funding body Arts Council England announced a future investment policy for supporting the growth of English folk music and dance. One aspect of this was the allocation of new funding to the English Folk Dance and Song Society to enable it to become a national development agency for folk music. Another aspect was the support given to projects designed to showcase the products of the contemporary English folk music scene in national and international music marketplaces. These included the showcase CD *Looking for a New England* (2009) produced with and distributed by *fRoots* magazine, the profiling of the *Looking for a New England* acts at the Arts Council's British Music at Womex Showcase, and a subsequent showcase of English folk music artists at the 2010 South by Southwest Music and Media Conference in Austin, Texas. Significantly, these activities highlight the integration of public subsidy, philanthropy and commercial interests, as they saw Arts Council England working in partnership with the membership organisation the EFDSS and commercial organisations *fRoots* magazine and the agency British Underground. Similarly, support given to English folk dance through the project 5000 Morris Dancers at the Southbank Centre, London (2010), involved Arts Council England, *fRoots* and the EFDSS and was professionally produced by Terry O'Brien of Playpen, a live music booking and artist management agency.

2.2.2 Folk in education

A further strand within the folk industry conferences focused on folk in education and included sessions on, for example, curriculum issues and the development of folk activity in schools. Not only did this strand underline the great importance of educational institutions as a source of employment for professional and semi-professional folk artists, but its language also highlighted an enduring discourse that views education as a prime site for a philanthropic encouragement of interest in tradition. A session on folk dance led by Laurel Swift, for example, offered to ask the question 'Where's the respect our traditions need and deserve?' (FolkArts England, 2007: 8). Another session, led by Lauren McCormick, explored 'the issues involved in encouraging a new wave of singers' (*Ibid.*). This echoes the focus of the first revival period on the embedding of folk arts in schools. Within the contemporary period of folk resurgence, activities focusing on learning, participation and the nurturing of a new generation of folk artists have been both significant and closely tied to the emerging folk industry. For example, the ubiquitous holding of 'workshops', in which both child and adult participants are able to study with professional performers, both provides opportunities for learning and furnishes those performers with an income stream and a chance to nurture a fan base and audience (Keegan-Phipps, 2008: 148).

Integral to this contemporary period of folk resurgence have been various moves towards the educational institutionalisation of folk music in England.[4] Of particular note is the growth of the folk development agency Folkworks. Established in 1988 in the North East of England, Folkworks grew to become an influential and high-profile agency for the development of folk music and, to a lesser extent, dance. A partner in the development of a prestigious new music centre in the North East of England – The Sage Gateshead – the organisation became integrated into the management structure of The Sage, and the Folkworks programme now operates from its landmark building on the banks of the river Tyne, a cultural centre of regional, national and international significance. Folkworks' educational activities include workshops, weekly classes, weekend courses and summer schools targeting both children and adults, as well as a young people's folk orchestra, Folkestra. From its northeastern base, its influence on the development of a new generation of folk performers has been evident throughout England and more widely within Britain.

One key development in particular has fed into the educational institution-alisation of folk music in England: the establishment in 2001 of an undergraduate BMus degree in Folk and Traditional Music, hailed as the first such degree in England. A joint initiative between Folkworks and the International Centre for Music Studies (ICMuS) at Newcastle University, and known to many (and henceforth here) as 'the folk degree', this four-year course offers a higher-education opportunity for folk and traditional musicians, with a central emphasis on performance. Tuition is given not only by ICMuS academic staff and Folkworks personnel but also by professional musicians, many of whom have a high profile in the industry. The course can be regarded as a potential launch pad for a career in professional folk music. Throughout the degree, students are given tuition in all aspects of a 'folk career', including arts administration, as well as opportunities to perform in professional contexts, such as showcase concerts within the programme of The Sage. Many groups and bands formed during their members' time on the degree course have gone on to perform professionally, and the degree course also facilitates social and musical access to high-profile folk performers that can help students to enter the folk industry as professionals. For example, multi-instrumentalist Ian Stephenson performed professionally during his time as an undergraduate, including as a member of the Kathryn Tickell Band. Tickell, probably the best-known contemporary Northumbrian smallpiper, was one of the foremost lecturers on the folk degree and has been the artistic director of Folkworks since 2009. The integration of folk degree and folk industry was illustrated at the 2009 Folk Industry and AFO Conference, where the promotional packs handed out to delegates included a free CD, *Folk Degree Sampler 2009*, showcasing a number of undergraduate performers (Newcastle University, 2009) and a two-track single previewing a band made up of folk degree students (SpinnDrift, 2009). Folkworks and folk degree-nurtured talent was profiled in busking spots provided at the conference for new performers to showcase their talents before the many promoters and festival organisers present. Alistair Anderson (co-founder of Folkworks and its artistic director until 2008), was also present at the conference. This is indicative of a growing infrastructure that prepares and presents folk-degree undergraduates for careers in the folk industry and, at the same time, supports the emerging industry's thirst for new, young performers – performers whose growing profile in turn acts as an advertisement for the educational institution through which they have achieved their considerable technical expertise and performance experience.

2.2.3. Publicity, marketing and promotion

The aspects of the folk industry discussed above coexisted in the 2007 folk industry conference with another, entitled 'publicity, marketing, media and promotion' (*Ibid*: 10). Here the sessions focused on topics such as: 'eMarketing success'; 'Using the internet to gain access to a young audience'; 'Broadcast media: new opportunities in a new climate?'; 'Developing a marketing strategy'; 'How to make the most of album sales: distribution in the 21st century'; 'Promoting folk in mainstream venues'; and 'Marketing artists'. These sessions were delivered by professionals from the music industry, broadcast and print media (including the BBC) and concert venues. We will focus here on publicity, marketing and promotion, before examining media issues more broadly in 2.2.4.

A notable feature of the resurgence in English folk has been the engagement of professional artists, particularly many younger artists (in their twenties and thirties), with music industry professionals in public relations and marketing. For example, promotional images have moved closer to those associated with the mainstream music business. Terry O'Brien of Playpen notes that when she moved from the mainstream music business to work with the young folk artist Jim Moray in 2002, professional artist management was very unusual in the folk world. Moray's album *Sweet England* (2003) was not only critically successful but also representative of a new, more professionalised, approach to the marketing of English folk music.

> The planning and approach to the album release, from an unsigned artist and their manager (I spent much of that year explaining the difference between agents and managers, which I certainly do less of these days) was also something new. [...] *Sweet England* also caused a real shift in the presentation of packaged folk music. Photography and artwork was created by David & David – their first project involving folk music. The imagery was imaginative, contemporary in many ways and of a standard more associated with mainstream music than folk. One look at the album sleeves for younger folk artists in the years that immediately followed showed that this album had raised the bar. (Terry O'Brien, Pers. Comm.)

Musicians Jon Boden and Tim Van Eyken both also identified David Angel's work on *Sweet England* as a significant moment for a shift in the imaging of folk. Van Eyken, for example, observed that prior to *Sweet England*, folkies had been unwilling to 'outsource', to go outside the boundaries of the folk world in search of professional expertise (Tim Van Eyken, interview, 2008). Boden notes that 'David Angel doing [Jim Moray's] ... photos and artwork has totally revolutionised the kind of quality of artwork in the folk scene' (Jon Boden, interview, 2008).

O'Brien observes that by 2010 she no longer needed to keep explaining to people the difference between an agent and a manager – suggesting that mainstream industry approaches were by that point more common and accepted within folk music culture – and Playpen was providing representation for a number of English folk professionals such as Jackie Oates, Sam Carter, Belshazzar's Feast, Spiers and Boden, Lisa Knapp, the Young Coppers, and the folk-themed visual artist David Owen. The presence of Playpen and other booking agents and artists' managers at the Folk Industry/AFO conference in 2009, including showcase concerts where their acts were profiled for festival bookers, illustrates the extent to which the programming of folk acts at festivals had become increasingly reliant on an infrastructure of professional agents and managers.

There are still exceptions, who persist in the 'do-it-yourself' approach formerly more characteristic of folk bands. One young band that successfully engages with the folk industry without using a professional agent or manager is the Essex band

Mawkin. Band member Dave Delarre noted that:

> [Alex] Goldsmith [a fellow band member] was at university at Buckinghamshire
> Chilterns [University College], doing music industry management, which
> was really helpful, because everything he'd learnt about contractual laws and
> negotiations, and how to deal with agents, and PR people, and marketing …
> everything, all of that kind of stuff that folkies don't know about, he kind of
> passed on to me … And then I … put it into practice with the admin side of
> things. (Dave Delarre, interview, 2008)

Delarre indicates, then, that despite an enduring sense that industry
knowledge is 'the kind of stuff that folkies don't know about', his band's do-it-
yourself approach relies nevertheless on a high level of industry expertise.

2.2.4 Media

At each of the Folk Industry conferences, a number of sessions were given over to
discussions of aspects of the media. Broadcast television and radio, print media,
technologies such as viral marketing and social networking sites were all being
discussed as ways of promoting folk. This highlights something of the place and
the significance of the media for the emergent folk industry in England. There
had by 2010 been a significant rise in the number of references to folk within
mainstream print, broadcast and online media, and many of our interviewees
pointed to the growth of media interest in folk as both reflecting and contributing
to this latest folk resurgence. 'The media' is, of course, neither monolithic nor
clearly segmented, but made up of institutions and platforms whose boundaries
are increasingly ambiguous and permeable, and whose impacts are increasingly
interrelated. Nonetheless, in keeping with an emic perspective on this element of
the folk resurgence, we will have recourse (as do the folk industry conferences)
to a conventional categorisation of media as we consider the place of television,
online media and radio in the consolidation of the emerging folk industry.

The televisual visibility of English folk has increased since 2000, with folk music
and dance becoming a more frequently featured part of cultural programming.
This is particularly the case for the BBC, where folk music regularly appears in a
variety of contexts, from arts programmes such as *The Culture Show* and the *BBC
Proms* to popular music shows like *Later with Jools Holland*. Whilst folk has been
less visible on commercial channels there are some notable exceptions, such as a
series of documentaries about English folk artists commissioned by Five Culture
(a partnership between Arts Council England and Channel 5, a commercial
terrestrial television channel). This series, which profiled a number of folk performers in England, has sometimes been invoked as a seminal moment in the
folk resurgence, both indicative of and contributing to a growing cultural interest
in folk. For example, Steve Heap (FolkArts England and General Secretary of the
AFO) spoke of his experience of the series' conception, as follows:

> Now, for twenty odd years, I've been in and out of radio and television studios,
> and media, saying 'folk music' … usually with a small 'f' and, in the earlier days,

quietly. And they've laughed and giggled and said, 'Morris dancers, and silly old men with beards and beer bellies'. At [a] meeting [...] less than a year ago, twelve top professional television people sat around a table, and discussed folk music at length, very seriously, and nobody laughed and nobody giggled, and nobody laughed about morris men – and they were discussed – and nobody said 'beer bellies', and ... that's a resurgence. That's people who previously didn't quite know what it was, taking it seriously. And understanding the potential. Some people only understand the commercial potential; other people can see the artistic potential; some can see the heritage potential, the community potential ... It's got lots of different branches to it, and more and more people are recognising it ... That's a resurgence. (Steve Heap, interview, 2008)

Television appearances not only circulate representations of folk music and dance widely but also have an impact on the size and broadening of audiences for events. Folk artists understand this. For example, a morris dance-based stage show, *On English Ground* was featured on *The Culture Show* (BBC) on 6 April 2006 (discussed in more detail in 3.7.3). The show's director Laurel Swift notes:

'And Sunday at Farnham ... all 200 of the flat-seating tickets he'd sold since the *Culture Show* appearance ... And the people we spoke to were all saying, 'Oh yeah, I came cos I saw it on the telly'. That was a lot of non-folkies and just random crowds. And I mean, it was great to be on the *Culture Show*, and it was great that we did it and they paid us in the end because I argued till I was blue in the face that it's not going to have much benefit for us as a promotional tool because it needs to go out in time before the gigs. And they were like, 'Telly doesn't make that much difference', and I'm like, 'You don't understand how little folk music's on telly'. And it totally showed – people do watch it. (Laurel Swift, interview, 2008)

Swift very clearly sees the value of the television feature as a potential promotional, ticket-selling tool. Similarly, Damien Barber speaks of the importance of being featured in the media, arguing, for example, that his media appearances have made his teaching work in schools easier to promote:

With the sword dancing ... I never used to have anything to show a school, apart from home video! Now I go into a school, and I set up a DVD, and I say, 'Right, this is what we do, this is when we were on telly at the BBC4 Folk Awards' – you know, 'Noddy Holder sat in the audience', or whatever – and 'This is when we did the thing with Paul O'Grady'. And it *means* something to those people, then. So instead of them saying, 'Oh, well, it's a bit folky, innit?', they go, 'Wow, that's really cool!', or whatever. (Damien Barber, interview, 2008)

The media appearances, then, allow Barber to assert the cultural currency of his sword-dancing activity: it 'means something' to people because it has been featured on television. The appearances are also mobilised as a sign of Barber's increasing professionalism, with the move from 'home video' to professional media product.

The significance of online media for the developing folk industry is underlined by the presence of conference sessions on email and viral marketing, internet radio, and the use of social media sites such as Facebook and MySpace. The spread and availability of online media apparently serve to democratise musicians' access to markets for their music. The networking site MySpace in particular was colonised by folk musicians at the turn of the twenty-first century as a place for putting band profiles and music downloads and for networking, all without a significant financial investment. However, such an online presence does not necessarily lead to music sales or a broadening of the market for folk music beyond its established audience, and our research interviews suggest that its main use has been as a billboard for posting information sought by promoters and existing audiences. In interview, musicians were most likely to point to live events as the most important way that new audiences discover folk music, whether through coming across it at a mainstream music event or through being introduced to it by folkie friends. Whether or not these narratives can be evidenced, it is clear that the social act of live audience membership is still privileged in discourse within the cultures of English folk.

It is generally accepted within the folk scene that commercial success with album sales requires engagement with professional distribution companies. The most significant of these for folk and traditional music in the UK is Proper Distribution. There has been some democratisation of access to these distribution channels. For example, a package, Proper Access, offered by Proper Distribution, allows for the distribution of relatively small quantities of CDs by small labels and unsigned artists who are 'just starting out' (Proper Distribution, 2010). In a similar way, the services provided by the American online retailer CD Baby are used by many folk artists as a do-it-yourself mode of distribution that gives them access to wider sales than they could achieve independently. Such democratised opportunities for self-distribution and promotion are underpinned by a discursive support for the 'little people' (i.e. new and unsigned bands overlooked by the big record labels), a discourse that is characteristic of (although not restricted to) the ethos of folk. At the same time, it might be read as realigning folk music with the economy of the larger music business, in which musicians need to invest both time and money in building their profile and popularity in order that the industry can assess their economic potential.

English folk music's strongest link with the broadcast media probably comes through its longstanding relationship with BBC Radio 2, the most listened-to radio station in the UK. Since its birth in 1967 the station has been the only provider of regular national radio broadcasts devoted to folk music, with its flag-ship 'folk and acoustic' programme, *The Mike Harding Show*. The institutional integration of media into the folk industry is illustrated in the involvement of the BBC in two of the largest folk festivals in England: the Sidmouth International Festival and the Cambridge Folk Festival. During the period of its sponsorship of the Radio 2 concert stage Ham Marquee at the Sidmouth International Festival from 1998 to 2004, performances were recorded by the BBC and broadcast on the *Mike Harding Show* (Schofield, 2005: 191). Similarly, the station has been title sponsor and, since 2009, principal media partner of the Cambridge Folk

Festival, for which it has had exclusive rights to recording and broadcasting from the festival, and where a media enclosure adjacent to the main stage serves as the base for live broadcasts.

Another phenomenon that demonstrates the integration of media into the web of the folk industry is competition: a competition culture has developed since 2000 around the BBC Radio 2 Folk Awards.[5] Covering a range of categories including 'Folk Singer of the Year', 'Best Traditional Track', 'Best Duo', 'Best Album', and 'Best Live Act', the awards are judged by a panel of experts in the field of folk and traditional music. Significantly, the awards reward both the social performance of folk (Folk Singer of the Year; Best Live Act; Folk Club Award) and the commodified folk recording (Best Traditional Track; Album of the Year). Highly regarded amongst programmers, artists and audiences, award nominations are displayed in bands' and artists' promotional materials, and guarantee both media exposure and bookings. The awards therefore play an important role in the professionalisation and marketing of folk music, as well as consolidating the links between folk and the BBC – a publicly funded institution. The Folk Awards competition demonstrates, then, the way that an increasingly commercialised folk industry also maintains a socially conscientious ethos through its reliance on a state-sanctioned institution with a culturally philanthropic brief.

Another competition, the BBC Radio 2 Young Folk Award, represents the bringing together of competition and industry celebration with educational institutionalisation. From its start in 1998 until 2005, much of the competition's organisation and its semi-final judging was conducted by Folkworks. The links between this competition and the folk industry are explicit, in that the prizes have included recording and performance opportunities – a recording session for broadcast on the *Mike Harding Show*, and performance bookings at the Sidmouth International and Towersey Village Festivals (two of England's largest folk festivals). Appearances on the judging panel of promoters such as Steve Heap and radio producer John Leonard (director of Smooth Operations, producers of the *Mike Harding Show*) illustrate that the judging criteria are likely to be informed by a sense of the saleability of the musical products being considered.

We have shown, then, how the Folk Industry Conferences bring together various strands from the web of the contemporary folk industry, where philanthropic and educational discourses intersect with growing professionalisation, commercialisation and integration of the media. The lists of delegates at the conferences also indicate the extent to which these have been a coming together of people associated with the various different strands of the folk industry, from professional promoters, managers, distributors and festival organisers to media professionals, managers of large and small events, folk artists and development workers. The coexistence and interrelation of these various strands are perhaps captured in the use of the expression 'folk activists' as a catch-all term for the various festival organisers, agents, artists, promoters, and music-industry and media folk present at the conferences – a term that imbues this whole range of industry personnel with an idea of 'activism' that recalls the more explicitly politically radical folk ethos of the second revival period.

2.3 The new folk club: the Magpie's Nest

At the BBC Radio 2 Folk Awards in 2010 the award for Folk Club of the Year went to the Magpie's Nest, a club in Islington, London, started by Sam Lee and Joe Buirski. In a context where, as noted in the introduction, the folk clubs that were so central to the second revival period had been experiencing waning numbers and an ageing demographic, the Magpie's Nest had been attracting attention as a new folk club, run by a new generation of folkies, that was in some ways reinvigorating the concept of the folk club for a new generation of Londoners. The Magpie's Nest demonstrates a convergence of folk ethos with new attitudes towards professionalisation and commercialisation.

The club was started in 2006 by Lee and Buirski, 'born in reaction to London's complete lack of places to see and hear good folk music in a contemporary environment with a crowd as young as it is old' (The Nest Collective, 2012). Lee had come from an art background, saying he knew nothing of the folk world beforehand (Sam Lee, interview, 2008). The venue, The Old Queen's Head, on Essex Road, Islington, was a pub being run by former nightclub operators who had since moved into gastro pubs and other venues around London. Through a personal contact, Lee and Buirski approached them with the idea: 'When we started they were, like, *folk*? [...] It was, you know, well alright because we've got Wednesday nights free but if football comes on you're out' (*Ibid*. Emphasis in original). The club was immediately successful and the owners liked it: 'suddenly we were bringing in a totally new audience from the area and all over London were coming for it. And they couldn't believe it' (*Ibid.*). Since then, Lee continues, 'we've become their biggest selling midweek night' (*Ibid.*). This indicates a commercial imperative underlying the establishment of the club. Even though the Magpie's Nest itself was not started primarily as a commercial enterprise, it was in no small part because of its success in commercial terms, bringing in a new audience, that it found its home. In fact, Lee notes, 'now they've started getting other people doing "acoustic folk nights" in there' (*Ibid.*).

It is also possible to see the club as taking advantage of a gap in the market for musical experiences in London. Existing folk clubs, with their ageing demographic and established populations, could sometimes feel inaccessible or daunting to new or younger people, despite their ethos of inclusivity. Lee saw the need for what he called a 'young person's environment' that would still capture the ethos of a 'real folk club' (*Ibid.*). With its banner of 'New Folk Old Folk No Folk', the Magpie's Nest offered an eclectic mix of music and a welcoming atmosphere to folk initiates and non-initiates alike.[6] A particular attention to the creation of the club's atmosphere was clearly evident at a visit to the Magpie's Nest in 2008. Ascending from the crowded Islington bar to an upstairs room, the staircase was lit with twinkling tea lights, and the club's room itself had been decorated with bunting and furnished with sofas. Lee and the other organisers were greeting people, and the atmosphere felt comfortable, welcoming and friendly. This decoration of the building and overt attempt to be welcoming is significant, because it underlines the recognition of the quality of experience that is being offered to the audience of the folk club. In a historical moment that has been characterised in terms of the 'experience economy' (Pine and Gilmore, 1999), the Magpie's Nest recognises well the need to provide an enjoyable and novel experience for its audiences:

> We specialize in creating exciting spaces and environments that let the power of this indigenous music shine through letting our audience be part of that experience and not just its consumer. (The Nest Collective, 2012)

This statement is interesting in that it asserts that its folk audiences are not 'just' consumers, but, we would argue, it implies too that they are *also* consumers, a notion that would be antithetical to the anti-commercial ethos of the second revival folk clubs. The success of the Magpie's Nest meant that Lee and Buirski's activities soon began to expand beyond the club in Islington. They had been building contacts and knowledge of the folk scene that enabled them to develop several different strands of activity including consulting on folk programming for festivals. They were taken on as 'folk developers' by Continental Drift – event producers operating a scheme funded by the Arts Council and the EFDSS at festivals such as Glastonbury – and they branched out into music promotion at other venues. In other words, they were soon engaged in several different commercial facets of the folk (and wider music) industry. By 2012 the Magpie's Nest had expanded to the point where it had outgrown its original concept and developed into two new organisations, with Lee forming 'The Nest Collective' and Buirski 'Two For Joy', and covering a range of music promotion activities, including and beyond the continuation of the original club (The Magpie's Nest, 2012). This development appears to usher in a new phase of professionalisation as Lee's Nest Collective lists a team of ten people with professional titles including Administration and Events Manager, Marketing Manager, Administrator and Funding, Camera Man, and Website Producer.

Speaking of the springing up of other 'acoustic folk nights' at the Queen's Head, Lee commented: 'I don't think any night quite has the sort of real folk element to it' (*Ibid.*). The Magpie's Nest is firmly rooted in the idea of this 'real folk element', emphasising some key aspects of the folk ethos embodied by the clubs of the second revival period. For example, the professionalised management structure alluded to above is framed within the construct of a 'collective', thus drawing on the non-hierarchical ethos of folk (see also the use of the term 'collective' discussed in 3.7.1). Key to this ethos is the notion of inclusivity, and a lack of rigid separation between performer and audience. The club nights always have an extensive 'open mic' session, in which audience members take the stage, a version of the 'floor spots' offered by folk clubs, and a practice that blurs the boundary between performer and audience. For Lee,

> the wonderful thing about ... folk clubs is the way that audience–performer relationship is very ambiguous, and the accessibility of the music is enhanced by that and just the atmosphere is right upon that. And I think it's really important because the reason I'm in the music – much [though] I love the music – is because of the social aspect to it. (Sam Lee, interview, 2008)

Hence, Lee speaks of his disapproval of the practice of musicians approaching the club merely as a platform to perform. Such musicians might perform a floor spot, hand over a promotional CD and then leave for another floor spot somewhere else in London rather than participating in the rest of the evening. Misunderstanding the Magpie's Nest as purely another venue for performance does not acknowledge the participatory aspects of its folk ethos:

> We're not just there to give a platform to people. It's about participation, everyone being part of the night. (*Ibid.*)

The emphasis on the social aspect of the folk ethos was, finally, demonstrated on our 2008 visit to the club, when the final parts of the evening developed into a spontaneously organised ceilidh dance.

The Nest Collective, successor to the Magpie's Nest, describes itself as follows:

> The Nest Collective prides itself in being a hub where both established stalwarts of the tradition, youthful successors and new challengers to the throne of folk meet and make merry. (*Ibid.*)

The success of the Magpie's Nest perhaps resides in its ability to bring together audiences, musics and discourses in a site where professionalisation coexists happily together with folk ethos.

2.4 The uneven grip of the folk industry

We have been highlighting the relatively comfortable coexistence of commercialism and folk ethos within the developing folk industry. This has been a significant trend within the cultures of folk music and dance in England, but we should note that it is not all-encompassing. For some individuals and events, the folk ethos is privileged over, or expressed in opposition to, the move towards commercialisation represented by the folk industry. This is particularly the case within cultures of English folk dance. With some relatively high-profile exceptions that will be examined in 3.5 and 3.7.3, the participatory culture of the various variants of morris, clog and sword dance continues largely to be underpinned by principles of amateurism and populated by non-commercial and do-it-yourself events. And alongside the relatively high-profile shift exemplified by the Magpie's Nest, the majority of folk clubs with their roots in the second revival period operate mostly unchanged as non-profit-making organisations run by enthusiasts, albeit maintaining a circuit that sustains many professional and semi-professional folk music acts. Festivals, rather than the existing folk clubs, have been a central site for the growth of the folk industry, as we have argued elsewhere (Keegan-Phipps and Winter, forthcoming). Some folk festivals do still remain, however, firmly at the 'anti-commercial' end of the folk spectrum, foregrounding the inclusive spirit of the folk ethos. Whitby Folk Week, for example, does not advertise headlining acts, in the manner of a commercial festival, but presents its guest list in alphabetical order, where known and unknown artists, professional and amateur, are listed alongside each other. England's folk culture also continues to be populated with participatory events that are not run for profit, in which nobody is paid and where the participants may pay a small fee to cover the costs of venue or camping. Durham Folk Party is an example of such an event. There is, of course, no binary distinction to be made between 'commercial' and 'non-commercial' events: pubs may host participatory singarounds or music sessions, for example, because of the additional trade that they bring, even if no money changes hands for venue hire or admission. Folk cultures exist along a spectrum in which discourses and processes of professionalisation and commercialisation interact at different levels and in different ways with the folk ethos. There is also considerable synergy, overlap and movement between events in different parts of the folk spectrum. For example, media-savvy professional folk artists may perform and participate at long-established folk clubs and less commercial festivals or dance out with morris sides as well as headlining at Cambridge, Towersey or Sidmouth. Whilst its diffusion through the folk scene is uneven, the growing folk industry has nevertheless been an inescapable and significant part of the resurgence of English folk.

2.5 Conclusion

The two case studies presented here, the folk industry conferences and the Magpie's Nest, both draw together the celebration of a developing folk industry with the powerful 'more-important-than-money' discourses of the folk ethos. On the one hand, the professionalisation of folk products and the commercial-isation of participation has seen folk music, for example, operating within structures more commonly associated with popular music. On the other, dis-courses and practices remain that maintain a central 'folk' identity. A valued sense of authenticity is retained through certain vital processes: the folk ethos is consolidated, for example, through an emphasis on inclusive participation that mitigates potential concerns about the 'selling out' of professionalisation, or the 'artifice' of media representation. Folk's underlying principles of amateurism, philanthropy, participation and non-commercialism continue to be asserted and it continues to be offered as a counterpart and an antidote to the perceived commercialisation of contemporary popular culture.

The extent to which commercialisation and professionalisation are reconciled with folk ethos can sometimes be striking. Where this happens, profession-alisation tends to be characterised as a means to a culturally valuable end, that of being 'taken seriously' by a mainstream music oriented media (and thus the wider society). Where the commercialisation of folk is celebrated, that is often done as an indication of success in the pursuit of cultural credibility and popularity for the folk arts. The resurgence is taking place within a cultural context where professionalisation and industrialisation are experienced as the natural order, and where attempts to reject that order would not only undermine the success of English folk music but actually erode its claims of authenticity or legitimacy as a popular movement.

The increasing commercialism within England's folk culture is one manifestation – and, simultaneously, one active vehicle – of a cultural identity in flux: it speaks to larger issues currently under negotiation within English folk music and dance – concerns for engagement with the contemporary, the urban, the 'real' and the progressive. These concerns will be examined in the following chapters of this book.

Notes

1 This is not intended as a comprehensive discussion of the two multifaceted periods of revival; for more detailed historical accounts, see: Boyes (1993), Brocken (2003), Harker (1985), MacKinnon (1993) and Sweers (2005).

2 See MacKinnon (1992: 70–6) for an account of the rise of the folk professional in the second revival period.

3 See Sweers (2005) and Burns (2012), for detailed consideration of the electric folk and folk-rock of this period.

4 See, for example, Keegan-Phipps (2007; 2008); Keegan-Phipps and Winter (forthcoming). For a broader discussion on the educational institutionalisation of traditional musics, see Hill (2009).

5 The Norwegian fiddling contests examined by Goertzen (1997) are an interesting case for comparison with the competitions discussed here.

6 In fact, despite Lee's discursive emphasis here on 'young' audiences, he also notes that the audiences for the Magpie's Nest include a wide demographic, including people in their forties to sixties who were new to folk.

3

The mainstreaming of English folk

The previous chapter explored some of the complexities of the relationship between English folk culture, its over-riding discourses and the professionalised industry with which it has become increasingly engaged. We have shown how many artists and participants have become more closely involved with commercial structures whilst folk culture simultaneously continues to present itself in opposition to capitalist motivations. This chapter will focus more closely on the creative outputs of the contemporary English folk resurgence. Specifically, it looks at folk artists' growing engagements with the cultural mainstream and will examine the extraordinarily wide variety of ways in which English folk music and dance is thus being represented, redeveloped and reinvented.

After a discussion of the idea of the 'mainstream', the chapter moves to an analysis of four case studies which exhibit different kinds of engagements of English folk with popular music or dance – the acoustic pop of Seth Lakeman, the electric folk of Jim Moray, the English ceilidh dance music scene, and the Demon Barber Roadshow's fusion of traditional dance with contemporary street dance. It offers a short examination of the referencing of historical popular cultures by acts such as Bellowhead and Jim Moray, before moving on to consider art-orientated folk music and dance in the output of four closely related acts – Chris Wood, the English Acoustic Collective, Methera and Morris Offspring. It will argue that the developing artistic engagement with multiple mainstream genres can be read as an assertion and an exploration of folk as a contemporary, popular and valuable phenomenon.

3.1 The idea of the 'mainstream'

> If folk has really gone mainstream in recent years, there can be no greater symbol than its increasing regular appearance in venues better known for their orchestras or rock and pop. (FolkArts England, 2007: 13)

At the 'Publicity, marketing, media and promotion' session in the 2007 Folk Industry Focus Days (see 2.2) representatives from two venues (Loughborough Town Hall and De Montfort Hall, Leicester) took part in a presentation to folk activists under the heading 'Promoting Folk in Mainstream Venues'. The idea that folk is 'going mainstream', expressed in the above quotation from the conference brochure, has circulated both within the folk scene and more widely. This conference session offered advice for promoters and artists in handling the transition of music from folk scene to mainstream context. Inherent in the notion of going mainstream is, of course, the distinction between the concepts of folk and mainstream culture (a gap that the session in question was designed to bridge). This distinction, as we have already discussed (see 1.2), has historically been fundamental to the definition of folk. Whilst the term 'mainstream' is used frequently in common parlance and is particularly prominent in discussions of the current resurgence in English folk, it is rarely examined as an idea. It is therefore appropriate that we take a moment to discuss what is meant by the word in this field, and in this book. [1]

In its common usage among our informants the idea of going mainstream is perhaps most closely synonymous with achieving greater public visibility to (and, implicitly, popularity with) audiences beyond the pre-existing boundaries of folk culture. It is generally used to characterise the kinds of folk industry processes discussed in Chapter 2, including engagements with institutions and processes of mediated popular culture, as well as others such as education and competition. Academic constructs of 'mainstream culture' are very often indirect – the secondary focus of engagements with particular sub- or counter-cultures. The appearance of the term in such contexts is, in fact, indicative of its synonymy with a notion of a dominant culture in line with a Gramscian hegemonic order.[2] As Pillai has pointed out, the model of 'mainstream/margin' is central to the idea of a hegemonic culture (1996: 68). So the construct of a mainstream plays a central role in, for example, the assertion of a music's sub- or counter-cultural identity, whether that be within academic writing or within the grassroots discourses around the genre with which it is being contrasted.[3]

To examine further the idea of the mainstreaming of folk, let us focus for a moment on the example of the 'mainstream venue' given above. The extract from the conference brochure cited earlier illustrates the generic expectations of mainstream venues, 'better known for their orchestras or rock and pop' (FolkArts England, 2007). The genre-led marketisation of performed music has resulted in such levels of categorical specificity as to ensure that a large proportion of music can see itself or be marketed as sub-or counter-cultural. Significant genres that are not required to identify themselves as such are – as the quotation would imply – first, orchestral music, and second, rock and pop. The latter category's place within the 'mainstream venue' is obvious: 'rock and pop' is the very epitome of contemporary mass-mediated, popular culture. On the other hand, art music (characterised in the same quotation by orchestras) is less able to declare a position within the popular culture of contemporary English society.[4] Rather, this reference demonstrates the socio-historical associations central to the actual and assumed functions of the mainstream *venue* within that society. Many such venues have names that refer strongly to historical links with products of high culture and high art: Opera House, Theatre, Concert Hall, etc. The references and histories inherent in these performance contexts serve to perpetuate strong associations with performance texts and products that have historically been given high cultural value.

The idea of the mainstream is, therefore, simultaneously and ambiguously related to both popular culture and high culture (and their products, referred to here as 'pop' and 'art'). It is engaged in the dissolution of generic boundaries at a structural level whilst simultaneously maintaining those boundaries through generic labelling of the acts. Such breakdowns in the categorisation of consumed culture are inevitable when the mainstream arts centre is predominantly a space for cultural engagement by 'omnivorous', educated, middle-class audiences.[5] The mainstream venue is, therefore, a space in which economic success and an ostensible disinterest in economic success are celebrated in combination. As we consider here the movement of English folk music and dance into mainstream contexts, this will involve examining its alignments with both of these aspects of the mainstream.

As noted in our earlier discussions of folk music as a concept (1.2), denotation of a folk or traditional culture is regularly identified in folk scholarship as an active rejection of the cultural symptoms of urbanisation, industrialisation and commercialisation throughout the nineteenth and twentieth centuries. Meanwhile, as Storey has indicated, such a process was instrumental in the arbitration of the alternative categorisations of high and popular culture (Storey, 2003). Whilst this suggests that any interaction between folk and its high or popular cultural counterparts must be contradictory and ideologically problematic, such synthesis has a history as long as that of the boundaries which its creators have sought to blur. In the early stages of the folk music construct, the material was sought with the express intention of developing new art music; in the latter half of the twentieth century, folk-rock explored the combination of folk materials and the new soundscapes of rock. Interestingly, though, the outputs of such creative sojourns did not result in something that was itself accepted by creator and audiences as *folk*. Vaughan-Williams' output was recognised by all as art music that drew inspiration from folk; Steeleye Span's work was part of a new genre that combined folk and rock elements. And here lies a key difference between these historical developments and the contemporary English folk resurgence. The artists who will be discussed in this chapter might all be said to engage in some form of cross-generic synthesis that looks beyond folk's historic boundaries. However, they also eschew any fusion-based labelling of their work (although media commentators may attempt such labelling as 'electro-folk' or 'folk-pop'), in order to alleviate the potential for confusion amongst uninitiated audiences. To artists and to English folk audiences, the work discussed in this chapter is all simply 'English folk'.

It might be argued that in contemporary Western culture the labels 'pop' and 'art' are no longer meaningful devices for the categorisation of cultural products, and a wealth of postmodern theory would support that claim. However, we shall persevere with these labels here for two central reasons. The first is a general matter of ethnographic expediency – the concepts continue to hold discrete meanings and play a role in the way that English audiences give taxonomy to their cultural experiences, as demonstrated by the citation above. The second reason relates more specifically to our analysis of the English folk resurgence. The division of folk acts into those orientated towards, or drawing on, popular idioms and those orientated towards high art may appear a little simplistic, but is still helpful since it acknowledges two sets of approaches to the contemporary performance of English folk that are – at their core – quite distinct in terms of style, content and discourse. Nonetheless, ambiguities in the margins between these two camps abound, particularly with regard to the construction or evocation of vernacularity and authenticity. Much is shared by acts representative of these orientations, including audiences, performance contexts and personnel, and all are generally referred to as 'English folk'. We therefore accept that our division of the case studies in this chapter, according to either 'pop' or 'art' allegiances, may potentially be somewhat problematic, but deploy it as a necessary way of applying some order to an extremely diverse gamut of stylistic practices.

3.2 Acoustic pop: Seth Lakeman

Seth Lakeman is a young singer-songwriter from Devon in the southwest of England. He comes from a family of folk musicians and achieved success as a solo artist around 2004. Previously, he had performed as part of the acclaimed group Equation (with his two brothers) and as an accompanying musician. In 2005 his album *Kitty Jay* received a Mercury Music Prize nomination, resulting in a considerable and fast rise in profile. He is one of the most popular English folk artists among audiences that do not otherwise identify with English folk. Lakeman is predominantly known for being a singer, fiddler and tenor guitarist, and for his close ties with Devon in general and the Dartmoor National Park area in particular – a place that features heavily in the subjects of his self-penned songs. Beyond heavily compressed, methodically produced, 'professional'-sounding recordings, Seth Lakeman's music employs a number of features that combine to effect artistic alignments and associations with popular music. Two such features are particularly central to the sound of Lakeman's output: the prominence of strummed stringed instruments; and the role of riff-based arrangements.

The instrumentation of Lakeman's music is a distinctive element of his work within the context of English folk music. Strummed strings – such as guitars, mandolins, bouzoukis and banjos – predominate in the music to an extent uncommon across the genre as a whole. Furthermore, there is a notable lack of free-reed instruments in his work – certainly no melodeons or concertinas are clearly audible – which causes the music to stand out from that of other artists of the contemporary resurgence. The instruments used combine with percussion (usually a standard drum kit) and bass to create a sound similar to that of the extended rhythm section one might expect to hear in acoustic guitar-based pop. However, the word 'acoustic' is important here, since it hints at an important way in which the music maintains a 'folk' aesthetic. There are very few instances of any obviously electrified instrumentation – the most likely electric instrument to accompany the standard drum kit would be a bass guitar, but for the most part the bass lines in Lakeman's songs are provided by an acoustic double bass, which is often clearly audible by virtue of its relatively high volume in the mix and wide frequency range.

Other key instruments also disrupt immediate associations with mainstream acoustic pop. For instance, beyond his reputation as a vocalist, Lakeman is probably most closely associated with the fiddle. Aspects of Lakeman's use of the fiddle will be discussed further in 4.6.1, but for now it is enough to point out that this plays a central role in audibly distancing his music from a broader acoustic pop genre. This is particularly the case where the fiddle is brought forward from the strummed strings, as in 'Lady of the Sea' on *Freedom Fields* (Lakeman, 2006), or even multi-tracked to provide a full rhythm accompaniment in 'Kitty Jay' (2004). Another of Lakeman's preferred instruments is the tenor guitar, which is very similar to a standard guitar, but has a slightly smaller body and four, rather than six, steel strings. This instrument is relatively rare in English folk music, but its significance lies in its visual aspect within the live performance context: here, it is particularly interesting – and, it could be argued, partly successful – due to its being simultaneously familiar and foreign to pop music audiences (like a guitar, but noticeably different), while being employed to fulfil the musical duties normally assigned to a normal six-stringed guitar with relatively little audible difference to the non-specialist listener.

The similarities with the predominating soundscape of Anglophone pop music are, however, more striking. The tenor guitar – along with the other guitar instruments played in Lakeman's work – is also usually played in a way expected of pop or rock rhythm guitar, commonly with an emphasis on the first, fourth and sixth quavers of the bar, in juxtaposition with the 'square' (four quavers + four quavers) rhythmic pattern of the percussion.[6] Riffs – often pentatonic or with modal flattened sevenths – and equally phrased harmonic progressions feature heavily in many of the tracks across his albums. Although backing vocals are not that common, when they appear they are often female, generally ethereal, and thoroughly separated from Lakeman's lead vocals in the mix, as one might expect of a pop track rather than a folk-song recording. Electronic effects, although rare, can sometimes be heard applied to the vocals (as in 'The Charmer', 2004), and Lakeman's voice generally has a relatively glottal, husky quality by comparison with most English folk singers. The overall sound of the recordings is similar to that of professionally produced pop songs by virtue of the high levels of compression applied in the post-production stage.

The 'American-ness' of Lakeman's delivery and arrangements is noteworthy. The general emphasis on a rhythm section of strummed and plucked strings holds strong associations with American Old Time and Country genres, particularly on the regular occasions where double bass, banjo and mandolin are foregrounded. Audible associations with American folk and folk-rock genres are amplified by: finger-picked chords on the banjo in songs such as 'The White Hare' (2006) and 'Poor Man's Heaven' (2008); electric slide guitar on 'Feather in a Storm' (2008); and the use of the harmonica on 'Crimson Dawn' (2008), the only instance of a clearly audible and identifiable free-reed instrument in Lakeman's music to this point. The conspicuous appearance of the Jew's harp in 'Race to be King' (2008) also suggests foreign (American, or possibly Australian) traditions. American traditions are further invoked in much of Lakeman's fiddle playing. Whilst many stylistic qualities are shared between American and English folk fiddle traditions (e.g. regular double-stopping, drones at the tonic and fifth, and movement between a melodic and a rhythmic accompaniment role), the sliding movement that appears regularly in Lakeman's melodic playing, from the flattened fifth up to the perfect fifth or down to the fourth, is audibly locatable squarely in the American Old Time and Bluegrass fiddling styles. Finally, the enunciation of Lakeman's vocals often include closed 'a' sounds (such as in the repeated word 'dancing' in the 'The White Hare', 2006) that are strongly reflective of an Americanised (or mid-Atlantic) accent. Whilst such enunciation is often a feature of a strong West Country accent, it is not really consistent with Lakeman's speaking voice, and the combination of this feature with the other aspects mentioned above suggest that this is not affected to express a local or regional identity.

As the comments above illustrate, the significance of American musical signatures is multifaceted. Many of the musical aspects that hint at American influences do not point directly to links with contemporary Anglo-American popular culture, but rather to American counterpart traditional musics, in a way that might be understood as – at least in part – a fusion of English repertory with stylistic features of one or more secondary folk traditions. However, it is important to recognise that any clearly audible reference to American culture brings with it strong connotations of globalised popular culture, due partly to the far greater role of American traditional musics (as opposed to English folk music) in the development of contemporary rock and pop, and also a widely held association of the globalised mainstream music industry with American cultural and economic input. In the light of other links drawn from the music of Lakeman, then, his role in the sonic alignment of English folk music with globalised, contemporary acoustic pop is both significant and complex. It is not, however, all-encompassing, since the visual representation of the artist emphasises nature, antiquity and the local in a way that starkly juxtaposes the modern, multinational characteristics of his music. Lakeman's album artwork generally locates the artist within the landscape to which he has developed a close association – Dartmoor and the Devon and Cornwall coastline. On the cover of *Poor Man's Heaven* (2008) Lakeman is pictured walking over a wind-swept cliffscape, whilst that of *Kitty Jay* portrays the singer crouching among moss-covered rocks. The contemporariness of the music on these albums is implied in the artwork only by the fact that the artist is clearly young, attractive and fashionably dressed and styled. Similar representations can be found on the album covers of many of Lakeman's contemporaries, but the following sections will explore deployments of album artwork that move beyond this portrayal of traditional musicians in traditional locations.

3.3 Electric folk: Jim Moray

Jim Moray is a young singer and multi-instrumentalist who began to gain in profile around 2002, receiving a nomination for the Horizon Award at the BBC Radio 2 Folk Awards in 2003, and releasing his celebrated first full-length album *Sweet England* in the same year. As discussed in 2.2.3, the album was considered a landmark for the developing folk industry, due partly to the professional aesthetics of the glossy and artistically composed artwork (by photographer David Angel), but also to the unusual nature of Moray's arrangements of traditional songs. Just as Lakeman's music makes close reference to the characteristics of acoustic pop, so Moray enjoys strong association with electronically generated sounds and recording methods. Since the release of *Sweet England*, Moray has regularly foregrounded his use of contemporary music technology to set his work apart from that of more 'traditional' artists. In particular, his live performances have made conspicuous use of a variety of pedal-boards, both to manipulate the sounds created by his electric guitar and to create and overlay an intricate array of live-samples; unsurprisingly, the range of technologically facilitated recording and electro-acoustic techniques showcased in his recorded output is even greater. That said, his methods for utilising recording technology in the arrangement of material vary considerably throughout his recordings. In the case of 'The Seeds of Love' (2003) the accompaniment to the track employs a considerable range of audibly electronic synthesiser-generated tones, including sine-wave style rapid – and obviously automated – arpeggiations; the rhythmic accompaniment is provided via a beat-track comprising bass, snare, and 'open' and 'closed' triangle samples, reminiscent of downbeat electronica artists such as Groove Armada or Massive Attack.

By contrast, the following track on the album – 'The Week Before Easter' – foregrounds a studio technique, rather than electronic sounds: the entire accompaniment is made up of multi-tracked vocal lines (apparently all Moray's own voice), beginning as vocable-based chords, and becoming more polyphonic as the track develops. The resultant soundscape is no less 'electronic' in its impact than that of the previous track. The lengthy and complex recording process – whether the result of computer sampling, repeated live recording, or a combination of the two – is immediately apparent even to the inexperienced listener, and the vocal lines are treated with audibly changeable (and in most cases considerable) amounts of reverb. The subsequent track on the album, 'Gypsies', offers another alternative treatment of traditional material. Here, the song is sung to a sparse accompaniment from a (mostly picked) electric guitar. The guitar is treated with relatively little distortion, but the fairly high-frequency range leaves the listener in no doubt as to the electric nature of the instrument. As the song develops, a jazz-inflected trumpet line adds to the texture, and the 'unnatural' relative volumes of the three elements (vocals, guitar and trumpet) emphasise the manipulations involved.

Across his outputs, Moray foregrounds (and thereby celebrates) the studio recording and production processes to an extent unique within contemporary

English folk music. Nonetheless, his popularity and profile are among the highest of any individual in the current resurgence. His reimagining of the traditional within the contemporary English folk scene is not confined to his musical arrangement: the visual aspects of his output have proven to be as revolutionary as his musical approaches. As discussed in 2.2.3, Moray's *Sweet England* is widely regarded by artists as a significant turning point in the imaging of the contemporary English folk resurgence. The cover picture (see also 6.2) shows Moray, in featureless black clothing, lying down – apparently asleep – in the leaf litter of an oak woodland.[7] Beside him lies an unusual, shiny chrome, electric guitar that he has regularly played live and is pictured playing in a number of promotional photographs. The neck of the guitar, which is orientated parallel to his body, rests on a stack of two thick, shabbily soft-bound manuscripts, whilst in the background there stands an attentive, still black dog, looking towards Moray and the camera. Moray's *Sweet England* album cover supports his creative explorations via the visual juxtaposition of nature (which can also stand for the rural historic, and therefore, for the antiquity of folk culture) with the chrome electric guitar – the contemporary apparatus of Moray's thoroughly modern musical interpretations.

3.4 Folk-rock: the English ceilidh band

Where the previous sections have discussed the outputs of individuals, this section will broaden the focus to take in a subgenre or context of folk music performance – the English ceilidh. The ceilidh was outlined in 1.6.2 as a participatory dance activity central to contemporary English folk culture. For the purposes of this section, we will concentrate on the nature of the music that accompanies the dancing – the music of ceilidh bands. The basic melodic materials on which such a band relies are generally drawn from a canon of traditional tunes or recent tunes composed in the traditional idiom. Occasionally performed in 'sets' of two or three for a single dance, the tunes are conceptually categorised by the musicians according to form and rhythmic attributes ('a 32-bar jig'; 'a 48-bar polka') enabling the appropriate musical accompaniment to be quickly and easily selected for the caller's choice of dance (dances are also categorised in this way). However, the presence of 'tradition' in the musical output of ceilidh bands is limited to this basic framework and melodic canon; how the melodies are harmonised, orchestrated or otherwise arranged is a matter of considerable variation from one band to the next, and the variety of solutions results in each group being associated with a particular 'sound'. There are, however, some features of instrumentation and style that are common to a large number of the more successful and popular English ceilidh bands. The most striking and ubiquitous of these features is the presence of a rhythm section consistent with a rock band, and comprising drum kit, electric guitar and electric bass.

Given the regular appearance of these instruments amongst the higher-profile professional ceilidh bands currently working, it would be reasonable to suggest that English ceilidh – as a *musical* genre – owes much to the folk-rock of the

1960s and 1970s, as documented by Sweers (2005) and Burns (2012). The context for its performance, however, makes certain formative demands on the bands in question. For instance, the music must necessarily be of a purely instrumental nature in order to fulfil its brief as an accompaniment to the primary activity of the event; for each set of dancers to work effectively as a group, their attention must be focused on the progression of the dance figures, rather than a song narrative. The lack of singing is particularly important because the caller continues to 'call' instructions over the music as the dance is going on, which would be less easily heard if the caller were forced to compete with a singer's vocals for the attention of the dancers. The melody instruments (normally including the melodeon, which will be discussed more in 4.6.2) are therefore particularly prominent within the overall sound of the ceilidh band.

On the other hand, the need for the dancers to be able to identify their place in the sequence of repeated events through reference to the musical accompaniment means that the band must provide a strong, unambiguous beat, with the structure of the tune clearly articulated through the arrangement. For that reason, the rock-based rhythm section performs much as it would in a non-folk context, with bass emphasis commonly falling on the first and third beats, and harmonic progressions characterised by even phrasing. The latter is something that often requires a certain amount of musical 'negotiation' (i.e. modifications to the standard tune), given the unequal harmonic periods suggested by much English folk music – something which will be discussed further in 4.4.1. As a result, the ceilidh band's function – to facilitate dancing – encourages the maintenance of a clear and conspicuous distinction between the constituent folk and non-folk (usually – but not always – rock) signatures. English ceilidh can therefore be characterised as a site for continuous and varied negotiations of what constitutes folk (as opposed to other sorts of music, specifically rock), and for the combination of folk with other genres in a way that encourages dancing and affords a band its unique musical identity.

Significantly for the purposes of this chapter, the engagement of folk music with other popular genres goes beyond the simple combination of folk instruments and tunes with rock rhythm sections. Ceilidh musicians are faced with a constant challenge: the music they play must necessarily meet the needs of dancers, requiring constant speed within a single dance and relatively little variation of tempo across the event's music as a whole. This, added to the musical requirements discussed above, means that ceilidh band musicians are constantly reflecting on – and often experimenting with – new ways of arranging the tunes they play in order to ensure that a gig is sufficiently varied as to hold a dancing audience's interest. Bands regularly find their 'sound' through successful experimentation of this sort, with an emphasis placed on originality. For this reason, recent years have seen ceilidh developing as an arena for folk-fusion as a musical challenge, leading to a number of well-known bands achieving extremely strong – and unique – musical identities. One such band is Whapweasel, which was named Best Dance Band at the 2005 BBC Radio 2 Folk Awards (the only year that the Best Dance Band award has been given). The band is best known for combining English folk tunes with a two-tone/ska rhythm accompaniment and arrangement. Whapweasel includes a brass section of saxophones and trombone, and a keyboard often deployed to provide a variety of organ sounds. This instrumentation, along with a general treble-accompaniment emphasis on second and fourth beats, provides an overall soundscape very similar to that of 1980s ska bands such as Madness or the Specials. Another example of this kind of hybridised ceilidh band is the Great White Steamchicken. Also playing concerts as a jazz band, Steamchicken combine the standard ceilidh repertoire with traditional jazz, jump jive and rhythm and blues, particularly through polyphonic foregrounding of their extensive brass section and harmonica.

As suggested above, often the development of these hybrids is initiated through trial and error, and discursive emphasis is placed on the 'compatibility' of different dance music genres through the sharing of a common goal. This is certainly the discourse of bands like Steamchicken, whose website claims that the band takes English folk tunes 'back to a time where dancing was fun and jazz was to dance to' (*Steamchicken*, 2011). The ceilidh band Glorystrokes, however, represents a rather more explicitly preconceived 'concept' hybrid, fusing as it does English folk dance tunes and melodeon with metalcore (a subgenre combining heavy metal and hardcore punk). The band builds its sound around heavily distorted guitar and rapid, double-pedalled bass drum; band members wear full face paint, punk hairstyles and black clothing; and staging usually includes high-contrast lighting and dry ice. The extent to which the alternative genre (metalcore) is embraced and meticulously recreated on stage (as well as the incongruity of such a sound with folk festivals in general, and ceilidh dancing in particular) ensures that a Glorystrokes ceilidh is founded on a strong sense of irony. The ironic content is heightened for the better-informed ceilidh-goer, since the main members of the band are well known for performing in a number of conventionally 'traditional' bands and contexts (although they are, of course, almost unrecognisable in their Glorystrokes face paint and pseudo-goth attire).[8]

3.5 Dance fusions: the Demon Barber Roadshow

A high-profile and sustained attempt to connect English traditional dance with popular cultural dance forms is represented by the work of the Demon Barber Roadshow, headed up by musician and dancer Damien Barber. A central characteristic of the Roadshow's live performances has been their staging of various forms of English folk dance performance, primarily longsword and rapper sword dance, Cotswold morris, and what the company refer to as 'hard-core dance', alongside the Demon Barbers' musical performances as an electric folk band. The Demon Barbers' dance presentations have evolved into a touring theatre show which stages a fusion of traditional dance with contemporary street dance. *Time Gentlemen Please!*, in which, 'clog, sword and morris meet B-boying, Popping and Krump', toured to mainstream theatres and arts venues in 2010–11 after a development period beginning in 2007 (*Time Gentlemen Please!*, 2011).

The profiling of English traditional dance for wider audiences outside the boundaries of the folk scene is an explicit aim of the Demon Barber Roadshow. For Barber, its central aim 'is to raise the profile of traditional English dance by promoting it to a wide as possible audience and by making it as exciting and accessible as possible' (Barber and Walker 2011). In other words, the aim is to popularise it. This popularising is approached, at one level, through professionalisation, and the production of the dance show as a polished event taking place in mainstream theatres and arts venues. Two of the main points of reference for *Time Gentlemen Please!*, are highly (and globally) popular commercial theatre shows that are based primarily on percussive, rhythm-based dance: on one hand the Irish Dance Spectacles exemplified by Riverdance and, on the other, the rhythm-based theatre show Stomp. These are referenced in the marketing materials for *Time Gentlemen Please!*: 'Think Riverdance with a false moustache and Stomp with bells on' (*Time Gentlemen Please!*, 2011). These points of comparison are also recirculated in critical responses to the show.[9] Julian May's comment, 'Someone should give this show a West End Run' , which is reproduced on the Demon Barber Roadshow's website, might be seen as an indicator of the kind of broad popular audience for which this show positions itself (*Time Gentlemen Please!*, 2011).

The traditional dance performers of *Time Gentlemen Please!* are skilful dancers whose levels of virtuosity in their own disciplines generally match those of the professional street dance performers and would not be out of place alongside the professional dance performers associated with Riverdance or Stomp. This is worth remarking on, because the participatory culture of English traditional dance is, in general, less conducive to the overt display of elite technical skill and athleticism than is, for example, the competition-based Irish Dancing culture that feeds shows like Riverdance (see Foley, 2001; Wulff, 2003). English traditional dance participation, and morris dance in particular, is more often characterised by a kind of defiant amateurism, and although it has been attracting new, younger participants in places, its culture is still generally characterised by an older demographic than that presented on stage by the Demon Barbers.

Like street dance, the mode of performance retains traces of vernacularity that speak of its everyday origins. For Barber, 'with the morris and the rapper you want it to … look like Joe Public is doing it on the street' (Damien Barber, interview, 2008). This is achieved, in part, through the frequent adoption of a posture that is less taut, elongated or stylised than that typically adopted by professional dancers in art traditions like ballet or contemporary dance, and closer to an everyday posture. It shares this with the street dance performers. The 'everyday' origin of both traditional dance and street dance – its folk authenticity – is, similarly, narrativised within the show by its setting within an English pub. It is also mobilised in the marketing discourses around the performance. Barber, for example, is quoted as saying: 'But a big part of the show is its community side. We are all old friends. Apart from the hip-hop dancers who joined a few years ago, we have known each other for 20 years' (Hall, 2011).

The popularising project is advanced here not only through presenting English traditional dance within a professional show in mainstream venues. It is most overtly approached through its juxtaposition and hybridisation with a popular contemporary dance form – street dance. The idea of the meeting and eventual mixing of English traditional dance and street dance is itself enacted in the loose narrative of the show, which, very broadly, has three street dancers enter a pub and encounter the traditional dancers. A series of dance episodes and battles ensue, and gradually they come together and the dance forms fuse.

Just as the musical hybridisations already discussed are often spoken of in a way that emphasises the underlying similarities between folk and popular forms, so the choreographic strategies of *Time Gentlemen Please!* emphasise the similarities between elements of its dances and those of street dance. As Barber puts it, speaking in the promo video for the show, 'the idea of this is really to see similarities between traditional dance and modern dance, especially street dance and clog' (*Time Gentlemen Please! Promo 2010*, 2010). These similarities are further discussed by the choreographer Bobak Walker:

> During the R&D period for the full show there were some amazing moments where the similarities between the two styles became clearer and more over-whelmingly obvious than either groups of dancers had expected ... I think we were all shocked at how these dances, seemingly worlds apart, were actually variations of the same movements. (Barber and Walker, 2011: 9)

Such similarities are clearly highlighted in, for example, episodes of unison dancing where street dancers and clog dancers all display the same fast rhythmic footwork, relaxed body posture and freely swinging arms, the main difference being their footwear – clogs for one, trainers for another. Similarities are drawn also by the adoption of the idea of the 'battle' as a choreographic device. The hip-hop battle in which individuals or groups compete vocally or in dance, has been a feature of hip-hop culture since its beginnings (Dimitriadis, 2009: 35). The use of this device in *Time Gentlemen Please!* may well dramatise some of the surface differences between the two dance forms, but by juxtaposing and framing them together it does also allow their similarities to shine through. It also has the effect of suggesting an equivalence between the two dance forms, especially given that one of the choreographic outcomes is fusion.

As well as highlighting formal similarities there is also an attempt to highlight historical connections between these dance forms. One character, whose dress (a basque) references the showgirl, and whose dance references the tap-dance styles of the 1920s and 1930s, does a dance battle with the clog dancers. This association with historical popular cultures in the figure of the burlesque dancer evokes also the imagery around Bellowhead's album *Burlesque* (2006), to be examined in 3.6.

In addition, connections between the traditional dancers and the hip-hop dancers are emphasised discursively in texts that circulate around the show. This is done through a discourse emphasising talent and mutual respect: 'It didn't take long, however, for mutual respect to show', writes Barber; 'everyone was quickly aware of the quality of the talent that was being thrown into the pot' (Barber and Walker, 2011: 7). It is also done through a discourse that equates these dance cultures as misunderstood subcultures. For Bobak Walker,

One of the important realisations for me was how English folk culture is treated in the media, often the butt of jokes and seen as a relic. I was very much guilty of this stereotype and dismissive of the whole culture before my chance encounter with The Demon Barbers and the group. Since then my understanding and outlook has completely transformed. Until recently I had missed that although Hip Hop is massively popular, there is still a huge misconception of what Hip Hop is especially outside of my own circles, and in mass media and for older generations. (*Ibid*: 9)

It is significant that one of the central elements of the Demon Barbers' performed version of English traditional dance is what they refer to as 'English clog'. The use of the term 'English clog' is interesting. Clog dancing can be found in various parts of the country (see 1.6.2) and is most associated with northern regional locations. However, the term 'English clog' is not generally used (rather, there are specific clog dance styles such as those associated with the North East and Lancashire). It appears to have been coined by the Demon Barbers to encompass the various styles of clog that they draw on, in line with the English theme of their dance show. In fact, their newly named and constructed 'English clog' is also influenced by elements of Irish and Appalachian traditions.

The Demon Barbers explicitly make the point that clog dancing was associated with popular cultural entertainment in the nineteenth century:

Clog dancing was entertainment for a lot of working class communities in northern England […] Similarly hip-hop and street dance was the entertainment for the American working class. They share lots of similarities in their roots. (Hall, 2011)

By invoking a roots story that emphasises English clog dancing's historical associations with working-class *popular* culture, Barber not only makes a link with the American-rooted popular dance culture of street dance, he also rearticulates traditional dance in terms of popular culture. Elsewhere, he argues that the activities of folk revivalists can cause it to ossify:

One of the frustrations of the revival of traditional dance is you get these groups who want to preserve the dances […] Traditional dance was always developing. People were always trying to do it better and faster, to perform quicker and jump higher, to move it on and do them better than the lads next door. (*Ibid*.)

Elsewhere, Barber remarks:

Unfortunately though, there has been a tendency by many folk organisations to only preserve them [traditional dances] and to perform them the way they've always been done. Ironically, the same process that has helped save them is quite often also responsible for stifling their natural development. A slow, steady development of a tradition is undoubtedly preferable but having missed out on the opportunity for this we hope that project's [*sic*] like ours will help make up for lost time. (Barber and Walker, 2011)

So, the narrative goes: folk dance tradition has lost its connection with the popular, due in part to the ossifying activities of revivalists; for the Demon

Barbers, moving the tradition forward involves reasserting its connections with popular culture. *Time Gentlemen Please!* is not simply aiming to popularise English traditional dance by showing it to mainstream audiences who might have been unfamiliar with it, by professionalising it, or even by attempting to explode unhelpful media stereotypes about folk dance. Its attempt to move the tradition forward requires an insistence on its status as a living form of contemporary popular culture, and it does this not only through the moments of fusion with street dance but by suggesting similarities and equivalence with it.

3.6 Historical popular culture(s)

A more explicit example of the discursive unification of folk and popular culture can be found in the title of Jim Moray's fifth album, *Low Culture* (2008). The title of Moray's album celebrates an explicit recognition of folk music's status as a vernacular activity of low cultural value within an implicitly elitist British society. Thus, it suggests the aforementioned bringing-together of folk and other forms of popular culture (notably pop music) in the face of a high-culture opposite. However, the reference to this high–low value system is a largely anachronistic one, at least in terms of spoken and written discourse: no contemporary cultural commentator would expect to use such terms except to critique the value judgement. This means that the title effectively indicates folk music's *historical* place in popular cultural performance, rather than its contemporary status, and that has a number of subsidiary effects on the impact of the title. Firstly, a subtext for this suggestion is the implication that folk is the forerunner of contemporary popular music. Secondly, as a functioning part of popular culture, folk can be expected to be – in fact necessarily *must* be – subject to ongoing processes of reinvention and modernisation that reflect developments in popular aesthetics. This discourse has been a common one among folk music performers and commentators for some time, but the quest for innovative musical manifestations of the principle has become a preoccupation common to many of the artists involved in the current resurgence. The music of the album *Low Culture* variously juxtaposes English folk songs with Southern African mbira, Indian-inflected glissando string lines and West African kora ('Leaving Australia'), and with the vocals of rapper Bubbz ('Lucy Wan').

The album also includes a much talked about rendition of 'All You Pretty Girls', originally a song by the British New Wave band XTC in 1984. In contrast with the reworkings of traditional material, here the object is the 'traditional-ising' of a relatively recent pop song. This is done by emphasising an acoustic aesthetic, through such methods as the inclusion of folk instruments (e.g. the melodeon and fiddle) that are not apparent in the original. Nonetheless, the track is musically fairly close to the original, which is itself a self-conscious parody of a sailors' song of the eighteenth or nineteenth century (as is clearly apparent from the costumes of the original XTC music video). In other words, Moray's 'All You Pretty Girls' is a folk version of a pop song that was written in the style of a folk song. Furthermore, Moray's cover falls short of embodying the 'folk-as-a-contemporary-pop-music' discourse examined in earlier sections of this chapter, since the material is not contemporary but taken from a specific period in pop *history* (the 1980s). This would suggest that these juxtapositions of folk with elements of popular culture are about more than merely bringing the material of English folk music up-to-date. Rather than breaking down the boundaries separating 'folk' and 'pop' as disparate forms of vernacular music, activities such as those of Moray effectively highlight, celebrate and reinforce the currency of those distinct terms.

The acknowledgment and celebration of a folk/pop dualism can be seen in the large number of instances where popular culture of specific periods of English, British or Anglo-American history are referenced (as opposed to *contemporary* popular culture). When images signal the specifically historical, Victorian and Edwardian England are often foregrounded. This is particularly the case where the photographic composition is set within an interior space, rather than an exterior landscape. For instance, the cover of the album *Songs* (2005b) by Spiers and Boden shows the duo sitting in what might be an attic space, on dusty period furniture, with a chandelier. The back cover of Tim Van Eyken's *Stiffs Lovers Holymen Thieves* (2006) shows Van Eyken with his band mates in a similarly dark and mysterious attic space: one of the group is holding the antlers of a stuffed stag's head, whilst another grips a candelabra. Amidst the antiquity of the surroundings and props, modernity is suggested by the musicians' clothing, which in one case includes a fedora hat and small, round-lensed sunglasses. Perhaps the most striking interior-set album cover by David Angel for this genre is that of Bellowhead's first album, *Burlesque* (2006), which shows the eleven band members in a large, empty Victorian building.[10] The space appears to be a dilapidated performance venue which includes a large gallery around three sides of the hall. In combination with the burlesque dancer in the foreground – dressed in corset, face mask and elaborate feather headdress – the implication is that this is a theatre of some description, and the viewer is instantly led to associations with the Victorian music hall. The dated theatrics of the venue are made explicit in the album's title. Note too the sharing of the showgirl reference with that made by *Time Gentlemen Please!*

It is important to note that historical references within the music and visual imagery of the current English folk resurgence can be plural and fragmented. Often, historical signifiers denote the broader cultural contexts of multiple periods of development in English folk culture. Bellowhead's musical attributes are a strong case in point. The intricate and carefully orchestrated arrangements of the eleven-piece group are successful in achieving a variety of subtly nuanced soundscapes. Nonetheless, the most striking of those soundscapes is that of a naïve, 'village band' sound. This impression is created principally through the instrumentation: the striking juxtaposition of folk instruments (specifically Jon Spiers' melodeon) with orchestral instruments (e.g. Paul Sartin's oboe and Rachel McShane's cello) and a Big Band brass section gives the impression that the group might be more a band of friends or convenient personnel than a carefully constructed ensemble. As has been discussed elsewhere (see 2.3 and Hield, 2010), such a portrayal of community is always likely to hold considerable cultural currency with a folk audience. Needless to say, whilst some band members happened to be friends (mainly those involved in folk music as performers in their own right), others were sought 'from cold' to fulfil a specific musical function. When asked in interview whether the choice of personnel was social or musical, the reply of the band's front man and founder member, Jon Boden, was emphatic: 'Musical … I didn't know half the band before pretty much our first gig, to be honest' (Jon Boden, interview, 2008).

A couple of specific instrumental features within the band's line-up are particularly important for achieving an *ad hoc* aesthetic, and are worthy of specific discussion. Firstly, such an aesthetic can be identified in the band's percussion, performed by Pete Flood. Flood's style is one that avoids reliance on a repeated rhythmic accompaniment for more than a few bars, and favours rhythmic complexity (relative to more common styles of percussive accompaniment in English folk music – namely those found in ceilidh).[11] Most significantly, this intricate style is applied to a conspicuous variety of unconventional percussion (including stomp box, toy glockenspiels and even a metal cutlery container – complete with knives and forks). On the other hand, the unique use of sousaphone for the creation of the band's bass lines adds to the 'village band' aesthetic by means of its conspicuous incongruity with this folk context and its marching band associations. The reasons for the selection of the instrument are explained by Boden:

> SKP: So was there a choice about having a bass brass instrument rather than just …? I mean, in a normal ceilidh band it would have been an electric bass, wouldn't it?
>
> JB: Yeah, yeah. We really didn't want it to be a folk-rock band […] I mean, we all like folk-rock, but I guess we wanted it to be a bit different […] Gid [Gideon Juckes] wasn't actually a Sousaphone player – he's a tuba player – and he was saying, 'why do you want a sousaphone? Tubas are much better instruments', and I was saying, 'well because it's bigger – it looks better' [*Laughs*]. I've got a kind of theatrical background, so I'm always quite focused on what it's going to look like or whatever, and a sousaphone does just look fantastic, whereas a bass is not a particularly visual thing. (*Ibid.*)

The desire for the band to differentiate itself from a folk-rock band is a significant indicator of the general plurality of the musical solutions explored within the current resurgence, whilst Boden's own interest in the theatrical hints at an important foundation from which to understand both the band's image *and* its sound.[12] Interestingly, there are a number of points in the band's output where the sousaphone (sometimes the helicon and, in studio recordings, the tuba) imitates the kinds of bass lines one might expect from a bass guitar, with very little attempt made to differentiate the instrument from a bass guitar musically. Furthermore, the emphasis on low frequencies in the amplification of the sousaphone at live performances makes the sound of the instrument at times almost indistinguishable from that of a bass guitar, which would certainly support the implications of Boden's comment that the decision to include it had much to do with its visual impact.

In much of Bellowhead's output these elements combine with a highly poly-phonic sound (the broader significance of which will be discussed in 4.4.3). At some points most instruments play rhythmically and melodically independent parts, whilst division of the band into sections via interlocking motifs is also common. The result of this combination is an overall soundscape that often implies a musical process that is at once carefully ordered and shambolic. More significantly for this chapter, it facilitates a variety of extra-generic associations. Perhaps the clearest and most regular of these is music theatre of the early to mid-twentieth century, such as that of Kurt Weill. The complexity of rhythmic and motivic structures in a number of tracks on the band's first album underpins this association, along with a relatively high level of chromaticism (e.g. 'Rigs of the Times', 2006). Theatrical arrangement is made most explicit in the programmatic Vaudeville comedy stylings of 'Flash Company' from that album (with its exaggerated time changes, wailing vocals, seemingly random interjections from muted trumpet and general party atmosphere).[13] The most striking appearances of sectional montage in the arrangements, meanwhile, are clearly intended to reference pop genres like 1970s disco, such as is the case in 'Fire Marengo'.[14]

A visual example of pluralism in the referencing of historical periods can be located in the artwork of Moray's single *Sprig of Thyme* (2004), which gestures to both the early twentieth century and the 1960s.[15] Here the cover of *Sweet England* is echoed with a number of key changes: the black dog has become a majestic stag; the guitar has been replaced by a sprig of thyme in the Moray's hand; and his featureless black clothing is now a khaki army uniform. Where before there were difficult-to-identify soft-bound exercise books, in this version of the scene there are LPs spread out underneath a brass bugle. The appearance of the stag is difficult to codify iconographically: it is often considered a symbol of early periods of British history marked by feudal society and baronial hunting activities; however, elsewhere it can be presented as a knowing symbol of nineteenth-century neo-gothic romanticism (hence the stuffed stag's head in the gloomy candle-lit interior featured in the album artwork of Tim Van Eyken's *Stiffs Lovers Holymen Thieves*). The army uniform is rather generic and difficult to date, but is of a smart cut with metal buttons and appears to be of the early twentieth century. Its antiquity is also hinted at by its appearance alongside the bugle. The singer's location, on the leaf-covered ground of a woodland (which also has a light covering of snow) could be read as evocative of the trenches of the First World War. Meanwhile, the LPs are carefully chosen: at the bottom of the pile is *The Best of the Bachelors Vol 1*; above that is June Tabor's *Airs and Graces* (1976), and on top (though beneath the bugle) are Moray's own albums, *I Am Jim Moray* (2001) and *Sweet England*. Beyond a postmodern self-referencing (more strikingly achieved through the revisited composition of the photograph), the appearance of Moray's albums in the pile (in LP format) can reasonably be read as an indication of his place within an unfolding history of English folk music, of which Tabor is an earlier installment. The significance of the Irish band The Bachelors in the pile is less obvious: popular throughout the 1960s, and firmly situated at the heart of the heavily mediated and establishment-sanctioned mainstream of that time, they are often thought of as a precursor of the boy band phenomenon. The inclusion of their 'best of' album here, then, is effective as a – perhaps slightly mischievous – nod towards a significant period in the crystallisation of popular culture as commercially driven and globally mediated. It can be further understood as an assertion of the need to reunite the 'pop' and 'folk' genres as a single category of vernacular music.

The argument is later made more explicit in the title and imagery of Moray's *Low Culture*. The artwork of that album – designed by English folk-inspired artist David Owen – shows a paperback book, the aged and faded cover of which is clearly designed in the iconic style of mid-twentieth century pulp fiction.[16] Inside, each track's name appears as the title on a different pulp fiction-style picture, which – one quickly understands – depicts a scene related to the narrative material of the respective song. Of course, it could be argued that rendering of the traditional song narratives in the terms of a second anachronistic literary genre can be read as an imagination of the ''twas-ever-thus' discourse. Owen's visual accompaniments to Moray's music would certainly appear to illustrate the common argument of folk singers that the over-riding thrust of ancient folk songs are 'timeless' threads such as love, sex and violence, that are still relevant to contemporary society (although contemporary expressions are less commonly couched in terms of incest, equestrian skills or colonialist profiteering!). However, such a message might have been successfully presented via an almost infinite number of alternative historical references – the choice of this imagery is significant. The significance resides in the fact that the 'trashy novel' represents a particularly iconic turning point in the mass-production of popular culture (or 'low culture' as the album title would have it). Therefore, rather than subverting or disrupting the cultural distance between folk and pop, this juxtaposition of ancient (or at least antiquated) narrative with pulp fiction imagery emphasises and ironically exploits the schism.

Crucially, the kinds of historical references discussed in this section can play a fundamentally different role from the more conventional signalling of nature and the English landscape that will be discussed in 6.2 and 7.2.1. The referencing of 'Victoriana,' vaudeville theatre, naïve 'village band', and disco in Bellow–head's *Burlesque* (for instance) represents a new conceptual link between English folk and a lost urban townscape. It is important to note that this evocation is not simply a return to the romanticised industrial histories employed during the second revival period of the mid-twentieth century. No 'noble worker' identities are presented in the music or imagery here. Rather, these are celebrations – in more or less sober forms – of English popular cultures past. And these are not just any popular cultures: most of the examples listed here specifically resurrect musical and visual icons of the popular cultures that previous folk revivals have actively moved to negate and from which revivalists had actively sought to be distanced.

So far in this chapter we have seen that the engagement of the contemporary

English folk arts with popular culture is multifaceted. It commonly takes the form of sonic and visual references designed to draw clearly identifiable links with popular genres previously considered external – even antithetical – to English folk music and dance. This act of fusing folk and pop is extended by a strongly related trend towards the exploration of folk as a form of popular culture in its own right, a trend that explicitly or implicitly critiques earlier revivalist attempts at isolating folk music and dance from the mainstream milieu.

3.7 Folk as 'art'

The performance of folk music and dance has become increasingly common in contexts generally reserved for 'art' music and dance (such as 'classical' or art music, and ballet or contemporary dance). On 20 July 2008, BBC Radio 3 hosted the BBC Proms Folk Day concerts in the Royal Albert Hall, with a selection of specifically *English* folk music ranging from orchestral works by Vaughan-Williams to performances by contemporary folk artists such as Bella Hardy and Martin Simpson, with Bellowhead providing a close to the proceedings.[17] On 6 April 2006, the morris dance company Morris Offspring received coverage on BBC2's *The Culture Show* for its first extended stage show, *On English Ground*, which premiered as a sell-out performance at London's Southbank Centre, before touring major arts venues in England; another key protagonist of the resurgence, Tim Van Eyken, played the role of the 'Songman' in the National Theatre's 2008 production of Michael Morpurgo's *War Horse*; while the Askew Sisters, a young duo from London, performed at both the National Portrait Gallery and as part of the National Theatre's foyer concert series during 2007–8. It is perhaps not surprising that certain aesthetic developments in the contemporary resurgence have lent themselves to positive reception in art-orientated contexts, and it is these developments that will be discussed in this section. It is essential to begin, however, by pointing out that the relationships we are about to examine contrast strikingly with those between English folk and popular forms discussed above: where the folk–pop relationships are foregrounded and celebrated by acts like Moray and The Demon Barber Roadshow, the folk–art relationships in the case studies that follow are subtle, tacitly implied, ambiguous and less clearly acknowledged or intended.

3.7.1 Chris Wood and the English Acoustic Collective

The name 'English Acoustic Collective' (herein EAC) is generally used to refer to the Trio made up of Chris Wood (violin, viola and vocals), John Dipper (violin) and Rob Harbron (English concertina), although the title originates from what their website refers to as 'a fluid group of composers, writers and choreographers whose work is grounded in a love for their common cultural inheritance' (*English Acoustic Collective,* no date). Most significant in the inception of this collective has been the annual summer schools in traditional music composition and performance organised by Wood, and at which both Dipper and Harbron were early attendees. However, when audiences and promoters refer to the EAC, they are almost invariably referring to the Wood–Dipper–Harbron trio. The discursive representations offered here are immediately striking: the use of the term 'collective' within the title of this 'fluid group' implies the collaboration of *artists* rather than craftsmen. The word also speaks of the 'art-ification' of other vernacular musics, particularly through the – now largely implicit – historical references to its use in the modern jazz and free jazz movements of the 1960s and 1970s.[18] In fact, the concept of intellectual discourse is central to the identity of the EAC, and to Wood as an individual musician. Wood's own explanation of the group's intentions set the tone:

> The EAC is a fluid group of composers, writers and choreographers whose work is grounded in a love for their common cultural inheritance. The work outlined on the site seeks to articulate and amplify the case for authentic and meaningful indigenous forms of cultural expression. It also investigates the creative 'wet edge' between the traditional and the contemporary. (English Acoustic Collective, no date)

These comments are expanded, and complemented by substantial quotes by the acclaimed writer Kazuo Ishiguro and cleric Dr John Sentamu. Where one might expect to see reviews from the most popular and recognised home for folk music in the national media (BBC Radio 2's popular *Mike Harding Show*), instead the erudite reviews of BBC Radio 3 presenters (Verity Sharp and Fiona Talkington) are profiled on the trio's website (*Ibid.*). Via a web link from the Collective's home page, the visitor can be taken to the *Journal of Music in Ireland*, the journal in which Wood's thoughts on the subject of Englishness and English folk music have been published (Wood, 2006). In the group's music, too, are manifest profound textual links with contemporary art music, offering up unspoken associations with wider cultural concepts of 'art music'.[19] It is the nature of such links that are investigated here, through the brief analysis of examples taken from their recorded works. Before doing so, however, it is worth making some general points about the musical language in which the EAC operates.

The EAC's music is generally diatonic or modal (the latter portion being commonly Dorian or Mixolydian), characteristics that are in keeping with the idiom – the English traditional repertory – with which they are dealing. However, the following examples will demonstrate how the group engage with a process of arrangement that enforces tonal ambiguity. This is achieved principally via the employment of what could arguably be described as EAC's key musical characteristic: the relative polyphony of the instrumental texture. Only very rarely does a clear monodic dichotomy of melody/chordal accompaniment – so standard throughout the arrangement of all folk musics across the British Isles – appear in EAC's performances and recordings. Another central characteristic of EAC's soundscape is the particularly 'clean', intonationally precise and sonorous fiddle sound produced by both Wood and Dipper. The pure timbre produced by the two players (and most likely attributable to a careful consistency of bow pressure) minimises the creation of pitchless, percussive sounds and secondary overtones more commonly heard in the playing of most English fiddlers, and is clearly distinctive in comparison with the more rhythmically inflected, 'bow-thirsty' playing of contemporaries such as Eliza Carthy or Jon Boden.[20] This clarity of tone from the fiddlers is often highlighted by the notable, relative absence of a bowed second, sympathetic, open string for harmonic emphasis or drone effect. In combination with relatively understated, sparsely textured arrangements, these stylistic qualities result in a restrained – almost chamber-ensemble – quality.

'Train Tune/Tom Cat', composed by John Dipper and recorded by the EAC on their album *Ghosts* (2004), encapsulates many of these characteristic features. Most significantly, the opening to this track provides a clear example of the complex of musical ambiguities that lies at the heart of the EAC's output. Firstly, there is a distinct lack of monody inherent in the arrangement: only a subtle difference in volume between the two polyphonic voices (concertina and fiddle) is present to assist the listener in discerning the 'tune' from the accompaniment (see 1.6). This uncertainty of the texture is compounded by a metric ambiguity: the tune is in the unusual – and, most notably from the standpoint of English instrumental folk music, *undanceable* – time of 5/4, and the grouping of crotchets oscillates between 2+3 and 3+2, resulting in a relatively complex, irregular phrasing. Finally, and perhaps most crucially, the melody's tonal centre is never harmonically asserted: as can be seen in the approximate transcription in figure 3.1., the 'A part' of the tune – that is, the first full 16 bars in the violin part (bars 17–32 in figure 3.1) – could be largely interpreted as being centred around an A melodic minor, albeit with consistently flattened sevenths and variable (sharpened or natural) sixths. Any tonality of this melodic line is, however, made ambiguous by the repetitive accompaniment figure played by Harbron on the concertina, which emphasises the flattened sixth (F♮) from the outset. The appearance of the note as a resounding pedal in the lower octave from bar 25, is so emphatic as to result in a false relation in bar 28. The B part is anchored more securely to a mixolydian mode centred on D, but this is accompanied by a relatively unusual harmonic movement between D major and F major, emphasising the regular flattened seventh, whilst systematically avoiding a more predictable dominant harmonisation (A minor).

The tune 'St. George's Day', written by Harbron and featuring on the same album, *Ghosts* (*Ibid.*), offers a far clearer assignation of melody (a single concertina line) and accompaniment (a pizzicato ostinato split between a detuned viola and violin), although it remains polyphonic and understated to an extent uncharacteristic of English folk music performance more generally.[21] The tune's form is also clearly recognisable as a standard 32-bar jig (e.g. in 6/8 time, and in AABB structure). Tonally, however, the melody alone can be regarded as somewhat ambiguous: it begins on a G, and phrases end on notes from the C and A minor triads, but is essentially in Dm and F – a fact only made apparent by fleeting signifiers such as the recurring mid-phrase Dm arpeggios (e.g. bars 18 and 22 of figure 3.2).

3.1 Extract from 'Train Tune' by John Dipper (EAC, 2004). Select transcription by Keegan-Phipps.

3.2 Extract from 'St. George's Day' by Rob Harbron (EAC, 2004). Select transcription by Keegan-Phipps.

It is, however, the nature, and also the performance of the pizzicato string accompaniment that is key to an understanding of the cultural associations invited by this piece. Primarily due to their relatively low dynamics, and the resultant limitations of the technique in unamplified – traditional, social – contexts, the plucking of strings is a fairly unusual occurrence in English fiddle music.[22] The technique is more readily identifiable with art music, whether historical or contemporary. Even more significantly, it can be argued that the repetition and angular nature of the pizzicato figure forges more specific associations with the works of relatively populist (or 'accessible') contemporary composers, such as Michael Nyman, Howard Skempton or Arvo Pärt. In total, the piece is fully tonal, but the pseudo-minimalist string accompaniment leads to transitory dissonances and reinforces the sense of harmonic ambiguity already implied by the linear characteristics of the melody. Unspoken relationships to twentieth-century art music are equally apparent in the opening to the track 'Albion', taken from Wood's solo album *The Lark Descending* (2005). Here, the two-chord repetitive figure is perpetuated to an extent reminiscent of minimalist works by Steve Reich, Philip Glass or John Adams. It could even be suggested that the relatively percussive strumming of the strings in 'Albion' results in an mbira-like effect similar to that present in many of the better known performances and recordings of the Kronos Quartet. In the case of 'St. George's Day' (English Acoustic Collective, 2004) the subtle alterations to the established pizzicato figure in bars 44 and 46 of the extract in figure 3.2 carry connotations of minimalist phase-changing.

The destabilisation of generic boundaries is a feature present not only in the textual foreground of contemporary English folk music. Just as the harmonic structuring and accompaniment of tunes is moving away from the established diatonicisms and monodies, so too are the larger-scale forms of performance developing beyond the expected. A folk performance, as with a folk CD, generally involves a programme made up of discrete 'sets of tunes' and/or songs (usually accompanied), but this most basic of conventions is also undergoing renegotiation, through the development of extended, semi-narrative musical products. One such work is *Christmas Champions*, a collaborative composition by Wood and the storyteller Hugh Lupton. The original piece, around twenty-six minutes in duration and commissioned in 2005 at the request of presenter Verity Sharp for Radio 3's *Late Junction*, explores the specifically English tradition of mumming – the itinerant performance of folk drama that has, in the distant past, been particularly prevalent during the Christmas period (combining as it does legendary and nativity narratives) but is now a relative rarity within the broader realm of the English folk arts. In its earliest form, *Christmas Champions* existed as a recording, combining Lupton's narration and Wood's music, and interpolating recordings of the reminiscences of one Herbie Smith, a regular mumming player during the 1930s. However, after receiving critical acclaim in the national media, the form was extended yet further into a touring show performed with Dipper, Harbron and Scottish singer Olivia Ross, which was performed first in December of 2007 (Lupton and the English Acoustic Collective, 2007) and was toured in a reworked form in December of 2008.

A key component of the show is the song 'England in Ribbons,' itself an extended work by Chris Wood; the song is introduced at various points within the show but receives a full exposition at the very end, reiterating the central sentiments of Lupton's narrative. As well as featuring in the original recording and in the subsequent show, this song also appears on Wood's solo album *Trespasser* (2007) as a track thirteen minutes in duration. This version is notably experimental in its use of multi-track recording techniques: Wood not only builds an almost orchestral body of string parts up through the multi-tracking technology at his disposal, but also uses his voice for instrumental effect (for instance, doubling the cello's pedal tonic, D♭). The result is an extremely full, thick texture – very different from the sparse textural characteristics of the EAC.

This full texture is, however, not replicated on stage for the *Christmas Champions* show: to do so would require the cumbersome and problematic (and, many folk audiences would argue, experientially obtrusive) involvement of backing recordings. Instead, a more sparse arrangement is performed by the three members of the EAC and Olivia Ross. The various incarnations of 'England in Ribbons' acts as a reminder that the 'arts' context is by no means confined within the physical boundaries of arts venues but is equally resident within the recorded artefact. This connotation of 'the arts' beyond the performative space of the concert stage is made yet clearer by Wood's relationship with BBC Radio 3, the programming for which is typical of the larger arts venues throughout the UK – focusing as it does on classical music, contemporary art music, jazz, world music and, increasingly, British folk music. Meanwhile, both 'England in Ribbons' and *Christmas Champions* as a whole are exemplary of contemporary English folk music's increasing engagement with the kinds of extended forms readily associated with the arts centres and theatres in which they are to be performed. This is not to suggest that extended compositions relating to folk music are a new phenomenon *per se*: the very *modus operandi* of the first English folk revival was the combination and reworking of collected folk material into large-scale chamber or orchestral works. However, these were only ever regarded as alluding to or engaging with folk music, rather than actually *being* folk music.[23] Previous examples have also been more clearly centred around an explicit art music discourse. The extended forms in which Chris Wood is involved are also a departure from strictly musical composition and performance: as well as engaging with recorded media, *Christmas Champions* is a directed show involving simple choreography and scripted dramatic interludes; the EAC were also, in 2006, the fore-grounded musical accompaniment to the full-length morris dance show, *On English Ground* in collaboration with the morris dance company Morris Offspring (which will be discussed in 3.7.3).

Perhaps the most important point to be made regarding the pizzicato strings in 'St. George's Day' relates to the way in which the track is performed by the EAC in a live concert context. We have reduced the viola and violin to a single stave in the transcription in figure 3.2, not simply because they combine to form a single, fluid line but also because they are simultaneously performed by a single individual – Chris Wood. Wood sits with the instruments balanced near-vertically, one on each knee: the neck of each is supported, close to the body, by the thumb and crook of the corresponding hand, whilst the fingers are used to pluck the open strings. This performance technique has an immediate visual impact, through its novelty both in folk music and art music contexts: audiences of either musics are quite unaccustomed to the sight of these stringed instruments being played in this way, and the method has become something that English folk music audiences now associate very strongly with Wood.

The use of this technique in the performance of 'St George's Day' can be interpreted in a number of ways. Firstly, it is possible to consider the method as a celebration of folk music as a 'homespun' genre. Through this interpretation, Wood's behaviour can be regarded as a 'naïve' exploration of the practical musical potential of the limited number of available instruments.[24] This 'do-it-yourself' approach to the use of instruments is particularly effective in the context of the English folk music resurgence, since it represents a visual and embodied manifestation of a home-made aesthetic, supporting a construct of authenticity that is regularly renegotiated and reasserted with relation to this genre. Perhaps, in response to the more 'artistic' elements of the trio's music, here at least is a valuable affirmation of the folk-musical identity, acting in contradistinction to the accepted, conservative practices of the arts establishment. An alternative reading of this technique, however, would be that it represents a celebration of experimentation: these highly recognisable instruments are used by Wood in particularly unrecognisable ways, through a notably self-conscious exploration of organological potential. This analysis would suggest that Wood's method of performance here can be seen as imbued with a post-modern esotericism similar to that present in John Cage's works for 'prepared piano'. Whilst apparently taking on 'Heath Robinson' characteristics in isolation, when considered in combination with the musical text and the cultural and commercial positioning of the group more generally, it could be argued that this experimentation actually reinforces – rather than repudiates – the EAC's alignment with the musical and conceptual values of twentieth-century Western art culture. Both sets of associations are simultaneously active within the musical event. The network of seemingly conflicting intertextual references and connections invoked here serves to demonstrate – and is, in fact, necessarily reflective of – the wider ambiguities of contemporary English folk music's movement into a mainstream environment.

As well as the implications of the EAC's specific textual characteristics, formal expansions and performance behaviours, it could be argued that more middle-ground associations with art music are at play in the instrumentation of the trio. The ergonomic characteristics of the English concertina, in particular combination with Harbron's performance style and ability, are such that it lends itself to polyphony in the tenor and (in the case of the baritone and bass concertinas, which Harbron employs occasionally) bass registers. It is no surprise then that, when both Dipper and Wood are playing violins – and even when Wood is playing viola – the resultant soundscape is remarkably similar to that of a string quartet: the ultimate art music ensemble. The group's physical presence on stage also reflects that of a string quartet: they invariably appear on stage in a relatively closed arch, with Wood and Dipper at either side of Harbron, almost facing each other (i.e. almost at ninety degrees to the audience). So the performance is, to some extent visually, as well as aurally, introverted: conceptually 'artistic'.

3.7.2 Classical folk music: Methera

The subtle links between the EAC's strain of contemporary English folk music and art musics obtained ultimate clarity when, in 2007, John Dipper and three other English folk musicians embarked upon a new project: a string quartet by the name of Methera. As might be expected, the group have generated a good deal of discourse relating to their choice of ensemble, much of which is underpinned by an assumption that the string quartet is an inherently natural, and effective unit:

> *Methera* unites the depth and integrity of traditional English music with the rich texture of the string quartet. Four fine young musicians with individual traditional styles meet in a unique classical constellation. (Methera, 2008b)

> It was a yearning for traditional music to be heard through the voice of the string quartet that compelled Methera into existence. It quickly became clear that Methera was about a meeting of musical minds.
> Four individual musical characters with our different stories to tell; the cohesive structure of the string quartet gives us the freedom to indulge in tradition and rebel against convention. (Methera, 2008c)

The essential, organic purity of the string quartet's 'rich texture' and 'cohesive structure' are not questioned in these statements; they appear, instead, to represent the rehearsal of a timeless, simple truth. Were it not for the – broadly well-known and acknowledged – traditional backgrounds of the individuals involved, the reference to a 'unique classical constellation' might even lead one to question with which conventionally labelled genre the group are seeking to identify. Interestingly, however, the musical language of their output is likely to be less aesthetically challenging to folk audiences than that of the EAC: their debut album, *Methera* (2008), is – proportionately – far more orientated towards diatonicism and a clearly monodic texture. Where textures become more polyphonic, the presence of the cello (played by Lucy Deakin) as a dedicated bass instrument often results in the strengthening of harmonic progression, and instances of octave-unison playing are surprisingly frequent.

As with the EAC, elements of Methera's performance practices are unique and key to an ethnographic understanding of the group's intertextual negotiations of the folk and art idioms with which they engage. The four performers play without scores (as is normal of a folk group – but not of a string quartet), but are not orientated towards the audience: they perform in a tight square arrangement, each musician facing inward, in such a way that one player has their back to the audience for the duration of a piece (or set). Between each discrete rendition, the members of the group stand up and move around the square, thus varying each member's orientation in relation to the audience. This physical arrangement of the musicians will often require a performer to look over their shoulder, temporarily re-orientate their body on their seat or briefly stand in order to announce the next piece, or otherwise address the audience. Such consequential requirements highlight to the audience not only the unusual nature of the arrangement, but also – by implication – the importance bestowed upon it by the performers. The importance of this inward facing configuration is also acknowledged through its depiction in the majority of the group's promotional photographs.

The cultural significance of this performance technique can be read in a number of ways. At a discursive level, the inward-looking formation places emphasis on the creative negotiations apparently taking place between the constituent parts of the group and a greater whole: attention is physically directed towards the liminal creative space between Methera as 'four individual musical characters' and Methera as the 'meeting of musical minds' within a 'cohesive structure'. The group's 'gig book' on their website offers audience members the opportunity to leave (positive) comments, many of which demonstrate inclination towards an engagement with this discourse:

- I loved the playful precision of your rhythms, and the column of sound that rose up from the middle of the square.
- You played together like one instrument.
- A really special, emotional experience – 4 as 1!
- Your music is so beautiful and your communication together fabulous – a quartet so without ego you didn't even introduce yourselves!
- A wonderful evening of spontaneous music-making.

(Methera, 2008a)

Certainly, Methera's act of sitting with one member presenting their back to the audience, takes the notion of introspective performance to a logical conclusion, but this, as with various elements of EAC's presentation, can be understood as engagement with and reference to both traditional and art culture. For instance, whilst the act of turning one's back on the audience may be read as an indication of artistic introspection and creative immersion, it can be argued that doing so in order to look directly at your fellow musicians is an invocation of folk music's perceived origins as a participatory, self-motivated activity, rather than an audience-orientated practice. The most 'grassroots' exhibition of this behaviour can be seen in the context of a pub session, where players are creating music for their own enjoyment rather than for the benefit of other patrons (i.e. not producing music for an 'audience' *per se:* see 1.6).[25] Through this reading, the audience is offered the privilege of bearing witness to a timeless, organic creative event, such as it would occur whether or not onlookers were present.[26] Through this action, Methera can be said to be actively constructing a form of social authenticity, thus claiming the string quartet for the creation and development of traditional music.

On the other hand, it must be acknowledged that the display of traditional music-making in such a 'backs to the audience' manner occurs nowhere else within the professional performance of English folk music. Furthermore, Methera's presentation foregrounds the occurrence of a – to some extent, spontaneous – performance process, rather than the musical text as a product. The very act of presenting the music as process rather than product in this way, and of developing a clear and unique challenge to performance conventions (conventions accepted within both contemporary folk *and* art music genres) is a practice that, of the two genres involved, is most easily associated with twentieth-century Western art music. The indeterminacy-based compositions of Riley and Cage provide obvious examples; the foregrounding of practical devices is also found in the methods of postmodern dance implicit in the title of a series of Contact Improvisation dance performances in 1975 New York, *You Come, We'll*

Show You What We Do (Banes, 1987: 66).[27] It is, of course, worth noting that much of the intended demystification of compositional technique that is inherent in such high-art events is not present in Methera's live performances: in fact, the emotive and often spiritual content of the audience responses chosen to appear on the group's website suggests an *increased* mystification of the communicative processes at work between the musicians. Nonetheless, the unusual practices involved in their live performance are comfortably experimental in a way that can enable their contextualisation on the arts-venue stage. In total, the artistic connotation of the string quartet is juxtaposed with folk-orientated elements, but this apparent challenge to genre culminates in the production of a relatively accessible, diatonic soundscape that serves to render the event culturally secure.

A point that we have deliberately neglected to mention thus far in this consideration of Methera is the important fact that the group rarely appears on concert stages of middle-scale arts venues (such as those on which the EAC regularly performs). Many of Methera's performances take place in smaller-scale venues, such as churches and village halls, with a large number taking the form of 'house concerts'. Such concerts consist of an individual in contact with the group hosting the performance as the larger part of a social event for an invited audience. The house concert takes place in the largest available room of the host's home; audience/guest numbers are therefore limited by the size of the space – usually to less than twenty. To avoid various issues pertaining to licensing and regulation, the audience are not charged on entry, but after the concert a suggested donation is invited, which is invariably paid (or even exceeded) by each audience member. The house concert as a performance context deserves more ethnographic investigation than is possible in our study; however, it is of particular interest here since it represents a subtle physical manifestation of the generic dissolution characterised by the music of the two groups discussed.[28] On the one hand, the small scale of the space and the low number of audience members result in an intimate atmosphere, enhancing the perception of authenticity, and offering the opportunity to bear witness to the musical event at the closest possible quarters. As with the group's non-presentational seating arrangements, the scenario offers a comfortable reminiscence of a perceived past in which traditional music existed as a domestic, amateur pursuit. One comment in Methera's gig book expresses this:

> It was just like a Thomas Hardy novel, travelling musicians playing in a thatched cottage. (Methera, 2008a)

The social element of the occasion is also emphasised: audiences often include groups of close friends, and post-concert socialising affords attendees the opportunity to converse – and enjoy a glass of wine and some food – with the performers. On the other hand, however, the social roles of a concert (audience/performer/host) are very present, and the established conventions of an arts-venue stage (attentive silence during – and applause after – each piece) are respected. Through adherence to such protocols, the event might in fact be read as an evocation of chamber-music recitals popular amongst the European bourgeoisie prior to the development of the public concert culture during the nineteenth century (see Weber, 2003). It is important to note that house concerts are mentioned by Locke as a specifically art music-orientated milieu in late nineteenth- and early twentieth-century America (Locke, 1994: 804). Certainly, the predominant audience demographic at house concerts appears to support this reading. Alternatively, such an event could be considered closely reminiscent of the patronage of itinerant court musicians throughout the Middle Ages; ultimately, the connotations of the process are historical, whilst those of the domestic space are vernacular. Thus, the house concert can be understood as an inherently 'artistic' context by contemporary values, but one that invokes the sense of authenticity more commonly associated with folk music.

3.7.3 Morris Offspring: On English Ground

The morris dance group Morris Offspring, led by dancer and musician Laurel Swift, began with a commission for a morris-based performance at the Sidmouth International Festival in 2003. Two short works choreographed by Swift, entitled 'Blue' and 'Red', had their premiere on the Arena Stage, where they formed the centrepiece of a show, 'Flame', that presented a range of folk dance acts and performers. 'Blue' and 'Red' went on to form the basis of a full-length evening show in collaboration with the EAC, entitled *On English Ground*, that played at the Southbank Centre's Purcell Room, London, in November 2005 and went on to tour arts venues in England in 2006. As mentioned earlier (2.2.4; 3.7), the tour received coverage on *The Culture Show* on BBC2 (2006). The success of *On English Ground* made way for a follow-up, *Rising* (2007) and, subsequently, *Must Come Down* (2011). It is *On English Ground* that will form the main focus of the analysis here. Whilst the Demon Barber Roadshow, discussed earlier, demonstrates the engagement of folk dance with popular culture, taking urban street dance as a point of reference, Morris Offspring's engagements with the mainstream adopt a different range of stylistic features and contexts more associated with high cultural forms.

The contexts in which *On English Ground* has been performed illustrate this association, from the profiling of the show at one of the key cultural venues of the capital city, the Southbank Centre, to its touring of major regional arts and theatre venues. This placing of morris dancing in theatres and arts venues is noteworthy, in that (like the Demon Barber Roadshow) it represents a significant recontextualisation of a dance form whose contemporary performance is still very much tied to the practice of dancing in public places, especially the street. In its routine incarnations, these contexts of performance are a key part of the meaning of the dance. Its new theatrical framing is underlined on the Morris Offspring website, which claims for it the status of an 'art form':

> This show sets out the relevance of this most spectacular element of England's cultural inheritance for a contemporary audience and demonstrates that the Morris and the music that supports it are as compelling as any other art form. (Morris Offspring, 2007)

When Swift was asked, in interview, if the group ever danced in the street, she replied: 'it's not our thing', although, she said, they had done so once or twice (Laurel Swift, interview, 2008). She explained further:

> If we want to dance in the street we want to do it really well, and we'd have to practise just doing that, and actually we'd rather concentrate on what we do. And that's a decision we've kind of made. (*Ibid.*)

There is a recognition here that the degree of specialisation involved in being a company who dance on the stage may preclude them from the normal morris dancing practice of street performance, thus separating the dance from everyday life. This relates, it should be noted, to Morris Offspring as a company, and not to the individual dancers within the company, who retain their activities with regular morris sides. As Swift puts it:

> The thing is that ... most of the team dance with other good teams – very, very good street teams – and why would you go and dance with Offspring when you could dance with them in the street? (*Ibid.*)

Whilst this separates, in the lives of individual dancers, the stage-orientated practice of Morris Offspring from the everyday practice of their 'street teams', the community-based, street-dancing folk ethos is nevertheless maintained, because for these dancers Morris Offspring is an adjunct to their regular dance practice, not a replacement for it.

Morris Offspring's reframing of morris can also be seen at the level of the performance text. Whilst rooted in Cotswold morris, the performance departs from the normal conventions in which an individual dance might last for around three minutes, danced to one tune. *On English Ground* is, in comparison, an extended, evening-length performance made up of several linked sections, and closely choreographed to the music of the EAC. This is very clearly a newly choreographed product, albeit one that is based on the characteristic steps and figures of Cotswold morris. This newly choreographed status marks it out, as the writing of new dances is not common within the culture of Cotswold, which has an established traditional repertory of dances.[29] Speaking about the process of choreographing (or, as she puts it, 'writing') these new dances, Swift says:

> I'd been sitting in Towersey [Festival] when EAC had been playing, and I just got this idea in my head of this stage that was kind of ... dappled blue lights, and these people just totally in white just floating across it in these, like, lots of lines and things going on. And that's what the whole thing came out of. (*Ibid.*)

This suggests a choreographic concept that was very much created with a theatre stage context in mind. It also implies a choreographic vision that 'sees' the dance, complete with costume and theatrical lighting, from an outside vantage point, the vantage point of an audience. Swift comments later that the dances are choreographed as if seen from above: 'It's always written looking down on it' (*Ibid.*), a notion that places the choreographer outside of the dance, looking on, from above as if in a proscenium theatre. Even though Swift also performs with the company, this notion of the choreographer/director as external brings it in alignment with the conventions of Western art dance, where works are overseen by an artistic director or choreographer.

The extended form of *On English Ground* deploys choreographic techniques whereby basic elements of Cotswold morris are extended into more complex group choreographies. Its characteristic stepping patterns progress through more complex and expansive floor patterns. Figures such as rounds (dancing round in a circle), heys (three or more men dancing in a figure-8 pattern), processions (stepping forward and back as a line) or back-to-backs (protracted versions of the common do-si-do) are extended and extrapolated upon. The symmetry that characterises Costwold morris dances is evident, but applied to more complex group formations. Swift explains:

> A lot of stuff is still in symmetry. Or in a procession. And everything is based on morris. So there might be some big huge movement, but it's basically a back to back ... You might have one circle turning this way and one circle dancing through and turning that way, or joining on, but it's basically rounds ... And lots of things like heys, an inner set and an outer set shadowing them, but it still all fits into six double steps two back steps and a jump ... you know it's a recognisable tradition. It kind of makes sense to a morris dancer. (*Ibid.*)

Whilst Swift here emphasises that this extension of the dance language of Cotswold morris stays close enough to the tradition to be recognisably morris dancing, still 'making sense' to a morris dancer, she also speaks of subsequent choreographic experiments undertaken by the group that clearly test the boundaries of how far that extension might go:

> I wrote a piece called 'The Game', which is basically a set of rules ... All the steps that you're doing are morris dancing; it's just that it's set out in a big grid ... Basically you add in dances. You're only allowed to move to the adjacent square to you and eventually you get to a stalemate position and that's when you win. (*Ibid.*)

This rule-based improvisatory choreographic structure brings to mind the contemporary art dance that grew out of the American postmodern dance movement beginning in the 1960s (see Banes, 1987), and found a British (and English) home since the late 1970s with choreographers such as Rosemary Butcher.[30] Whilst it may indicate something of the art-dance trajectory of Morris Offspring (regardless of whether or not such references were conscious or intentional), 'The Game' may have been an experiment too far for some:

> Everybody hasn't quite got their heads around it ... They're going, 'Well, why is this morris dancing? I don't see.' So, we're working on that one at the moment. That's been the most contentious thing we've ever done, because the team's kind of gone, 'I don't understand why this is morris dancing', and I've kind of gone, 'I don't understand why it isn't'. (*Ibid.*)

Finally, consider the ways in which Morris Offspring presents its performers. They are costumed in a way that refers to, but significantly alters, the traditional Cotswold morris costume. The opening section, 'Blue', has the dancers costumed in white long-sleeved shirts and trousers, and black shoes. In comparison with traditional Cotswold sides, where white shirts and white or black trousers are overlaid with often colourful accoutrements such as sashes, ribbons, rosettes and waistcoats, as well as hats, flower-bearing hats, badges, and so on, the Morris Offspring costume feels minimalist and almost austere, signalling a kind of 'stripping back'. This stripping back extends to one of the most significant characteristics of their costume, which is the lack of bells, and in some elements of performance, the absence of handkerchiefs. Bells and handkerchiefs are iconic signifiers of Cotswold morris, central to the public perception of the genre, and their absence here is noteworthy. For one, it raises the movement to an additional level of abstraction. This is particularly the case with the absence of handkerchiefs, because the dancers still perform the arm movements and hand gestures as if they were present. The visual and sonic absence of bells lends to the performance a quality of (literally) quiet restraint, and a seriousness that perhaps speaks of the desire to offer a representation of morris that will encourage people (audiences beyond the folk world in particular) to 'take it seriously'. Let us not forget that the bells that adorn the legs of Cotswold morris dancers, and the handkerchiefs that they wave are the target of much of the cultural ridicule of the tradition. Describing the experience of dancing in the street without bells, Swift notes:

> When we go and dance in the street with no bells – especially when Rob and Miranda were playing for us – it's concertina and fiddle and quite quiet. And sometimes you could kind of create this vacuum that draws people in and people just passing. The crowd would go quiet because they could see something was going on and they wanted to know. But sometimes it means you get totally ignored. (*Ibid.*)

This suggests that the absence of bells (which are one of the ways that morris dancing creates a spectacle to grab the attention of audiences in the street) creates a viewing context that is more akin to the engrossed audience in the theatre (going quiet and being 'drawn in') than to the uncontrolled audience of the street. Swift observes that the lack of bells actually began as an act of disorganisation: 'we didn't wear bells for the original gig because I forgot. I just forgot that morris dancers wore bells!' (*Ibid.*) She goes on with an explicit recognition that Offspring are engaged in an 'artification' of morris dancing: 'But then we kind of thought about it and went "well actually, it makes it more arty".' (*Ibid.*) Bells are not absent throughout the whole of the performance, but the absence of them in some sections highlights the way in which Morris Offspring, in recontextualising morris for the art context of the concert stage, divorces it from its carnivalesque roots and offers it as a serious art form.

3.8 Conclusion

When Jools Holland introduced a performance by Bellowhead on his television show in December 2006, he said, 'the first rule in music is that there are no rules whatsoever!' The phrase is, of course, anathema to the theoretical principles of social and cultural scholarship. One would probably receive a good deal of scorn for sitting at the piano during a 'free' jazz improvisation session, and incessantly repeating the theme of a popular television show. 'Free' does not necessarily mean 'free': there are always rules. However, the sentiment of the comment could in fact prove interesting as a model for our understanding of artistic processes within the current English folk resurgence. What this chapter has aimed to illustrate is the considerable extent of diversity that characterises the current resurgence. Multiplicity in the presentation of English folk music and dance is a strong theme within the contemporary moment, and can be analytically approached in terms of the making and breaking of 'rules'.

As discussed in the introduction to this chapter, the historically definitive rule – dictating a separation of 'folk' from popular or high culture – has been subverted before, whether by Steeleye Span or Benjamin Britten. Certainly, a rejection of that schism is also clearly present in much of the music being produced in the current English folk scene. But such a contravention of old rules is often accompanied by the making of new rules: the folk-rock movement, for instance, followed a relatively clear musical path, developed new conventions of musical fusion, and thus progressed as a self-contained movement within which a number of common musical characteristics can be traced. If any convention can be identified in the music and dance of the contemporary resurgence, it may be a tendency amongst artists to continuously seek out new methods for modernising or otherwise modifying traditional English folk materials or practices. Each of the major artists or acts that draw together folk and pop or art musics, dance or imagery do so each in their own distinctive way.

We have, however, demonstrated how some examples share certain similarities. For instance, as we have shown, those versions of contemporary English folk music that reference popular culture tend to do so in ways that simultaneously reify and subvert the conventional distinction between the categories. The juxta-positions in the work of the artist David Owen, for instance, are wholly reliant on the relative immobility of the culturally accepted boundaries between folk and pop. Owen's back-catalogue includes tongue-in-cheek manipulations of existing images to portray such unlikely and disparate icons of popular culture as Morecambe and Wise, Morrissey and a Star Wars storm trooper as morris dancers.[31] These images are not about the timelessness or universality of folk themes – they are simply strong symbols of a popular culture conventionally separate from folk music and dance, and the playful celebration of that separation is a key part of the substance of the artwork. In contrast, any boundaries between art and folk are subtly and tacitly defused through the work of musicians such as Chris Wood and Methera. Movements in the direction of classical music aesthetics are submerged relatively deep in the associative and structural fabric of, for instance, EAC's output, and when boundary-crossing becomes more obvious (as in Methera's instrumentation) they remain relatively unmentioned in the surrounding discourse. This differentiation of pop-orientated and art-orientated folk might go someway towards justifying our identification of two discrete camps, but we are happy to recognise that anomalies disrupt the idea – Lakeman's soundscape of mid-Atlantic strummed pop, for instance, appears no more explicit in its challenging of boundaries than any of the art-orientated examples we have offered here. The central purpose of this chapter has been to demonstrate the bewildering range of stylistic approaches to the performance of contemporary English folk, characterised by ambiguous overlappings of aesthetics, potential meanings and effects.

As explained in 1.5, the diversity of approaches to the contemporary performance of English folk music and dance is one of a number of reasons for our rejection of the label 'revival' with reference to the current English folk scene. The celebration and application of contemporary (or recent) popular cultural imagery, musical signatures and dance styles in the English folk culture at present would also appear to negate use of the phrase 'revival', or – at the very least – critique conventional use of the term. In her survey of music revivals, Livingston argues that these movements are 'characterised by their historical references and rejection of mass culture (considered a hallmark of modernity)' (1999: 81). Clearly, although historical allusions remain a central part of the English folk culture (and, it could reasonably be argued, of any 'folk' culture), a number of culturally central musicians and dancers are presenting their output in ways that seek to *equate* the traditional material with popular culture rather than explicitly reject the latter in favour of the former. While Seth Lakeman draws folk and pop together with an 'acoustic pop' aesthetic that subtly and implicitly realigns English folk music with Anglo-American pop (via American folk and country), figures such as Jim Moray or David Owen celebrate the sights and sounds of popular culture in extremis, embracing the 'inauthentic' reproduction and kitsch of twentieth-century popular culture in order to reframe folk as one facet of vernacular cultural expression amongst many others.

The rejection of compound niche descriptions like 'folk-pop' or 'jazz-folk' in favour of plain old 'folk' is not simply a question of semantics – it is a significant acceptance that folk is behavioural as much as it is textual or stylistic; that it is not bounded purely by material content or by performance approach. Alternatively, a 'classical-folk' label would be redundant on the basis that the boundaries between art and folk music and dance are being eroded implicitly, without announcement or celebration. When folk festival audiences listen to a concert set by the EAC, followed by a performance using live sampling by Jim Moray, and then adjourn to the ceilidh tent to dance to Whapweasel, they are complicit in a tacit acknowledgement that folk is – to some extent – inherently processual, based upon – but never constrained by – intangible concepts of history, participation and identity. In this context folk is, therefore, an ideological construct that transcends style, instrumentation, performance practice and even musical or choreographic material, although all of these features are effective and available for the negotiation of meaning within that construct.

Notes

1 For an unusually explicit discussion of the terminology, see Morgan and Leggett (1996).

2 For discussions of the concept of hegemony and its adoption within cultural studies to inform particular understandings of popular culture, see Storey (1997: 123–30); Storey (2003: 48–62).

3 An obvious example can be found in Halnon (2005).

4 Recent attempts by opera and classical singers to reach 'mainstream' audiences serve to emphasise this point (e.g. Luciano Pavarotti's successes after the use of his recording of Puccini's 'Nessun Dorma' for the Italia 1990 World Cup; more recent stadium performances by Russell Watson; Charlotte Church's early career; and the current popularity of Katherine Jenkins). For a historical discussion of opera's relationship with, removal from and recent returns to popular culture, see Storey (2002).

5 In their largely quantitative survey of musical consumption in England, Chan and Goldthorpe identify an omnivore-univore reading where 'omnivorousness is taken to express a new aesthetic – perhaps less inclusive than it may at first appear – that is itself exploited in status competition' (2007: 14). This reading would seem to corroborate succinctly the observations on the mainstream that are offered here.

6 Lakeman also strums the tenor banjo in a similar way in a number of his songs, a relatively unusual use of the instrument in English folk music, although also occasionally featuring in the playing of Benji Kirkpatrick when performing with Bellowhead.

7 The cover image can be viewed at the artist's website, www.jimmoray.co.uk/discography. php; at the time of going to press, a higher resolution image is also available at http://goo.gl/MOV4I.

8 For a variety of promotional and live-gig photographs of the band, see their website, www.glorystrokes.com and MySpace page www.myspace.com/glorystrokes.

9 See for example Hutera (2011).

10 The *Burlesque* cover image can be viewed at Bellowhead's own website, http://bellowhead.co.uk/releases.html, and http://goo.gl/XG8J0.

11 This assessment is based not only on his work with Bellowhead but also on his drumming for Tim Van Eyken's *Stiffs Lovers Holymen Thieves*.

12 Composing for theatre productions is a second source of income for Boden.

13 Programmatic arrangement returns in a pantomime form for 'Cholera Camp' on the album *Matachin* (2008), highlighting the disturbing nature of the song's lyrics.

14 For another example of disco-inflected folk, see also Mawkin:Causley (2008: 'Come My Lads').

15 Again, the cover image of *Sprig of Thyme* can be viewed (and compared with that of *Sweet England*) at the artist's website, www.jimmoray.co.uk/discography.php, and at http://goo.gl/eB4Mq.

16 See, for images, www.jimmoray.co.uk/discography.php, and http://goo.gl/KXvp5

17 See BBC (2008).

18 The term has often been used to refer to Ornette Coleman's Double Quartet, and most significantly appeared as an adjective in the title of that group's pioneering debut album: *Free Jazz (a Collective Improvisation)* (1960).

19 Here, we are using the term 'textual' in the most general sense – that is, pertaining to the nature of the audible construct. In actuality, the majority of the discussion in this article will be directed towards instrumental music.

20 See Eliza Carthy (2005); John Spiers and Jon Boden, *Bellow* (2003)

21 The pizzicato figure is built through a combination of the lowest three strings on the

viola (tuned down a tone, to B♭, F and C respectively), and the equivalent strings on the violin.

22 We use the term 'fiddle' here, as it is commonly used in English folk music culture, to denote a violin or viola (although it usually refers to the former). The term is often used specifically to acknowledge the instrument's use in the traditional genre: if one plays the 'violin' one is probably playing 'art music', whereas if one plays the 'fiddle' one is most likely to play a folk or traditional repertoire. This use of the term as a contradistinctive device is by no means limited to England, but is worth clarifying.

23 Likewise, the interaction of folk musicians with art music towards the end of the second period of revival resulted in extended works such as Alistair Anderson's classically tinged *Steel Skies* (1982), but this was specifically Northumbrian rather than English folk. The close relationship between Northumbrian folk music and art music contexts and performers has been cultivated since, by both Anderson and Kathryn Tickell (Newcastle University, 2008a, 2008b).

24 In fact, this 'limited' instrumentation is something of a self-imposed constraint. Although all three individuals are polymath in terms of their instrumental performing abilities, the only regular change in instrumentation within the context of the EAC is Wood's moving between fiddle and guitar.

25 For more on the session context in English folk music, see Stock (2004) and Keegan-Phipps (2008).

26 There is much of interest regarding tourist or audience perceptions of a traditional musical event's authenticity and perceived spontaneity in Stevenson (2004).

27 Banes quotes Steve Paxton, a central figure in the Contact Improvisation movement, as having explained: 'We're focused on the phenomenon, rather than on the presentation' (Banes, 1987: 67).

28 A detailed survey of the phenomenon is, sadly, beyond the scope of this book; anecdotally, it would appear to be something of a recent cultural import from America, where it also has close ties with folk musics.

29 It is more common in other forms such as border morris, where the more recent reinvention of the tradition has required – and thereby exalted – the creation of new dances.

30 Paradoxically, the work of Butcher and others was innovative partly in that it frequently took art dance out of the theatre and into public spaces, whilst the work of Morris Offspring innovates by doing the opposite.

31 These and other works can be viewed at the artist's website: theinkcorporation.co.uk.

4

An English style?

Central to any formation or consolidation of identity, national or otherwise, are processes of differentiation. The differentiations inherent in the present resurgence of English folk are, for the benefit of our understanding of the movement, two-fold. Primarily, the movement must necessarily be concerned with the essentialisation of those concrete aspects of the English folk arts that are identified with Englishness. In other words, a successful negotiation of English identity through the folk arts cannot be achieved without an acceptance (overt or tacit) of what artistic or stylistic elements make them *English*, as opposed to American, European or – most importantly in the case of folk music – Celtic. Closely interrelated to that essentialisation is a differentiation of the English folk arts from conceptual and generic 'others' by fixing artistic differentials between English *folk* and alternative types of artistic performance. Of course, while processes that distinguish Englishness can appear quite separate from those that distinguish folkiness, these processes are entwined at the wider cultural level, since the specification of folk continues to carry connotations of the national, the authentic, or – at the very least – the local. To balance the previous chapter's focus on the blurred boundaries between English folk and other genres, this chapter is mainly concerned with examining those characteristics of contemporary English folk that are accepted as definitively English, and thus speak directly to the broader concept of Englishness as it is constructed in this context.

The processes of differentiation mentioned above have operated differently for English folk music and folk dance. The variants of English folk dance have historically been, and continue to be, clearly and unambiguously identified as English, to the extent that morris dancing, in particular, has often been referred to culturally as 'quintessentially English'. They are sufficiently distinctive and unlike the folk dancing of other cultures that they do not have the need to differentiate themselves from, say, forms of Irish or Scottish folk dancing. Furthermore, English folk dancing is, paradoxically, characterised by its diversity. Cotswold morris is iconographically, choreographically and somatically distinct from, say, border morris, molly, any of the varieties of English clog, longsword, rapper or indeed ceilidh dancing. The processes of the resurgence may have led to an increased cultural profile for English folk dancing, but they have arguably not led to the development of new English styles of dancing analagous to the development of an emergent set of English styles of folk music. For this reason, this chapter will focus on English folk music.

Having examined the diversity of approaches and cultural engagements that characterise the recent resurgence of English folk, in this chapter we will now provide an examination of possible commonalities across this diverse genre. We will highlight some of the key elements of English folk music practice that have been foregrounded, or have developed in profile and significance, within the current resurgence. The list is by no means exhaustive or universally applicable: often, individual artists or groups have emerged as exponents of one or two of these characteristics, whilst engaging less with others. However, overall, the following sections cover general artistic trends within the music of the English folk resurgence that are observable – in differing combinations and to differing extent – across the outputs of the resurgence's key protagonists.

4.1 Discovering English folk music

We start by considering two anecdotes that offer windows onto a wider process whereby a distinctively English identified folk music has come to be more widely explored, searched for, or recognised. In doing so, England is characterised as culturally distinctive; in particular, it is presented as distinct from its nearest neighbours in the UK and Ireland.

Speaking in interview of his participation, along with other young English musicians, at the 'Ethno' festival in Sweden in 1997, musician Tim Van Eyken observed:

> That was quite an eye opener. We were the group from England and hadn't really made any distinction between English repertory and Irish. And we got there, and there was a group from Ireland there. So we prepared some Irish material, you know, and we performed that. And they were quite pissed off. Which we thought was ridiculous, but actually, you know, on reflection it wasn't ridiculous at all … There were lots of countries represented there, everybody playing their music. It's a great thing to make you think, 'Okay, actually what is English music?' (Tim Van Eyken, interview, 2008)[1]

Van Eyken was speaking of the emergence of his own interest in English music. Here he recounts a moment in which, encouraged by an 'eye opening' context which required him to look at his music with an outsider's eyes, he was led to consider the question: 'what is English music?'. This anecdote is interesting for several reasons. For one, it identifies a moment – in 1997 – which is recounted as a catalyst in the movement of some significant players in the new professional wave of English folk music towards something defined as English music. Notably, other participants in Van Eyken's 'group from England' included Laurel Swift and Rob Harbron, both of whom also went on to become key figures in professional

English folk music (and, in the case of Swift, dance). Secondly, it is interesting that, even in this context (the aims of which include intercultural learning and exchange), this group is described as not having made a distinction between English repertory and Irish at this time. This speaks of the extent to which the practice of folk music in England was, for these young musicians at this time, not strongly focused around an exploration of a specifically English tradition. Thirdly, it is interesting because it was the reaction of the Irish group (who were, it is implied, disgruntled because of a perceived appropriation of Irish music by these English musicians) that seems to have opened Van Eyken's eyes. There is a sense here, then, that this particular individual's turn towards English music was born not only out of a personal desire to explore it but also out of a situation in which the English musician is challenged, within a wider context, to find his own musical roots.

This previous lack of discrimination between English and Irish music speaks of a cultural context in which, in the years immediately preceding the resurgence, Irish (as well as Scottish and generically celtic) music had dominated the professional folk stage in England. Festival headliners, for example, were much less likely to be English-identified. Irish traditional music and dance also had a higher profile within popular culture with global phenomena such as Riverdance and supergroups like The Chieftans. It is hardly surprising, then, that people not involved in the cultures of folk music or dance might have taken the higher-profile Irish folk arts as a point of reference for folk. Sue Coe, talking about a pub session that centres around northern English tunes, noted in interview that: 'people come through the room the session is in because that's where the loos are. They used to say always every time, "Oh this is really great. Is it Irish?"'. She went on to observe: 'Now that is not happening as much recently … Whether it's just that we've saturated the local community … we are English! It is English!' (Interview, 2008). Whilst these musicians had been playing English tunes in the pub for many years, the change that she perceived was in the wider public perception of what they were doing. 'I do think it is changing,' she said, 'There is a wider perception out there that there is English folk music' (*Ibid.*).

The identification of musical traditions that are defined as English does not necessarily imply some kind of purity. The year 2007 saw the publication of *Hardcore English* (Callaghan, 2007), 'the first new tune book that the English Folk Dance & Song Society has published for some considerable time', and designed as an overview and guide to 'the current understanding of English traditional dance music' (*Ibid*: 7). In an introductory section entitled 'So What's England?' Callaghan points in particular to the considerable blurring of boundaries between the various dance musics of Great Britain and Ireland. He does, however, insist that, even though a search for purity of repertory might be fruitless, 'what *is* interesting, however, is to observe which tunes took root where, and how their peregrinations affected their essence' (*Ibid*: 10). Here, then, bound by a relationship with place, is a subtle and qualified investment in the concept of a discrete (if not 'pure') instrumental repertory, and it is performance of this repertory that will serve as the central focus of the following sections.

4.2 Englishness in English tunes

In the case of music, tendencies in the current movement are towards a rise in profile and status of instrumental music and musicians. It must be noted that, within English folk-music culture instrumental music and song are very closely linked: many musicians, at both grassroots and professional levels, engage in both activities, and the two repertories are often to be found cohabiting within performance contexts such as pub sessions and stage concerts. Relatively little evidence exists of the compartmentalisation of instrumental and vocal activities such as is more apparent in the other traditional music cultures of the British Isles. Within this context, however, there has been a significant growth in the number of professional musicians and acts that foreground instrumental music: the concertina player Rob Harbron, the fiddler John Dipper, and the groups Mawkin and Methera all enjoy considerable successes without any strong singing profile (although Harbron's vocal activities have increased in recent times with the groups Kerr Fagan Harbron and the Fay Hield Trio). Many more English folk musicians have strengthened associations with particular instruments that eclipse the profile of their singing activities (as in the case of melodeon specialists like John Spiers and Tim Van Eyken).

It could be argued that this growth in the profile of instrumental music is part of a wider quest for English folk to obtain a cultural status equivalent to that of the instrumental traditions of Ireland, Scotland and Northumbria. English instrumental music had been – for some time – less popular amongst English folk audiences than that of Ireland, Scotland and Northumbria, but this began to change in the early years of the twenty-first century. In the case of these 'rival' folk musics, despite each having strong vocal traditions, it is the instrumental forms that have been most successfully exported and achieved the highest profiles. It is, perhaps, possible to suggest that this is in part related to the problems posed by lyrical content. Apart from the obvious issue of language and dialect comprehension, which has almost certainly been a factor in – for example – the global popularity of Irish instrumental music as compared to Irish-language song such as sean-nós, there is also the issue of anachronism. Castle-inhabiting Lords, wandering fair maidens and other historically rooted characters and narratives loom large in the English folk song repertory; also historically rooted are the various metaphors, innuendos and other plot-furthering devices. Whilst such subject matter may be celebrated by those audiences heavily invested in the currency of its 'authenticity', the uninitiated and casual listener may be less receptive. For many, not only is the language of these songs irrelevant (or even incomprehensible) to the contemporary listener, but the content has also become so closely associated with previous revivals that it can appear clichéd and cannot easily be liberated from the heavy mockery aimed at those movements prior to the current resurgence. A challenge set by the Channel 4 television show *Big Brother* for its contestants in 2004 illustrates the inalienability of traditional song content and revivalist contexts (Keegan-Phipps, 2008: 249–50). During the week in which the Glastonbury Festival was being held, the programme challenged the contestants to write folk songs. The songs were required to include the lyrics 'pipe', 'Shrewsbury', 'fair maiden', 'barley', 'heritage' and 'bicycle', and were to be sung around fake campfires by the contestants, who were also required to wear fake beards, Aran sweaters and sandals (items perceived to be the sartorial calling-cards of the 1960s revivalist).

It is therefore possible to understand English instrumental folk music as an opportunity to maintain engagement in traditional music performance that avoids the revivalist associations and perceived lyrical irrelevances of many traditional song texts. Nonetheless, the extent of the growth of the instrumental form of English folk should not be over-emphasised: song is still considered central by many participants in English folk music culture. Song is regarded as particularly important within the culture of English folk clubs, making the rise of instrumental music an arena for quiet conflict between key representatives of the old and new generations (the former being the more represented in clubs nationally). Dave Delarre explained in interview the difficulties experienced by his band Mawkin when attempting to secure bookings with one local folk club organiser:

> Apparently there was a few people from the committee and the club members who had asked for Mawkin to play at the club, so she said, 'Yeah, that's right. Yeah, we've had a few people actually come to us and say they'd really like you [to perform]. And we'd really like to have you down, but erm, we heard that you don't sing? [*surprised tone*]' I was like, 'Yeah, that's right. We're an instrumental band, and we just play kind of English music, mainly, and we throw in the odd French tune, the odd Scottish tune…'
>
> 'Aah, but you don't sing?'
>
> 'No, we don't sing.'
>
> 'Oh, well we worry that you won't be able to entertain our crowd for long enough, erm, before they get bored of just tunes.'
>
> And I said, 'But your crowds have asked you to book us … they're not concerned'. She said, 'Yeah, but there's a few of us on the committee who are a bit concerned that, because you don't sing, a lot of people will be put off by the fact that you don't sing, and won't turn up.' And I was like, 'But, there's people in your club who have asked us to play, and on the committee that have asked us to play.'
>
> 'Yeah, but at this time, we just feel that, you know, you're not best suited to our club.' Put the phone down, you know. I was just like – you're having a fucking joke! [*Laughs*]. I mean, what more can you do?! (Dave Delarre, interview, 2008)

Response by English folk music audiences to exclusively instrumental English folk music has until recently contrasted sharply with those responses to other, non-English traditions – particularly Celtic traditional music repertories. Delarre's experiences emphasise this:

> They're just really weird! Because, you can go and see Flook [an instrumental band with a predominantly Irish repertory], and they'll just play tunes at you for an hour and a half, and people will fucking love it and they'll think, 'Yeah, great, woo', and it's the same people who are going to Waterson:Carthy. You're not telling me that's a different crowd – there's not that many people in folk music,

you know. So what's wrong with them appreciating *English* instrumental music? I think it's something that's been abandoned by us for the past hundred years or so. There's a wealth of English morris tunes that are brilliant to play, that are starting to get some recognition thanks to Spiers and Boden bashing them out and stuff like that, and Eliza and that group. (*Ibid.*)

Keegan-Phipps (2008: 90–1) has argued elsewhere that the emphasis on instrumental music and musicians in the folk music culture of the North East of England is key to its cultural distinction (or 'separation') from *English* folk culture – this separation will be returned to in 6.3. Delarre might just as reasonably have cited one of the most successful folk musicians of that region, Northumbrian piper and fiddler Kathryn Tickell, who has enjoyed considerable popularity with folk and mainstream audiences nationally, but who does not generally sing.

The narrative offered by Delarre suggests that the profile of English instrumental folk music within the folk community is in flux. Understanding the significance of this cultural shift requires an understanding of the common musical characteristics of the repertory, and of those other (Celtic) repertories with which it is most regularly compared. A comparative analysis of the English instrumental folk repertory (i.e. English tunes) pivots on two key features: first, the relative variegation of note durations, and second, the relative predominance of diatonicism (particularly major tonality) rather than pentatonicism or modality. Both of these features can be clearly seen in the typical English polka 'Bonny Breast Knot' (figure 4.1), when considered in comparison with a Celtic tune such as the popular Irish reel 'The Maid Behind the Bar' (figure 4.2).

'The Maid Behind the Bar' is indicative of Irish traditional (instrumental) music's inclination towards a uniformity of note durations (specifically the proliferation of quavers) and a common pentatonically inflected melodic structure, although many Irish tunes are in a full major or mixolydian mode. Here, it is helpful to borrow from Hughes (2008) the idea of 'pentacentrism', where a melody is structured around five central tones but is embellished with notes from beyond that pitch set. Speaking very generally, Scottish tunes tend to share these characteristics, although 'minor' tunes (that is, tunes where the third degree of the scale is flattened) are sometimes in the aeolian mode (rather than dorian, as in the case of most 'minor' Irish tunes), and pentacentric tunes are more likely to emphasise the interval between the second and fourth degrees of the minor scale, often omitting the third entirely (e.g. A-B-D-E-G). Also, in Scottish traditional music the Highland Piping tradition has canonised 'variation sets' (tunes where subsequent parts of a tune are melodic variations of the first). This feature is shared with a large number of older Northumbrian tunes, due mainly to the border piping tradition of the North East region. The dance tunes of the Northumbrian repertory contain a good deal more diatonicism, with quick, arpeggio-based passages, and accidentals that sometimes denote brief modulations to the dominant; they are, however, predominantly quaver-led in terms of note duration, as with the Celtic repertories. Performers of these Celtic and Northumbrian repertories share a common language of ornamentation, particularly relating to the rearticulation of notes greater than a quaver in length.

4.1 'Bonny Breast Knot' (basic tune). Transcription by Keegan-Phipps.

4.2 'The Maid Behind the Bar' (basic tune). Transcription by Keegan-Phipps.

Ornamentations such as 'cuts' and 'rolls' (realisations of which are similar to 'mordents' and 'turns' in the Western classical vocabulary, hence the suggested ornaments in figure 4.2) are particularly significant in 'breaking up' crotchets so as to disrupt any sense of static resolution and thus maintain the regular, driving momentum of the predominating quaver movement.

Of course, this is a very general summary of some key features – selectively pertaining to distinctions between these repertories and English folk music. It should be noted that all of these repertories include slow tune types (waltzes, airs, slow hornpipes, etc). In such cases, the proliferation of quavers is considerably less, and there is a wider variety of note durations. Nonetheless, the modal qualities referred to above are often still present. Moreover, they are less common in performance, often performed to inject a temporary change of mood in a programme that is otherwise typically dominated by the faster jigs and reels.

It can be reasonably argued that the popularity of Celtic and Northumbrian tunes amongst England's folk audiences during the 1980s and 1990s has much to do with their respective musical features identified above. Two general features of these repertories are particularly significant. Firstly, tunes that are commonly characterised by a rarely broken driving quaver rhythm, when punctuated by well-executed ornamentation, and performed at a swift pace (e.g. minim = c.120 bpm), present a good deal of opportunity to demonstrate virtuosic musicianship to a non-performing audience. Secondly (with relation to the Celtic repertories), tunes that are pentatonic or modal (especially those that include flattened sevenths) can be audibly – although rarely consciously – related by that audience to the common melodic properties of Western rock and pop. Such associations between Celtic and riff-based Western popular musics have been consciously explored and exploited by fusion acts such as the Afro Celt Sound System, Capercaillie, and the Peatbog Faeries, to name just three, but they can also be heard less explicitly in the performance of more 'traditional' groups such as Altan and Session A9. So the inherent qualities of the Celtic and Northumbrian repertories enable audiences to draw two vital and very positive associations. On the one hand, the repertories embody visible and audible virtuosity (especially through prestidigitation and general speed of movement) that suggests skill. On the other hand, their respective melodic structures are fundamentally accessible to audiences who are encultured within the aesthetics of Western and popular musics.[2]

English traditional tunes – for the most part – do not share either of these musical features and, therefore, do not enjoy their attendant associations. English instrumental folk music contrasts with these repertories in the aspects of rhythm and mode. The repertory is characterised by tunes that employ a range of note durations, with the majority of English dance tunes running the gamut from minims to quavers, with crotchets being the most frequent. As has been briefly mentioned in 1.6.2, the English instrumental repertory is essentially made up of music composed for dancing; since the dancing in question (morris and ceilidh) is generally formation-based set dancing, the movements are relatively large and slow in comparison with those of the Scottish and Irish competition dance forms, and the music is therefore suited to performance at an appropriately slow and steady pace. In the case of a polka (a 4/4 tune type, and the most common in the English dance repertory) this would be around minim = 100 bpm. Although performance of tunes away from dancers (e.g. in sessions or concerts) might involve playing at a faster pace, a significant deviation from a 'danceable' tempo is considered undesirable (i.e. untraditional) by many English folk musicians. Also in line with their relationship to step-hop dance moves is the fact that the variegated note durations of English tunes combine to form fairly simple rhythms that emphasise the down beats; syncopation is a rare occurrence. Finally, English instrumental tunes are generally diatonic: whilst many English tunes are in a dorian mode, the majority operate completely within a simple major scale. The combination of these musical factors means that the basic, common English instrumental tunes are often very simple to the ears of English audiences (as in the case of the tune 'Bonny Breast Knot', figure 4.1). They are not particularly difficult to remember or play, with the majority of the repertory accessible for performance by any intermediate-level instrumentalist. Perhaps more crucially, they do not *sound* difficult to play – the technical demands of an English polka are less likely to impress a listening non-musician than those of an Irish reel, for instance.

The resurgence, however, has seen significant changes in the ways in which English instrumental music is performed and, therefore, how it is perceived. Numerous trends have had the effect of developing a musical lexicon through which virtuosity and associations with popular culture have been nurtured in alternative ways, and it is these trends that we shall go on to examine here. However, it is worth emphasising that, since this lexicon has become available to the accompaniment of song as well as instrumental tunes, its significance is pervasive throughout contemporary English folk music performance.

4.3 'Playing around the tune': variation and improvisation

It is unsurprising that, during the course of the resurgence, the rise in status and profile of English instrumental music has been accompanied by the developments of technically demanding approaches to its performance. Of these approaches, one of the most significant has been an emphasis on variation. The act of varying each rendition of a tune (particularly through apparently spontaneous improvisation) has, in recent years, come to be seen as a constituent element of a good English instrumental folk performance.

The techniques involved in this practice revolve mainly around the endeavour of adding passing notes and arpeggio- or scale-based decoration to the tune's basic elements. Auxiliary notes will often reference or reinforce the harmonic structure implied by the original tune, or else that of a new arrangement, and notes of the main tune itself will sometimes be substituted with alternatives concordant with this harmony. Similarly, variation may be achieved simply through the accentuation, repetition or transformation of a particularly rhythmic element of the tune. A transcription of a sample rendition of 'Bonny Breast Knot'

4.3 Sample version of 'Bonny Breast Knot' as it might be played in performance.

that employs these techniques can be seen in figure 4.3 (compare with figure 4.1).

In group performance, this technique is likely to result in – sometimes multiple – counter-melodies, with the simultaneous sounding of the basic tune and variants that effectively harmonise that tune. This is particularly clear in the heterophonic texture of numerous performing groups at the forefront of the resurgence. The key individuals involved in the EAC have been highly influential in the propagation of the technique, but the wider emphasis placed on this particular strain of 'spontaneous', creative activity has increased and become synonymous with a specifically *English* style. Much as improvisation is seen as the technical cornerstone of jazz, the ability to spontaneously vary, harmonise and 'play around' the standardised form of a tune is becoming regarded as an important skill amongst English folk musicians. That said, there appears to be tacit agreement that this improvisation should not totally obscure the tune proper, and a number of those instrumentalists deemed especially inventive by audiences and commentators (such as Spiers and Boden) do not foreground this particular technique to such an extent, although it is certainly present.

Whilst varying the tune in the ways discussed above has become a clear feature of instrumental music in the contemporary English folk resurgence, the practice is rarely the subject of discussion, particularly amongst non-musician audiences. Variation has, however, become the subject of instructive discourse in workshops and other educational events. For instance, at the Fiddles on Fire

Festival – a series of workshops and concerts hosted at The Sage Gateshead – in 2005, Rob Harbron gave a workshop entitled 'Making a tune your own', in which he demonstrated possible methods for varying or altering a tune. The process of 'playing around a tune' is also used extensively as a vehicle for educational differentiation within a workshop of mixed-ability students: once students of a higher level have learnt the tune being taught by the workshop leader, they are able to apply simple methods of variation and development (such as the use of drones and passing notes), whilst allowing the less advanced students to (simultaneously) continue consolidating their knowledge of the tune itself. Here, then, it is possible to see the consolidation of a musical technique within the English folk music culture partly facilitated through its compatibility with contemporary educational practice.

The title of Harbron's workshop ('Making a tune your own') hints at an important reading of this trend towards spontaneous improvisation: namely, it speaks to a continuing rise of individualism within English instrumental folk music (and English folk music more generally). The comparative ability to vary a tune in the ways discussed above is a deeply personal one; the increasing cultural value of that skill emphasises the role of the individual in interpreting – rather than simply performing – the traditional material. Apparently instantaneous variation not only demonstrates the musician's internalisation of that skill but also represents the most immediate form of self-expression available within the performance of the repertory.

Thus, the performance of an English style has, in this instrumental arena, become more clearly denoted as a skilled, individual activity; the practice of 'playing around the tune' has afforded English instrumental music a new virtuosity through which can be presented a performance skill set considered distinct from Irish, Scottish and Northumbrian traditions, whilst being equivalent in technical difficulty. It should be noted that the art of spontaneous variation of tunes is considered an important skill amongst instrumentalists in the Irish and Scottish traditions, but we would argue that it is not foregrounded to the same extent musically or discursively. At a practical level, it might be argued that it is more difficult to vary the tune dramatically in these traditions due to a relative lack of 'space' created by the dense quaver rhythms. The nature of an improvisatory skill set within English folk music instrumental performance allows for the virtuosic performer and the novice learner to play together (be that in a workshop, a session or a more presentational context) in a heterophony that is becoming established as a dominant sought-after aesthetic of English instrumental folk music.

4.4 Arrangement

The way in which folk material (songs and tunes) are harmonically or texturally presented can be seen as a key arena of development in the resurgence. As Chapter 3 has demonstrated, the ways in which traditional material has been approached have varied substantially between the many artists involved in the performance of English folk music and dance. As we have shown, no clear overarching trends can be identified in the musical specifics of contemporary English folk music and song arrangement. Rather there exists a plethora of techniques that provide acceptable settings of the material, whilst simultaneously signalling towards exterior cultural and musical domains. However, the need to arrange in new, 'exciting' or even 'funky' ways is very commonly acknowledged, implicitly by musicians and more explicitly by commentators. The selection of audibly stimulating methods for such musical presentation of traditional material has, of course, been a consideration for English folk musicians that surely predates the Sharpian revival. But the intensity, variety and discursive profile of this goal has increased considerably over the course of this resurgence. Multiple methods are employed to this end, to greater or lesser extents by different artists, and can be roughly categorised in the following ways.

4.4.1 Funky chords

The phrase 'funky chords' is often used by musicians as a catch-all term for any harmonic element of a premeditated arrangement that successfully undermines the conventional diatonic harmonies prescribed by the inherent features of English traditional music. Due to some of the innate musical properties of English folk, along with the ergonomic characteristics of the melodeon (which will be discussed in 4.6.2), the application of alternative and unpredictable chord progressions represents a significant challenge within English folk music performance, and engagement with that challenge has been consolidated as more central to English traditional performance practice in recent times. As was shown at the beginning of this chapter, there is a predominating diatonicism among English melodies; an important consequence of this feature is the clear melodic signposting of a diatonic harmonic accompaniment. Specifically, the melodic structures of many English tunes incorporate clear arpeggios which connote particular harmonies; also, through pitch and rhythmic emphasis, such tunes very clearly prescribe [V-I] cadences at the ends of each phrase. The last bar or half bar of each part will commonly indicate a harmony of chord [I] by ending emphatically on the tonic, often preceded by the mediant. The subverting of these diatonic features has become a preoccupation for many artists, although responses to the challenge range considerably. Very often, a conventionally placed chord [I] might be substituted for a less predictable chord [IV] or [vi] so as to remain consonant with a tonic in the melody, resulting in an almost subliminal impact on the listener. At the other end of the spectrum, an arrangement might introduce a more chromatic harmonic accompaniment that produces an unsettled soundscape, peppered with dissonances and false relations (this is particularly the case with the carefully orchestrated and theatrical arrangements of Bellowhead, and also in many of the song arrangements by Mawkin:Causley).

It is important to note, however, that the destabilisation of English folk's diatonic foundations is regularly achieved via means other than simple, monodic harmonisation. Ostinato figures – commonly referred to here, as in popular music, as 'riffs' – are regularly used to vary the accompaniment of a tune or song. Likewise, pedal notes – sometimes referred to here as drones – are often employed, resulting in frequent dissonance. A pedal note that is not of the tonic triad is particularly successful at building a sense of tonal ambiguity, before resolving with the next verse of a song, or part or exposition of a tune. We have seen this most clearly in the music of the EAC (see 3.7.1), but riffs and non-tonic drones can be seen to some extent across all facets of the resurgence in English instrumental folk music and song.

4.4.2 Punchy rhythm

Much discourse has assigned great importance to 'rhythm' as an indicator of quality among the various soundscapes of the resurgence, although the exact nature of 'good rhythm' is never made entirely clear. One act that is regularly praised by audiences for injecting punchy rhythm (the word 'funky' is often used again here) is Spiers and Boden. Notable within their music is the great frequency with which marcato-like accents are employed by both musicians within their instrumental playing, and the diversity of rhythmic phrases created by these accents. A stark shortening of some crotchets is common not only in the music of Spiers and Boden but also in that of many other acts, including Chris Wood, Tim Van Eyken and Faustus, and can be seen as a celebration of the diversity of note durations mentioned earlier in this chapter as a central ingredient in English instrumental music. Particularly clear in the former's output, however, is the addition of a method of irregular phrasing (especially through the playing of the left hand of John Spiers' melodeon) that contributes to the rhythmic interest of the sound: for instance, that accompaniment will often group the crotchets of two bars in groups of 3-3-2, in such a way as to result in a strong sense of syncopation.[3] Often this is an apparently spontaneous phenomenon, as can be heard interspersed throughout the 'Sloe Gin Set' and 'Jack Robinson/Argiers/Old Tom of Oxford' (Spiers and Boden, 2003), although in the final tune of the latter track it also features as a clearly rehearsed 'break'.

Another common feature of the duo's music is the (more regular) emphasis of the off-beat (usually the second and fourth beats in the four-beat bar) by whichever instrument is taking an accompanying role – as in, for instance, the melodeon's left hand in 'Sportsman's Hornpipe' and the fiddle in 'Monkey-Cokey' (Spiers and Boden, 2005a). Prior to – and during – the resurgence, this technique of accompaniment has played a strong role in the explicit fusion of English traditional material with reggae, as can be seen in the cases of bands Edward II and Whapweasal.[4] If the emphasis of the off-beat is embellished by the inclusion of non-traditional instruments – particularly percussion (in a ceilidh band, for instance) – most listeners and musicians recognise the link to reggae, two-tone or ska. Played in the context of Spiers' and Boden's inherently 'traditional' instrumentation, however, such associations are not really present; rather, audiences are more generally aware that the music is rhythmically changed and stimulating. The duo subtly emphasise the rhythmic aspect of their music by the occasional use on stage of a stomp-box – a slightly raised, resonant platform on which Boden stands and stamps his foot while playing. In a four-beat tune, he stamps on the first and third beats, which often produces an effect similar to that of a club-dance track's incessant bass pulse (as opposed to the rock or pop feel of most ceilidh bands, for instance, where the bass would fall on the first beat, with the snare commonly articulating the third beat).

4.4.3 Polyphony

An implication of both of the above categories is that the performance of English folk is becoming more polyphonic in texture. Even where only two instrumentalists are involved, as in the case of Spiers and Boden, every opportunity to maximise the number of instrumental voices appears to be exploited, and the heterophonies created by variation serve to increase the density of the sound. Extensive polyphony can be identified in the work of the EAC, as has been discussed in 3.7.1. In the case of Bellowhead, the eleven band members play complex arrangements that move between homophonic chordal accompaniment, interplay between sections of instruments, and contrapuntal polyphony in which the musical line of each individual musician is distinct from the next, in terms of both pitch and rhythm; an excellent exposition of this textural range can be found in 'Rigs of the Time' (2006), but clear examples can be found throughout the band's albums – *Burlesque* (2006) and *Matachin* (2008). As the largest group of instrumentalists, Bellowhead are a strong illustration of the esteem in which polyphonic arrangement is now held, but this soundscape can be found to lesser extents in the works of many other key acts (for another example, see Mawkin:Causley's 'Mariners', 2008).

It should be noted at this point that a central development in the emphasis on polyphonic texture is the increased use of intricate and inventive percussion, such as that performed by Pete Flood as a member of Bellowhead, and also as percussionist on Tim Van Eyken's album *Stiffs Lovers Holymen Thieves*. The style and nature of Flood's percussion (such as polyrhythms involving cutlery, megaphones and children's toys) is particularly significant, since it draws together Bellowhead's expertly naïve (or even near-shambolic) music-hall or 'village band' aesthetics (see 3.6) with the developing trend for textural complexity.

And, certainly, the musical features discussed so far in this chapter can be collated as representative of a general move towards a complexity of texture. English folk music is undergoing a change in which we can see a significant rise in the audible profile of multiplicity, whether it be premeditated (through a process of arrangement) or improvised (through spontaneous, individual variation of the basic musical materials). However, it is probably helpful to consider these ideas as ends of a spectrum, rather than absolute, discrete practices. Much variation and improvisation comes about as a result of revisiting, internalising and even rehearsing patterns. The process of arrangement can range from stipulating each note to be played by each musician in a formal way – as in the case of Bellowhead (Jon Boden, interview, 2008) – to acknowledging a general structure within which individual musicians can maintain some creative autonomy. For the majority of smaller, more traditional groups, the appearance of effortless spontaneity is a significant part of the overall aesthetic (although there are others), and so much that is premeditated is designed to appear unplanned. Only close attention to repetitions over multiple performances reveals rehearsal, but even this may be deliberate or unintended, and varies considerably between individuals. Ultimately, the methods by which the aesthetic is achieved are far less significant than the aesthetic itself.

4.5 Canon formation

A significant point to consider in relation to the setting of traditional material in the current resurgence has to do with the selection of repertory – or more particularly, the formation of canon. The range of approaches to the arrangement and stylistic presentation of material – detailed in this chapter – has grown exponentially over the course of the resurgence, but the range of traditional material performed has not increased in quite the same way. Whilst it would be inaccurate to imply that the English folk repertory has come to venerate a restricted canon of songs and tunes, there are a number of items of traditional material that have received a disproportionate amount of exposure in recent years

One such example is the traditional song 'John Barleycorn'. The song depicts the gruesome murder of the eponymous hero; Barleycorn is actually a thinly veiled metaphor for the barley used to make beer, and the details of his murder are a dramatised account of the beer-production process. The song is widely regarded as ancient in origin, with a number of variants collected and located in manuscripts during the successive periods of revival; during the folk-rock era of the 1970s 'John Barleycorn' was subject to interpretations by bands such as Steeleye Span and Traffic, and a number of acts associated with that movement have recorded and performed the song since (e.g. Pentangle, Jethro Tull, Oysterband and Fairport Convention). Since 2000, it has been reworked by acts spanning the full stylistic gamut discussed above, and ranging from the highest to lowest in profile. Versions produced during the resurgence have variously included electronic sampled beats (in the case of the Imagined Village, 2007), guitar riffs and rock harmonisations alternating chords [I] and [IV] (Tim Van Eyken, 2006), Gambian drumming (Boka Halat), paired back acoustic guitar and vocals (Chris Wood, 2005) and church-organ-like homophonic village-band accompaniment (The Lark Rise Band, 2008).

It would be wrong to suggest that anything inherent in the song's melody or structure has lent it to the receipt of so much attention, although we shall discuss further the kind of England that the song helps to portray in 6.2. 'John Barleycorn' is one of a number of songs that surface regularly (others include 'Worcester City', 'Three Black Feathers' and 'Lord Bateman'), but share little except their perceived antiquity. Certainly existing literature on the revival of folk musics has documented and theorised the creation of canons in ways that continue to be relevant here (see for instance Bohlman, 1988: 104–21). It is likely, for instance, that a general sense of reverence towards certain songs is present amongst many of the musicians active in the current resurgence, based on personal history and memory. Some explanations of canon formation are, however, perhaps out of date. It is probably incorrect, for example, to assume that a canon is forming here through dissemination, as in previous revivals: where once grassroots musicians were reliant on limited sources (recordings, manuscripts, etc) for repertory, now considerable amounts of material – resulting from over a century of collecting activity – are available online or in hardcopy, in recorded or transcribed form. Keegan-Phipps (2008), Hill (2009) and others have discussed how educational institutionalisation of folk music may contribute to canonisation of repertory amongst learning amateurs, but as this chapter has shown, amongst recording professionals individuality or non-conformism appears to be a stylistic preference within the resurgence. If these musicians wished to avoid the repertory recorded by their peers, they would certainly be able to select alternative material without much difficulty. We must assume, therefore, that any conformities in repertory are in some way significant. We would suggest that this kind of regularly repeated material acts as a form of accepted, acknowledged tabula rasa upon which new methods of arrangement can be presented to knowing audiences. The impact of innovations in style is to some extent reliant upon a growth in the cultural capital of material that is pre-existing, 'authentic' and familiar: settings can only be recognised as 'new' where the material being set is deemed sufficiently 'old'. And at a time where audiences are broadening to include newcomers with more limited knowledge and experience of repertory, the process of ensuring that the majority are familiar with a song – and confident of its antiquity – must necessarily result in the favouring of a few 'standards'.

4.6 A national instrument?

4.6.1 'Fiddle-singing'

A performance activity that has become particularly iconic within the relatively short period of the current resurgence has been the act of 'fiddle-singing' amongst a number of English folk music's central protagonists. The term (sometimes appearing without the hyphen) is being used increasingly by artists, promoters and writers within the folk music industry to refer to the individual practice of singing and playing the fiddle simultaneously. Of the current wave of fiddle-singers, Eliza Carthy and Nancy Kerr are perhaps the earliest high-profile figures to be closely associated with the activity, but since then many of the musicians to appear at the forefront of the resurgence in English folk music have identified closely with it, including Jon Boden, Seth Lakeman, Chris Wood, Paul Sartin, Bella Hardy and Jackie Oates. For the most part, fiddle-singing actually involves the singer performing a song whilst playing an accompaniment on the fiddle via the bowing of (normally) two strings. The strings are open or stopped to create intervals of between a third and a sixth; thus they are used to indicate or reinforce predominantly diatonic harmonic progressions as support for the song's melody.

Whilst it is possible to perceive such a performance as the fiddle's utilisation purely for the purposes of accompaniment, similar to the role of the – elsewhere ubiquitous – steel-string acoustic guitar, it is also possible to identify semiotic significances in this performance method that extend beyond the function of harmonisation. For instance, since the violin is perceived as predating the steel string-string guitar, the fiddle has connotations as an older – and, therefore, more 'authentic' – instrument. The guitar is particularly closely associated with the second period of English folk revival (c.1950–70) as well as an icon of the American folk movement; in contrast to the fiddle, then, it can be seen as symbolic of a late-twentieth century counter-culture and representative of an 'inauthentic' cultural modernity. The fiddle, meanwhile, is more harmonious with the antiquity – or, perhaps more accurately, temporal ambiguity ('timelessness') – that is so central to the discourse and iconography of the latest resurgence.

The fiddle is also perceived to be amongst the most difficult of the instruments within the pantheon of Western folk musical instruments to master. Even amongst those members of the folk audience that would profess no musicality or musical experience, there is a general awareness of the technical challenges faced by the learning fiddler. Most are conscious of the small and necessarily instinctive adjustments in finger positioning required to achieve accurate intonation, whilst some more experienced listeners or musicians will also be able to identify bowing as something requiring a good deal of technical skill in order to reach even a basic level of competence. The playing of the fiddle and singing simultaneously, then, represents a clearly challenging technical display on the part of the performer, and the wider perception of the comparative skill levels involved must certainly be a contributory factor to the rise in celebration of the activity in recent years. Just as the level of improvisation inherent in the skill of 'playing around a tune' has been embraced and internalised as England's own form of musical virtuosity, distinct from those of neighbouring traditions, so too has the specific practice of fiddle-singing become regarded as a technical demonstration of a specifically *English* kind, even though the activity is also commonplace in various musical traditions across America. It might be argued that here the Englishness is inherent in the contradistinction of this performance technique with perceived common practice in Celtic musical traditions.

Beyond this distinctiveness of the activity, the nature of fiddle-singing may also be read as demonstrative of wider value judgements related to folk music culture in England. Most significant, for instance, is the fact that the two practices combined in fiddle-singing have – at least in the recent history of Western classical music culture – been separated activities, each regarded as sites for specialised study on the part of the musician. The combining of these elements is, then, highly symbolic: it emphasises the functional – even utilitarian – qualities of the fiddle and the voice. Such qualities carry with them a strong association with the economical deployment of musicianship, something that is seen to be a central characteristic within grassroots music-making of a historical, pre-modern cultural context. Thus, it can be argued that the combining of the fiddle and the voice results in the reassignment (particularly of the former) as a tool of the folk musician's trade, rather than a specialised – implicitly professionalised – activity. Performance of this kind then connotes a craft, rather than an artistic pursuit, and so emphasises links with perceived social, behavioural and contextual authenticities. Thus, subtle associations with concepts of 'art' are apparently disrupted here as they are in the performances of Methera discussed in 3.7.2.

4.6.2 The English melodeon

The melodeon has been ubiquitous at the grassroots level of English folk culture for much of the latter half of the twentieth century.[5] It has played a particularly central role in the accompaniment of traditional dance, owing to its relative volume, versatility (in providing both melody and harmonic accompaniment) and portability. It is now one of the most common instruments to be found at English folk music sessions and morris dance events. It is interesting to note that, despite this fact, it is the instrument least likely to be correctly identified by those English people who do not take part in or identify with English folk culture. Although its place at the heart of grassroots English folk performance is now well established, its growing profile as a virtuosic instrument of the concert stage has been a key feature of the current resurgence, a feature arguably started by the likes of John Kirkpatrick in the 1970s and 1980s, continued by Andy Cutting in the 1990s and furthered more recently by artists such as Tim Van Eyken, John Spiers and Saul Rose. To understand its developing role as an icon of English traditional music and dance culture, it is helpful to know something of the ergonomic elements of the instrument's construction and performance.

The melodeon is a diatonically arranged, bellows-operated, free-reed instrument that can be found in numerous folk traditions across the globe,[6] where it is variously referred to as: an accordion, a diatonic accordion (often to distinguish it from a chromatic form of free-reed instrument); button accordion (to distinguish it from the keyboard-arranged piano accordion); or simply a squeeze-box or box (where there is no requirement to distinguish it from another bellows-based free reed instrument). Globally, the melodeon exists in numerous forms, comprising different tunings and various numbers and arrangements of buttons, all of which impact on the number of keys and modes available to the performer, and the relative ease of their availability. The larger the number of rows of buttons under the fingers of the right hand, the larger the number of ergonomically accessible diatonic keys for playing melodies, whilst the same is true of the chords in the left hand. The greater the number of buttons, however, the larger, heavier and (on average) more expensive the melodeon. The common selection of the type of melodeon is therefore dependent on the conventions, performance contexts and repertorical demands of each of these various music cultures. However, the unifying principle amongst this group of instruments is that they are bisonoric: most of the buttons under either hand (i.e. on either side of the instrument) produce two different notes, depending on the direction of the bellows (whether they are being squeezed or opened, technically referred to as the 'close' and the 'draw', or informally referred to as the 'push' and the 'pull'). In English folk music culture, by far the most popular and significant form of the instrument is the 'D/G' melodeon: that being a melodeon with two rows of buttons on the right hand (melody) side, that sequentially provide the notes of D major and G major scales, respectively, as well as four accidental notes over the top two buttons (see figures 4.4 and 4.5).

As can be seen in figures 4.4 and 4.5, the buttons are arranged such that those of each row produce the notes of the D major and G major triads respectively when the bellows are closed (excluding the top button of each row, these being reserved for the most commonly required accidental notes). Meanwhile, the bass notes and (tenor range) chords in the left hand are ergonomically arranged to coincide consonantly with the melody notes. However, this arrangement is based on only the most basic of [I-V-I] alternations in harmony. So the instrument would appear, at first glance, to be highly restricted in its musical potential.

These restrictions can, however, be sidestepped via certain techniques. For instance, several melody notes in the right hand can be achieved via movement of the bellows in either direction, through 'crossing rows' (e.g. when playing a tune in G major, one can cross to the D row in order to play an A whilst closing the bellows), which maximises the options for harmonising. For instance, while playing a tune ostensibly in G major, one can cross rows in order to play a G on the draw, and thereby harmonise it with an E minor chord (which is only available on the draw). Crossing rows is particularly important for producing unaccented passing notes. However, this is not always possible – C♮ only appears in the G row, and can therefore only be produced on the draw; more significantly, D appears in both arpeggios, and so can only be produced by closing the bellows. Meanwhile, the left hand can produce more chords than is at first apparent by playing non-corresponding bass notes and chords: so, for instance, by playing the A bass note with the C major chord, one is able to create an A minor chord with the seventh. The same technique can also be used to produce B minor with a seventh; E minor over an A bass (effectively A major or minor with an added seventh and ninth) and C major over a D bass (effectively D major or minor with an added seventh, ninth and eleventh). But such exercises are complex, since the requirements of the melody can limit the chords available, and vice versa.

As has been suggested above – the melodeon, in one form or another – is by no means limited to the English folk music repertoire and culture: a form of the instrument allowing melodic chromaticism by virtue of the two right-hand rows being tuned a semitone apart (e.g. C♯/D) is common in Irish traditional music, where it is referred to as a diatonic or button accordion; two- and three-row melodeons tuned to fourths are also prevalent in Breton instrumental traditions, as well as in Italy, and across North and South America. So how does the rising profile of the melodeon contribute to the ongoing negotiation of *Englishness*, specifically? In answering this question, it is important to remember that the most significant cultural differentiation is that asserted between English folk music and its closest (and globally more popular) neighbour – Celtic traditional music. Here, the differences between the respective performative qualities of this instrument in English and Irish traditions are particularly important.

Much about the distinction grows out of the respective extents to which the left hand is employed. In the heavily melody-orientated instrumental culture of Irish traditional music, the role of the left hand (in terms of playing bass notes and chords) can be regarded as largely subservient to that of the right, and where other instruments are present to provide rhythmic and harmonic accompaniment

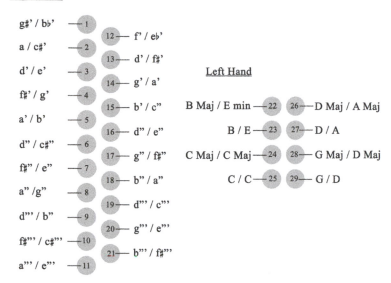

4.4 The arrangement of buttons on the standard D/G melodeon. Melody notes are located on the right hand, bass notes and chords on the left. The authors have numbered the buttons for use in conjunction with figure 4.5. The hands are presented the opposite way round here to simulate viewing the instrument from the front.

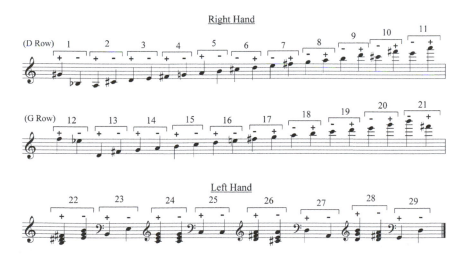

4.5 The arrangement of notes on the standard D/G melodeon, as represented on the stave. Notes are bracketed together to indicate that they are produced by a single button (the numbering of the brackets corresponds to the numbering of the buttons in figure 4.4). The symbol [+] indicates that the note or chord is produced by closing the bellows; [–] indicates that the note or chord is produced by opening the bellows.

(as is commonly the case in the form of a guitar or bouzouki), the chords and bass notes of the left hand are often not employed at all. In the professional performance of English instrumental folk music, however, it is far less common for the melodeon to play only the melody. Rather, the properties of the left hand are treated as part of the instrument's very *raison d'être*; in larger groups it may appear alongside a guitar or bouzouki (such as in the Demon Barber Roadshow or Bellowhead), but in smaller ensembles it can often represent the sole provider of tenor- and bass-range harmonic and rhythmic support to tunes and songs (most clear in the music of Spiers and Boden).

A key element of the melodeon's crystallising role at the centre of contemporary English folk culture lies in its iconic qualities, and in the bodily dimensions of its performance. The extent of physical movement in the upper body is relatively great compared to the performance of the instrument in Irish traditional music, or of other free-reed instruments. Since the bass and chord buttons of the left hand are usually heavily involved in English melodeon performance, the minimum amount of air required is considerable. Also, the direction of the bellows is constantly changing as required by the musician in order to achieve the desired melody notes and chords. The fact that – outside of the pub session – the instrument is almost always played standing up both allows for and contributes to the formation of the performance as a highly physical one, and therefore a visual as well as aural experience for audiences.[7]

The combination of the fiddle and melodeon now holds a secured place at the forefront of English folk instrumentation, thanks primarily to the duos Chris Wood and Andy Cutting, and Spiers and Boden, with these instruments also playing the central melodic roles in groups such as The Demon Barbers, Jim Moray's bands and numerous ceilidh bands. The instrument's visibility in the stage context has become increasingly significant in consolidating its role not only as an icon of Englishness but also as a symbol of folk music, folk culture and a folk aesthetic. In the live performances of acts where creative alliances with pop genres are clearest, the melodeon plays an important role in the visual achievement of an unambiguous identification with English folk music. This is particularly significant in the case of numerous ceilidh bands, where the other melody instruments are often non-traditional, as in the brass instruments of Florida, Steamchicken, and Whapweasel; it's clearer still in the case of more self-consciously overt 'fusion' ceilidh bands such as GloryStrokes, where the melodeon is the only visual clue that the band is not a straight-forward metalcore band.

Along with many forms of squeeze-box, the vast majority of melodeons currently available in the UK are made by manufacturers based in France (Saltarelle), Italy (Dino Baffetti; Castagnari) or Germany (Hohner). The latter's contribution to England's melodeon market is particularly significant: Hohner's Pokerwork model is not only one of the cheapest full-sized instruments available new (at around £500), but also one of the most instantly recognisable and popular models amongst melodeon players.[8] The majority of these musicians endow the instrument with the status of a venerable workhorse, held in fond esteem as an iconic tool of the English folk musician's trade, being loud, sturdy and low in price. This *Pokerwork* recently began being mass-produced in China, but its standing amongst English folk musicians (even non-melodeon players) remains that of a quintessentially English instrument, or at least of an instrument imbued with quintessentially English characteristics. The largest Hohner melodeon dealership in England, The Music Room, heralded the Pokerwork's new incarnation with a statement from a popular and long-established exponent of the English melodeon, John Kirkpatrick, in which he reaffirms the 'Englishness' of the instrument:

> I have just had a go on one of the new Chinese-made Hohner Pokerwork two-row melodeons. I have to say I'm absolutely delighted to see them back in circulation. There is a general feeling of unease about the new version of this trusty old war-horse. [...] The Chinese Hohner still sings with a lovely clear, bright voice – it is still the perfect sound for carrying over a rowdy morris team out in the street or a noisy hall full of ceilidh dancers. The tremolo tuning breathes warmth and life into the playing, and immediately imparts a quality of Englishness that the far more expensive models, with their currently fashionable dry tuning, simply never achieve. (The Music Room, no date)

This testimonial is an enlightening window onto the construction of Englishness in English folk music – at least as it is regarded by John Kirkpatrick, a leading and influential participant in morris and folk music culture since the 1970s. The 'trusty old war-horse' discourse here asserts the significance of the Pokerwork in the psyche of the English melodeon player, but central to that significance is the functionality of the instrument. It is significant that the evaluation of this melodeon is partially gauged according to its appropriateness for the accompaniment of ceilidhs and morris dancing – both grassroots, amateur and (relatively) participatory activities. The functional demands of public, socially located performance contexts are seen to be met in this instrument, a feature that is clearly important to Kirkpatrick. However, it is the tuning of the Pokerwork's reeds that receives a special, explicit mention as a site of Englishness. Kirkpatrick's reference to 'the tremolo tuning' relates to the fact that the Pokerwork has, like most melodeons, two reeds for each note. The closer in pitch these two reeds are tuned, the more 'pure' the tone produced, whilst the greater the distance between the pitches of the two reeds, the greater the 'tremolo' effect (or 'beat') produced. The former sound is referred to as 'dry tuning', the latter as 'swung tuning'; the Pokerwork falls very clearly into the latter category, something that Kirkpatrick sees as distinguishing it from the more 'fashionable' (not to mention more responsive, more versatile and more expensive) Italian and French melodeons.

The Pokerwork's status as an institution amongst English folkies was made clear when, at Whitby Folk Week in 2007 it was the subject of a special concert. The concert was humorous in its content (it opened with a tongue-in-cheek catwalk-style 'beauty pageant' of musicians – including Kirkpatrick – and their Hohner melodeons), and was designed to celebrate the long and close relationship grassroots and professional musicians have had with the instrument, for better or worse. The show was very well attended and particularly informal in atmosphere, and whilst some of the content poked fun at the instrument's shortcomings, it was clearly founded on a sentimental veneration of the brand and many of the performances during the concert featured highly virtuosic players. The English-ness of this German-originating, Chinese-manufactured Hohner Pokerwork lies not then in a conventionally locatable authenticity based on antiquity, or even on strong associations with an influential individual, but in the instrument's longevity and ubiquity as an enduring underdog among melodeons of vastly superior quality. Its success is born out of the fact that it is *sufficient* in all essential departments, but also affordable, and therefore available to all; thus, to revere the Hohner Pokerwork is to celebrate an authenticity inherent in the inclusivity of amateur, grassroots music-making – an activity that is still seen to be at the heart of contemporary English folk culture by the vast majority of those involved. In this way, it might even be considered a tacit celebration of popular culture writ large. However, the visual aspects of the Pokerwork signpost a historically located popular culture (the pokerwork design from which it takes its name is an Arts and Crafts-style gold and black pattern that covers the body of the instrument), locating it among the examples of the Victoriana sometimes referenced in the current resurgence. Its inclusion is quite congruous within the village-band and music-hall aesthetic of Bellowhead, and not only through its visual features but also through its characteristic 'chorus'-like swung tuning.

4.7 Conclusion

The stylistic developments of the resurgence offer musical echoes of the mixture of contradictory discourses illustrated in Chapter 2. Just as the burgeoning folk industry exhibits discourses of both commercial celebration and social inclu-sion, so do the various aspects of the emergent English style emphasise both the virtuosity that tends to accompany professionalisation or commercialisation and the inclusive, anti-elitist stance so fundamental to the idea of folk. Many of the characteristic features of this emerging English style mediate between these two pulls. This mediation is embodied in both fiddle-singing and the melodeon, which have emerged as iconic English practices and instruments, respectively. It can be also seen in several of the stylistic features discussed; for example, the art of 'playing around the tune', which provides a clear direction for advanced musicianship that is also inherently non-elitist, in that it does not remove the more highly skilled performer – conceptually or physically – from the communal, inclusive contexts of participatory performance.

As English folk music has increasingly asserted its own identity, so the Eng-land that is imagined and performed through it is constructed as culturally distinctive, with not only its own repertory but also its own characteristic styles. It is the particular character of this England that will be further examined in Part II of this book, along with the conceptions of Englishness that are associated with it. We begin, in Chapter 5, by examining the context within which the English folk resurgence is situated.

Notes

1 The Ethno festival is an annual summer music camp for traditional musicians aged 15–28, taking place in Belgium, Croatia, Cyprus, Czech Republic, England, Estonia, Macedonia, Slovenia, Sweden and Uganda (Ethno, 2012).

2 Again, the latter is less applicable to Northumbrian music, which tends to be more diatonic.

3 Interestingly, this 3-3-2 rhythmic phrasing – albeit at the quaver level – has played an important role in the music of Seth Lakeman (2004: 'Kitty Jay'; 2006: 'Lady of the Sea'), but here the aesthetic homology with Western pop is clearer, given the wider soundscape and instrumentation of Lakeman's music.

4 Numerous other ceilidh bands have also made – and continue to make – reference to reggae in many of their arrangements. For many ceilidh musicians it is seen as a humorous game – something of a tacit 'running joke' – since it can be achieved fairly spontaneously by a treble instrument dropping out of the melody and emphasising the second and fourth beats of the bar. However, the two acts mentioned here have been more concerted in making their links with reggae consistently explicit.

5 For much more information and useful links relating to the melodeon, see http://info. melodeon.net. For many images of melodeons, it is worth exploring the stock-list websites of leading vendors of the instrument, namely The Music Room (http://goo. gl/70tUC) and Hobgoblin Music (http://goo.gl/2Qy6d).

6 For more on this, see *The World of Music*, vol. 5, no. 3 (2008).

7 For more on this, see Keegan-Phipps (2008: 254–63).

8 Again, high-resolution images are easily available from stockists such as those listed in note 5.

II

Nation and identity

5

The English context

We noted in Chapter 1 that the surge of interest in English folk arts has happened in the context of a growing broader interest in Englishness. This has a political dimension – see, for example, the findings of the Future of England (FoE) Survey (conducted in 2011), which suggests that there has been an emergent sense of an 'English political community' (Wyn Jones *et al.*, 2012: 2). English voters, the findings of the survey suggest, appear to favour 'distinct government arrangements for England as a whole' (*Ibid.*). The survey's findings also suggest that changing attitudes about how England should be governed are tied up with changes in attitudes to national identity, with a sense of Englishness becoming more important for many. While most people have a dual sense of English and British identity, 'there is evidence to suggest that we are witnessing the emergence in recent decades of a different kind of Anglo-British identity, in which the English component is increasingly considered the primary source of attachment for the English' (*Ibid*: 3). We have also already noted in Chapter 1 the increased currency of cultural expressions of Englishness since the mid 1990s, including and beyond the folk resurgence that is our concern here. The reasons for this developing interest in all things English are multiple and complex, and a full analysis of the situation is beyond our remit, but it is worth summarising some important features of the British political and cultural climate that provide a context for the growth in popular expressions of Englishness.

Significantly, if unsurprisingly, many of these features feed into a wider (English) public concern that English identities, traditions, etc, are being consistently or increasingly undermined, either by people or by somewhat disembodied political developments. Kenny and Lodge identify an increasing celebration of English identity, and a belief that that identity goes unsupported by those in positions of power: 'the wider usage of specifically English symbols, the public celebration of English traditions, and a growing sense that Englishness is disapproved of by the political elite and most public authorities, have all become more prominent in the last few years' (2009: 223). This is interesting, since the majority of the political elite in Britain are English (Gordon Brown's brief tenure as Prime Minister, 2007–10, notwithstanding). It would seem, then, that one perceived threat to English identity and traditions originates from within, rather than from without, as might normally be expected where a national identity is being asserted. Nonetheless, however strong the discursive emphasis on the role of the political establishment in the suppression of Englishness, it is generally – often more quietly – acknowledged that Westminster's impact on the situation is often largely indirect. That is to say, accusations levelled at the UK government regarding an institutionalised 'disapproval' of Englishness are based on a general concern that the government has mismanaged – or continues to mismanage – processes that involve influences originating from outside of England's borders. We shall now introduce briefly the more significant of those processes.

A commonly aired explanation for the flowering of interest in Englishness is the ongoing process of UK devolution – that is, the devolution of political power from a centralised British government in Westminster, London, to the Scottish Parliament, and the Northern Irish and Welsh National Assemblies, respectively (Kenny and Lodge, 2009: 223). The Northern Irish Assembly is a return to a system of devolved government as part of the peace process following 'the inter-regnum of "direct rule"' (Wyn Jones et al., 2012: 4). The deferring of policy-making to the Welsh Assembly and the Scottish Parliament are more significant for our discussions here since they are more widely discussed (publicly and academically) with relation to present issues of English national identity, not least of all because these institutions represent the breaking up of Great Britain (of which Northern Ireland is not a part). The devolution of political power to Scotland and Wales, accelerated by Tony Blair's first Labour government, has been significant to the ongoing rise of awareness amongst the English of their national identity for a number of reasons, often expressed in terms of a general disenfranchisement of the English, both as a cultural group and as an electorate. Wyn Jones et al. argue on the basis of survey evidence that an English backlash against the anomalies and apparent inequities of a devolved UK has begun to take shape. For example:

> The English increasingly believe they get a raw-deal from the devolved settlement, with 45 per cent of voters in England saying that Scotland 'gets more than its fair share of public spending' – the number agreeing with this has almost doubled since 2000 (Wyn Jones et al., 2012: 2).

The processes of devolution have led to anomalies such as different levels of free-at-the-point-of-delivery public services being available in different parts of the post-devolution UK. For instance, England is the only country where a charge is levied on National Health Service prescriptions. Rises in university tuition fees only apply to English students, not to those from Scotland or Wales. The perceived inequities arising from this have been repeatedly attacked within the English press. For example, an editorial in the Telegraph sought to highlight what it described as a 'manifest injustice' regarding the Scottish parliament's continued policy of imposing tuition fees on students resident in other UK countries whilst not applying them to Scottish (or EU) students:

> It is especially galling in England, where taxpayers make a generous contribution to the Treasury's subvention to Scotland's public spending. After all, if Scotland

was independent and relied solely on its own taxes would it be able to continue a policy that is no longer affordable south of the border? (Telegraph View, 2011)

The asymmetry of the devolution process is most clearly illustrated by an issue now commonly referred to as the 'West Lothian Question'. This issue – named after a question raised by the Member of Parliament for West Lothian in 1977 – is a questioning of the fact that ongoing devolution has enabled Welsh, Scottish and Northern Ireland MPs to vote in Westminster on legislation where the outcome of the vote will only affect England. That is to say, MPs from Scotland, Wales and Northern Ireland can continue to vote in Westminster on issues that their respective national assemblies will decide independently (i.e. without the input of English MPs). Dissatisfaction in some quarters over the fact that Scottish and Welsh MPs have a disproportionate influence over policy in England (which includes legislation on health and education) was aired by the journalist and life-peer William Rees-Mogg in an article in *The Times* days after the 2005 general election, in which he claimed that 'The people of the UK's biggest, richest country won't accept second-class status much longer' (Rees-Mogg, 2005: 20). In September of 2011, the government announced the setting up of a parliamentary commission to consider in detail the West Lothian Question (BBC News Scotland, 2011). Such a commission was always likely under a Conservative-controlled administration, since the vast majority of Conservative constituencies are in England, with the party wielding relatively little power in the other nations. However, the significance of this constitutional status quo goes beyond party politics and underpins a sense of a marginalisation of the English – whose population is by far the largest of the British nations (around ten times that of Scotland, the next largest). Survey findings suggest that there has indeed been a growing sense, amongst the English, of the anomalies and perceived inequities resulting from the devolution process, and it is tentatively suggested that the popular proliferation of symbols of English national identity is in part a response to devolution (Wyn Jones *et al.,* 2012: 5). As Kenny and Lodge argue, however, to suggest that the rise in public celebrations of Englishness is solely underpinned by a 'grievance-fuelled politics of resentment' arising from devolution would be a partial account (2009: 223). We will go on in a moment to examine other key elements of the context, but first it is worth making some comments about the symbolic significance of devolution for the English.

Whilst (pre-devolution) the Scottish and Welsh electorate have been rep-resented within the British parliament, the location, structures and member-majority of that parliament have been English. The development of devolution has, therefore, been deeply symbolic. On the one hand, the English have been forced to recognise themselves as different from the Welsh and Scots, whose respective moves towards independence have been – unsurprisingly – accompanied by a considerable mobilisation of celebratory nationalist discourse in those countries. On the other hand, the English have also been required to acknowledge their role as a dominant power whose annexing of these nations over many centuries is slowly being undone. Devolution represents arguably the greatest symbol of the undoing of English, rather than British, imperialist oppression. That is not to say that any Englishmen or women that we have encountered believe that England deserves to maintain sovereignty over Scotland or Wales – far from it – but rather, it forces the English people to acknowledge their historical position within British politics. This is not a comfortable realisation, for its significance resonates beyond Britain's shores. For some decades the English have been able to mitigate a sense of postcolonial guilt through the acknowledgement that they were only one constituent part (albeit the strongest, leading part) of the British Imperial machine. Perhaps the proliferation of Highland bagpipes in the Punjab might reassure an English person that responsibility should be shared for the operation of the British Empire over the course of the eighteenth, nineteenth and early twentieth centuries. Devolution deconstructs this refuge: the renewed vigour with which Welsh and Scottish identities, languages and cultures have been celebrated as part of the devolution project in recent years implies a historic suppression (whether direct or hegemonic) of those things by a parliament under English control. It is therefore a stark reminder of the historical role of the English within Britain. The continued claims to – and fetishisation of – Irish and Scottish heritage by many Americans, along with celebration of independence from the British (but fundamentally English) monarchy, allows even the most powerful of the world's superpowers a degree of protection from this kind of cultural shame.

The second aspect of the context relates to the influence of the European Parliament. Unease about the extent to which sovereignty is being slowly devolved to a federalised Europe has been a common topic within the tabloid press over the last two to three decades. During that time, the news media have devoted considerable coverage to stories where European (or European-led) legislation has clashed with what are seen as common or traditional features of British culture. A particularly good example of this has been the press coverage of the imposition of the metric measurements of weight upon British shopkeepers (who have historically always used imperial measurements). Again, some sections of the right-wing tabloid press are a rich source of such stories: where traders have refused to change their practices to satisfy the legislation, putting them at risk of ruinous fines and criminal records, they have been referred to by the *Daily Mail*, for example, as 'metric martyrs'. Stories of these – and other – clashes of EU directives with the common practices of England or Britain were particularly regular in the years 2004–8, and a popular notion that British lifeways are under threat from the EU continues to resonate.[1] Whilst there is no clear evidence to support the view that Britain is inherently Eurosceptic (many are able to see benefits of membership in the European Union), a negative image of the European Parliament predominates in the British media (Glennie, 2011). More general concerns stem from a sense that the European Parliament is relatively distant and anonymous in nature, along with a sense that British interests will be insufficiently served or represented.

Debates and discourses around immigration have historically been a key site for the formation and maintenance of British and English national identity, articulating as they do notions of insiders and outsiders, voicing anxieties about the impact of incomers on national identity, and constructing national identity in relation to the figure of the 'immigrant other'. Historically, in Britain and England, anxieties concerning immigration and national identity have been expressed in relation to successive waves of migration from sources that include the former Empire and Europe. In the period under consideration here, anxieties about migration into Britain (and England, in particular) have been a ubiquitous theme across the country's broadcast and print media, where it is regularly presented – especially by the more right-wing broadcasters and publications – as being unsustainably high and as in some way endangering the fabric of English society.[2] Such presentations take a number of forms, from commentary on immigration policy to concerns about the policing of England's borders. The 'illegal immigrant' is a regularly revisited figure within the media, and representations of such a figure are the object of regular articles in the right-wing tabloid press (see, for example, A. N. Wilson in the *Daily Mail,* cited in Perryman, 2008: 29). The nature of the discursive figure of the immigrant shifts and changes with time. For example, amidst headlines speaking of an alarming rise in unemployment, the *Daily Mail* (a common source of anti-immigration discourse) recently published an article headed 'Secret Report Warns of Migration Meltdown in Britain' which demonstrates concerns specific to its context in 2011:

> A massive rise in immigration next year could trigger a devastating crisis in Britain's schools, housing and welfare services, according to a secret Government report leaked to *The Mail on Sunday*. The document reveals that every Government department has been ordered to draw up multi-million-pound emergency plans after being told public services face catastrophe as a result of the hundreds of thousands of Eastern Europeans pouring into Britain. (Walters, 2011)

An entrenched popular concern is that immigrants fail to successfully integrate into British society, and that this failure is characterised by a lack of English-language skills, along with a lack of understanding of – or respect for – British cultural and social values. These concerns contributed to the initiation in 2005 of the Life in the United Kingdom Test (frequently referred to as the UK or British citizenship test), a test administered by the UK Home Office, and intended to test would-be settlers. Passing the test is a requirement of any immigrant seeking to remain in the country.[3] Fears that immigration is threatening the cultural identity of the nation were manifest in 2011, when Prime Minister David Cameron argued the need for potential immigrants to be tested on British history (Whitehead, 2011). Whilst we can see that migration into Britain and England still functions for some as a source of anxiety regarding its ostensible impact on a national identity that is construed as fixed or pre-existing, at the same time the successive waves of migration, particularly those from the former Empire, have contributed to substantial shifts in national identity within Britain and the recognition, as the Parekh Report puts it, that 'England, Scotland and Wales are multi-ethnic, multi-faith, multicultural, multi-community societies' (Parekh, 2002: 2).

The final key element of the context for the upsurge of interest in Englishness is globalisation. Of course, the issues of migration and European influence discussed above are both related to globalisation, but concerns for an English identity are often couched in terms of a more general sense of cultural homogenisation brought about by the seemingly insidious and unstoppable forces of global communication and commerce. This discourse is developed clearly in Kingsnorth's book, *Real England: Battle Against the Bland* (2008), which links global capitalism with a cultural standardisation process that has the potential to eradicate the sense of England as a distinct place (and, implicitly therefore, the English as a distinct people):

> The things that make our towns, villages, cities and landscapes different, distinctive or special are being eroded, and replaced by things which would be familiar anywhere. It is happening all over the country – you can probably see at least one example of it from where you're sitting right now. The same chains in every high street; the same bricks in every new housing estate; the same signs on every road; the same menu in every pub. (Kingsnorth, 2008: 6)

Discourse on the impact of globalisation on Englishness tends to focus on the 'high street' element of this narrative, and to identify the United States as its source. The chains most often cited are American giants like McDonald's and Starbucks, whilst indigenous brands that loom much larger in the British high street, such as Tesco or Sainsbury's, tend to have a lower profile in the argument.

It must, of course, be remembered that none of these factors affect concerns regarding English identity in isolation from one another: shifting patterns of migration and EU federalisation are local manifestations of the broader globalisation process; devolution is partly significant because it highlights boundaries that articulate cross-national inequalities in relative levels of migration, or in the impact of cultural imperialism upon local culture. Nor are these factors experienced in any uniform way – different aspects are important to different people at different times and in different places. English people living in areas with large migrant communities may consider immigration to be the principal motivation for a growing interest in an English identity. A market trader may see EU legislation as a particularly concerning threat to a sense of Englishness, and an English person working in Scotland may find their national or cultural identity challenged by the progress of devolution more directly than most residing in England.

We must also acknowledge that these factors do not affect Englishness in isolation from a wider British identity. The idea of Britishness has also experienced a recent rise in profile with, for instance, a spate of television programmes celebrating Great British cookery, geography, history and institutions.[4] Responses to issues such as globalisation, immigration or the political growth of the European Union can take the form of discourse around either Britishness or Englishness. However, it is worth noting that, where Britishness is celebrated, the identity frequently stems from a discourse the origin of which is located tacitly – but unmistakably – within England. In other words, whilst Welsh male-voice choirs and Highland piping may have a highly visible role to play in the pantheon of British culture, the erection of that pantheon now tends to be a somewhat English preoccupation. Celebrations of Britishness rarely emerge from Scottish or Welsh media. Devolution represents a break-up of a British identity into constituent parts, and must therefore, to some extent, counter Britishness directly. However, Kenny and Lodge (2009) contend that roots of the developing awareness of English identity pre-date devolution, and that the subject needs to be understood as more than just a response to those changes in the UK's governance arrangements. They argue for taking a more historical perspective on these contemporary assertions of Englishness, seeing them as the 'latest chapter in the story of English self-assertion and examination' (2009: 225), and recognising that 'the case for an independently constituted English patriotism was made in powerful ways by figures as diverse as G. K. Chesterton, J. B. Priestly, Stanley Baldwin, George Orwell, Tom Wintringham, E. P. Thompson, Enoch Powell and Tony Benn, throughout the last century' (*Ibid.*). Nonetheless, it is fair to say that these earlier champions of Englishness are rarely cited in the contemporary public discourse on the subject.

As we have shown here, the wave of interest in, and identification with, Englishness with which we are concerned can be understood in the context of a very complex, multifaceted and interconnected set of historical and contemporary political and cultural contexts. These contribute to what might be seen as a reactive inclination towards expressions of English identity. These range from the expression of Englishness as a cultural (rather than an overtly political) identity to a variety of explicitly political positions which extend from left-wing 'reclamations' of English patriotism (e.g. Bragg, 2006) to far-right racist assertions of English 'racial' purity (e.g. British National Party, 2010). It is the role of English folk music and dance in voicing and shaping this nexus of multiple English identities that is the central focus of this book. In the following chapters we will concentrate more specifically on questions of identity, examining the ways that England and Englishness are being constructed within the folk resurgence.

Notes

1 For an example of the discourse, along with details of the tentative resolution to the internal conflicts, see Drury (2008).

2 Although immigration has, of course, had a significant impact on the other countries of the UK, the English tend to consider themselves most seriously affected by the issue, since this is where the majority of immigrants arrive and settle.

3 The test has been roundly criticised in various sections of the press, where complaints have been raised about the accuracy and relevance of the information on which it is based. Research by a publisher of British citizenship test study guides found, for example, that only 14 per cent of British respondents achieved a pass score on a sample set of questions from the test, coming sixth in its 'league table of Britishness' (Life in the UK, 2012).

4 Examples include: *Great British Menu* (BBC2); *The Great British Bake-Off* (BBC2); *Coast* (BBC2); *Jamie's Great Britain* (Channel 4); and *Britain's Best Dish* (ITV).

6

A place called England

I rode out on a bright May morning
Like a hero in a song
Looking for a place called England
Trying to find where I belong
(Maggie Holland, 1999: 'A Place Called England')

In February 2000 Maggie Holland received the BBC Radio 2 Folk Award's 'Best Song of 1999' for 'A Place Called England'. The explicit association of English folk music with the idea of 'looking for England' still had currency a decade later, when the magazine *fRoots* released two CD samplers of contemporary folk artists entitled *Looking for a New England* (2009) and *Looking for a New England 2: The Other Traditions* (2010), these titles being a reference to the 1983 song 'A New England', written by Billy Bragg. The artists associated with the resurgence do not always make such overt capital out of the idea of a search, but when people participate in English folk music and dance, when they go explicitly or implicitly looking for England, what ideas of England do they draw on, imagine and circulate? And when the English folk arts are written about and otherwise represented in contemporary culture, what understandings of England are mobilised?

In *The Nations of Britain*, Christopher Bryant observes that 'when the English do think about England there is more than one possibility with which to engage' (Bryant, 2006: 159). Or, as Andy Medhurst puts it, in *A National Joke*, Englands exist 'on multiple planes and in confusing profusion' (Medhurst, 2007: 62). Bryant identifies, for example, four broad ways in which England has been, and is, characterised: 'English England', which looks back to an England older than Great Britain 'with all the attributes the English suppose to be peculiarly, quintessentially, emblematically or just evocatively English' (2006: 162); 'British England', which is invoked when England is conflated with Britain; 'Little England', often deployed since the 1960s as a pejorative term to denote an inward-looking England intolerant of outside engagements such as, for example, immigration from the former Empire, alliances with Europe, or processes of globalisation; and, finally, Cosmopolitan England, an idea of England that is both outward-looking and contemporary in its orientation, culturally and ethnically diverse, acknowledging the diversification of the people, and 'the enrichment of its economy and culture from sources abroad' (Bryant, 2006: 192). Other imaginations of England include the concept of 'Merrie England' that overlaps Bryant's 'English England' and is referenced by Judge (1993) and Boyes (1993) to understand ruralist notions of England historically circulated through the folk arts. As Bryant notes, the various constructions of England have their historical continuities but are also ever-changing, as new generations engage with them. Whilst we will outline along the way some of the constructs of England historically associated with the folk arts, and to some extent still written into them, our main focus will be on how these are articulated in the contemporary context. The primary emphasis is on constructions of England as a place rather than on the overlapping concept of Englishness as an identity, which will be addressed in Chapter 7. There is no one consensual or monolithic version of England that is produced around the contemporary English folk arts. There are, however, some dominant versions of England that are strongly associated with them, and that they sometimes also work to disturb. It is these dominant constructions of England that we will outline here.

6.1 Historical legacies

One of the most powerful constructs of England associated with the folk arts is that of England as rural idyll. In 2008 the BBC broadcast the first series of *Lark Rise to Candleford,* a Sunday-night period drama adaptation of Flora Thompson's three novels set in the rural Oxfordshire of the late nineteenth century.

> The BBC's adaptation of Flora Thompson's *Lark Rise To Candleford* delighted millions of Sunday night viewers with its endearingly quaint portrayal of a Victorian rural community. Back in 1981, the same series of books were the inspiration for two National Theatre stage productions. And in his search to find music as quintessentially English as the rural idyll of Thompson's childhood, playwright Keith Dewhurst turned to folk legend Ashley Hutchings, esteemed founder of Fairport Convention and Steeleye Span. (White, 2008)

Music making and social dancing play an integral part in the fictional world that the above reviewer refers to as a 'quintessentially English ... rural idyll', some of whose characters appear to sing, dance, play fiddle or melodeon as naturally as breathing. Folk music (also described by the reviewer as 'quintessentially English'), also plays a key part in the soundtrack, which features renowned performers of English folk music active in both the previous period of folk revival and the most recent resurgence. The Lark Rise Band, led by Ashley Hutchings, also released an album, *Lark Rise Revisited* (2008), and toured a concert performance coinciding with the television broadcasts, and featuring 'music, words, dance and song from the book and the plays, celebrating a lost way of life so memorably captured by Flora Thompson' (The Lark Rise Band, 2012).[1] A quote from Thompson appears on its website, juxtaposed with an image of the English flag of St George:

> The hamlet stood on a gentle rise in the flat, wheat-growing, north-east corner
> of Oxfordshire. We will call it Lark Rise because of the great number of skylarks
> which made their springboard and nested on the bare earth between the rows of
> green corn (Flora Thompson, quoted in *Ibid.*).

As many commentators from Raymond Williams (1973) to Jeremy Paxman (1998) have pointed out, the image of the countryside has often come to stand as an image of England itself. The idea of folk has played a key role in supporting and circulating this idea. The association of folk with a utopian imagination of a disappearing or bygone rural England has, since its consolidation in the revival period of the late nineteenth and early twentieth centuries, been one of its fundamental features. The England that was seen to be disappearing in the wake of processes of urbanisation and industrialisation, and whose songs, dances and stories were deemed in need of recording and 'revival' by collectors like Cecil Sharp, was a rural England. As we discussed in 1.2, rurality was, indeed, an important element of Sharp's pioneering definition of 'the folk'. The idea of a rural folk culture was the 'other' against which the notion of (an urbanised, industrialised) popular culture was produced at that time.

The 'myth of an England essentially rural and essentially unchanging' has probably been most trenchantly criticised by Wiener, writing in the context of the Thatcherite years, who sees the glorification of the countryside as a symbolic rejection of industrialisation by a patrician culture (Wiener, 2004: 55).

> An 'English way of life' was defined and widely accepted. It stressed nonindustrial,
> noninnovative and nonmaterial qualities, best encapsulated in rustic imagery –
> 'England is the country', in Stanley Baldwin's phrase (by his time already a cliché.
> This countryside of the mind was everything industrial society was not – ancient,
> slow-moving, stable, cozy and 'spiritual'. (Wiener, 2004: 6)

So the definition of folk was caught up in the first revival period with a bucolic imagination of England, with what Boyes has memorably termed an 'imagined village' (1993: 65). Boyes examines the idea of 'Merrie England' that is circulated through this period, tracing its ideologically wide appeals in that particular cultural and historical context.

> To conservatives, the concept implied a reversion to the historical balance of
> contented class relations, a pastorale, where the middle as well as the labouring
> classes happily accepted their allotted places. Removal of the consequences of
> capitalism also characterised the just and joyous, de-industrialised common-
> wealth represented by the 'Merrie England' of socialists like William Morris and
> Robert Blatchford. All that might be projected into 'Englishness' ... was at stake.
> (*Ibid.*)

In identifying the struggles for control of the first folk revival, Boyes points to its differing interpretations, particularly the divisions between Cecil Sharp's vision, couched in a 'language of control, authority and nationalism', and the socialist approach of Mary Neal, the founder of the Esperance Guild of Morris Dancers. Sharp, as Boyes puts it, 'won the battle' (*Ibid.*: 83). The points that we would emphasise here are not only the centrality of this rural imagination of England in the consolidation of the idea of folk in the first revival period, but also its power to speak to the concerns of its time, and to appeal across a wide ideological spectrum, a point that we will be returning to in Chapter 7. In the discourses that we have referred to, it is a vanishing or vanished rural *past* that is being invoked through the folk arts, although of course references to a rural present can also call up such associations, through the strong culturally established implication of timelessness that is carried in the idea of rural England.

Whilst the association of the idea of folk with varying imaginations of rural England has been a foundational and powerful one, it is not all-encompassing. English folk has also, through its development, been associated with those realms of the urban and the industrial that are set in opposition to the rural within the discourses of the first revival period. The association of folk with the urban is particularly the case in the second revival period. A. L. Lloyd, for example, a collector and performer of folk songs, embraced the idea of an urban folk music and documented industrial folk songs. Lloyd criticises Cecil Sharp's imagination of the folk community as isolated from and innocent of the processes of industrialisation and urbanisation:

> Now it is true that early in the century when Sharp was cycling along the lanes of the West Country in search of songs, class differences were clearer than they are now and a wide gulf separated the pen-and-ink man from the man with bowyangs of binder-twine. But a whole class, in Western Europe, in England, in Somerset moreover, entirely shut away from and uninfluenced by the world of the educated elite, surely that has not existed since the Middle Ages, if then? Were Sharp's countrymen quite out of the orbit of the newspapers, railways, pillar-boxes, medical prescriptions, lightning conductors, fit-up theatres, romantic novels, *Hymns A. & M.*, to name but a few factors that might break down old 'primitive' ideas and replace them with modern ones including some in the service of squire and stockbroker? (Lloyd, 1967: 14)

This may be a somewhat schematic characterisation of those two revival periods (the first rural, the second urban in its imagination of the folk), but it is nevertheless helpful for contextualising the articulations of the rural and the urban that run through the current resurgence. As we move on, then, to examine this most recent resurgence of English folk, we will bear in mind these historical associations that are written into its texts and practices. Concepts and definitions of England are changeable over time, as Matless (1998) notes of the shifting definitions of rural England since the 1920s. Similarly, Raymond Williams argues that 'Old England, settlement, the rural virtues – all these, in fact, mean different things at different times'. He goes on: 'We shall need precise analysis of each kind of retrospect, as it comes ... each of these stages is worth examination in itself' (Williams, 1973: 21–2). So let us turn, then, to this most recent stage.

6.2 England as rural idyll

Of all the folk arts it is morris dancing, and Cotswold morris in particular, that has, since the first revival period, most regularly been invoked to stand for England and Englishness. Its continued currency as an 'icon of England' in the early twenty-first century can be seen by the entry in the 'Icons: A Portrait of England' website, where it is characterised as a national dance for England:

> As well as national costume, national dishes and a national sport, a nation should have a dance. Argentina has its tango, Poland the polka and England has the Morris. (Icons: A Portrait of England, 2009)

It is a particular rural vision of England that is summoned up by images of white-clad, handkerchief-waving Cotswold morris men on village green or outside local pub. Such representations are in line with what Wiener and others have called the 'Southern Metaphor' of England, in which it is the rural south, or 'Deep England', that has sometimes come to stand for the nation (see, for example, Wiener, 2004: 72; Shaw and Chase, 1989: 75). A more detailed scrutiny of the multifaceted practices of contemporary English folk music and dance reveals, however, a more varied set of engagements with the idea of the rural – and, in relation to it, the urban – and a more heterogeneous picture of England.

As we have seen in the example of *Lark Rise to Candleford*, the powerful association between folk and the imagination of a pre-industrial rural England does still have considerable purchase at a popular cultural level. This popular television series is infused with precisely that kind of nostalgia for a disappearing rural golden age that characterises the first revival period; in fact its fictional world is set in that very age and its plot deals with those very processes.[2] An association of the folk arts with the idea of a rural England can be seen in much of the folk music and dance of the early twenty-first century. To an extent this is inevitable, in that much of the source material – dances, tunes, songs – on which it draws has its rural origins embedded in it. For example, as discussed in 4.5, many albums released by the contemporary wave of folk artists include songs from the canon of English folk song that was consolidated through the two revival periods of the twentieth century, and largely originated with the collectors of the first. It is no surprise that one of the central songs to feature in the contemporary repertory is 'John Barleycorn' – that which most explicitly offers a representation of an England that is deeply and fundamentally rural.

Turning to the iconography of the resurgence, images of rural England are a continuing theme. Echoing the historical rural setting of *Lark Rise*, the two films mentioned in 1.6.2 have contemporary settings that are explicitly or implicitly celebratory of the English countryside. *Morris: A Life with Bells On* is filled with lingering panoramic shots of the countryside – of Dorset and Wiltshire, in this case – and visually celebrates such icons of timeless English rurality as the pub and village green. *Way of the Morris* is more explicitly nostalgic in its characterisation of English rurality, with a narrative that features its urban narrator-director in a journey towards a reconciliation with his rural family and village roots and the morris dancing tradition that is connected to them, and drawing heavily on personal nostalgia for a rural childhood, often evoked through the use of Super 8 home-movie footage. The film is set in the Oxfordshire village of his youth, and the rural context for the dancing is of primary importance. 'When it works it works in situ', he says in the closing sections of the film. 'When it works it works in context. When it works it works because you're watching it while standing outside a public house in the place where the dancers come from holding a pint of locally brewed foaming nut brown ale in your hand' (*Way of the Morris*, 2011).

Images of rural England are also a significant theme in album and website artwork associated with contemporary English folk music, some of which has been discussed in 3.3. From the abstract rural imagery adorning the Askew Sisters' *All in a Garden Green* (2007) or the cottage exteriors and interiors featuring on albums by Methera (*Methera*, 2008) or Tim Van Eyken (*Stiffs Lovers Holymen Thieves*, 2006, to more geographically specific rural images such as the Devon countryside of Jim Causley's *Fruits of the Earth* (2005), or the West Country map of Seth Lakeman's *Freedom Fields* (2006), the covers of folk music albums still regularly play on the folk-rural connection. This is not simply a case of the southern landscapes of 'Deep England' being offered as standing for England as a whole, however. Whilst many of these images of the rural, such as Lakeman and Causley's, do indeed reference southern English landscapes, many are so abstracted as to be non-specific and there are significant examples of northern rural landscapes too. Particularly significant perhaps, given the high profile of the Carthy family within English folk music, is the North Yorkshire moors landscape portrayed on the back cover of Eliza Carthy's album *Rough Music* (2005).

There has also been a movement towards the construction of highly self-aware, knowing or ironic references to folk's longstanding associations with ideas of a rural England. Take, for example, that visual iconography that is associated with the influential album and website artwork of the photographer David Angel (introduced in 2.2.3). These pictures imagine England in a less direct and more poetic manner than do the English landscapes that adorn some album sleeves and websites. These magical and artfully staged images hint at a mythic and enchanted England of fairytale forests, crumbling country houses, metaphorically resonant animals – bees, pheasants, stags. Jim Moray (*Sweet England*) poses on a forest floor; Tim Van Eyken's *Stiffs Lovers Holymen Thieves* features musicians posed in gloomy and candle-lit neo-gothic interiors suggestive of a country house and featuring such props as candelabras, a pheasant and a stuffed stag. Jim Causley's *Lost Love Found* (2007) has the musician dramatically posed as a sleeping youth on top of a beehive, entwined in ivy. Although the England that they invoke is mythic and non-specifically historic, in the mode of Merrie England, these are also absolutely contemporary images, closer to those of fashion shoots or popular music marketing than to the images that have conventionally graced the covers of English folk albums. (See also 3.3 for a discussion of their contemporaneity.) They are highly theatrical and overtly staged images. Their figures are posed within formal compositions as if in a painting, film or photographic set, surrounded by carefully positioned props; the colour palette is often dark and painterly. The artful staginess of these images draws attention to their constructedness, their performative quality, and suggests a reflexive or ironic distance from anything so naturalistic as the ruralist Merrie England discourse traced by Boyes in the first revival. The England that is evoked may well reference a mythic Merrie England, but these highly constructed images speak at the same time of a contemporary, knowing and sophisticated deployment of visual codes in the marketing of a new generation of English folk artists.

Similarly complex imagery adorns the album cover of Jim Causley's *Fruits of the Earth*.[3] Here, Causley's location within the landscape is represented literally (and ironically) in a depiction of the singer rising, naked and tree-like, from the turf of a field in the rolling English countryside, apparently offering up an apple for the viewer. This tongue-in-cheek representation of Causley's identification with rural Devon is a continuation of the prevailing discourse on his website, subtitled 'Devon Incarnate,' and adorned with the green and white flag of the county. Although Causley's music is relatively traditional in comparison with that of artists like Jim Moray or the Imagined Village, the digital manipulation of the photography on this cover is strikingly modern. When asked if his intention was to depict himself as being rooted in a tradition or a locality, his answer combined discourses on the traditional and the contemporary in a marked way:

> Actually, the first idea for that cover is, erm, I'm quite a fan of Cindy Lauper. My sister was a bit older than me – almost ten years older – and so when the eighties were going on she was a teenager and stuff, so she made me watch top of the pops … eighties pop music. Anyway, Cindy Lauper released an album called 'At Last', and it was her coming out of a manhole cover so you only saw the top part, and it's almost like mermaids. And I liked the idea of that – of coming out … and we were into the whole slightly pagany things. I'm not as bad as some people, but I wanted to hint at that as well. And I suppose it's my first album and the whole idea of emerging … And the apple was that I had the wassail song from my village in it, so the apple's quite a big symbol. And I wanted it to be of where I was from.
> (Jim Causley, interview, 2008)

The subtle reference to a significant visual encounter with contemporary popular culture is likely to have been lost on much of its audience, but it is important inasmuch as it speaks of a trend that we have already noted, for folk artists to engage with, reinvent, critique and subvert the materials of that popular culture, and to otherwise blur the boundaries that have culturally separated those materials from the genre of English folk music since the end of the folk-rock era (see Chapter 3). That is not to underplay, however, the significance of Causley's final statement, 'I wanted it to be of where I was from'.

6.3 England as a patchwork of distinctive places

Within the English folk arts there is often a particular insistence on the regionally and locally distinctive character of England's folk music and dance. This means that when England is pictured, spoken about, and otherwise invoked, this is often done through references to specific regions or places within England. The musician Pete Coe, for example, acknowledges this when he points out:

> If you went around the festivals and said, 'Where do you come from?', I'd say 'Cheshire'. I wouldn't say 'England'. Or 'I live in Yorkshire now'... It's the regions in England that people would focus on rather than being 'English', as it were. (Pete Coe, interview, 2008)

The period since the 1980s has seen the publication of a number of largely eighteenth- and nineteenth-century English musicians' tunebooks. These are books of tunes collected in or associated with specific places. Callaghan notes that the publication of *A Sussex Tunebook* (Gammon and Loughran, 1982) was 'the first time that an authentic repertoire of working village musicians playing for local traditional dances had been made available to musicians interested in the native English repertoire' (2007: 7). Examples of the subsequent raft of publications include collections of tunes identified with or collected in Somerset (Woolfe, 2007), Hampshire (Shatwell and Sartin, 2006), North Yorkshire (Bowen *et al.*, 1998), Lincolnshire (Sumner, 1997), and the north of England and borderlands with Scotland (Seattle, 2008). As already noted in 4.1, a key publication in this regard has been *Hardcore English* (Callaghan, 2007). The importance of the local provenance of tunes within this English collection is highlighted there through the inclusion, within that overview of English traditional musical sources, of a map of England showing the locations of principal sources of tune collections.

In the realm of professional folk music, which circulates nationally and sometimes internationally, many contemporary artists have developed and marketed a musical identity that foregrounds or is identified with a specific locality within England. Seth Lakeman's CD artwork and website picture specific locations in the southwest. *Freedom Fields*, for example, includes a historical map of the West Country. Mawkin takes its name from an old Essex dialect word referring to an unkempt person, or scarecrow. The continuing significance of locality for contemporary English folk can be seen in the series of television programmes produced for Channel 5 in 2008, *My Music*, which profiles five folk artists by the device of placing them in their 'home regions'. As folk activist Steve Heap puts it, 'you've got Seth Lakeman doing Dartmoor, Kate Rusby doing Yorkshire, and Eliza Carthy doing North Yorkshire' (Steve Heap, interview, 2008). Similarly, a strong local identity is one of the central features of the shanty-singing group Fisherman's Friends from Port Isaac in Cornwall, a group of singers who signed a record deal with Universal in 2010, and whose marketing literature describes them as 'Port Isaac's Fisherman's Friends' (Port Isaac's Fisherman's Friends, n.d.)

The programme notes on what are presented or received as 'English' albums very often detail the provenance of a range of tunes and songs associated with varied parts of England. Faustus, for example, cite oral sources and manuscripts associated with the West Country, Kent, Wiltshire, and Hampshire. The Askew Sisters' CD liner notes also feature detailed documentation of a range of musical sources collected and published across England, such as Playford's *The English Dancing Master* (1651), the *Penguin Book of English Folk Songs*, the William

Dixon manuscript (1732) and Dave Townsend's *English Dance Music* (2007). The England invoked in this way is a collage of specific and culturally distinctive locations and places brought together by the artists.

English folk dance tells a parallel story, with England's many different dance traditions being closely associated with specific locations, often down to the level of a particular village. In the realm of popular cultural representations of folk dance, this is illustrated in the picture of England offered by a BBC television documentary, *Still Folk Dancing ... After All These Years* (2010). Presented by the Northumbrian folk singers and clog dancers Rachel and Becky Unthank, and billed on the BBC website as 'a journey around the towns and villages of England to experience its living folk dance traditions in action', this portrait of English folk dance is constructed as a series of visits to different regional and village traditions (BBC, 2010). These include: the clog and rapper sword dancing of the presenters' native North East of England; the Britannia Coco-nut Dancers of Bacup, Lancashire; the Mayday celebrations in Padstow, Cornwall; the Morris Men of Moulton in Northamptonshire, Bampton in Oxfordshire, and Saddleworth, Oldham; traveller step dancers in Stowmarket, Suffolk; and the Abbots Bromley Horn Dance, Staffordshire.

The uniqueness of these different local dance traditions is highlighted within the commentary, in which the presenters frequently observe that what they are watching is very different from their own native (North East) tradition. It is significant too that the presenters, who are professional folk singers and also perform the clog dances of their own region, are offered here as on a journey of discovery of the rest of England. It is telling that dancers from one region are portrayed as initially unfamiliar with the dances of the other regions of England. It produces a picture of England as composed of distinctive places, each with its unique cultural traditions. So unique, in fact, that they can appear arcane and unfathomable to outsiders, even outsiders versed in other folk traditions of England.

Within this programme, the ties between dance tradition and place are repeatedly emphasised. 'It [traditional dance] gives you a real connection to where you live,' says one of the presenters in the opening to the programme. The tie between dance and place is usually asserted as forged over time, through reiteration: 'It's amazing', says Rachel Unthank, 'to think that these dancers have been coming through these gardens every year for so many years' (*Still Folk Dancing ... After All These Years*, 2010). Historical linkages are evoked by sepia photographs and black and white film footage of earlier performances of the same dances in the same places.

The Abbots Bromley Horn Dance is claimed to be an unbroken tradition: 'This tradition was never revived,' says the presenter. 'It's continuous. It goes back hundreds of years through generations of local families and ... it's the oldest dance that England has'.[4] But the links between folk dance and place are not always described as being so long-established. Other dances profiled in the programme, it is explained, are Victorian or more recent inventions – the Golowan festival in Penzance, for example, was started only 20 years prior to the making of the programme. As Rachel Unthank puts is, 'it's an invented event, based on tradition but *for Penzance*' (our italics). As a recently invented tradition, Golowan highlights how traditional dances and their related festivals do not only speak of the uniqueness of a local culture, its rural or industrial past, they are also mobilised to *constitute* that culture as unique. The dance itself can be seen as the very thing that makes a place special and distinctive. A Bacup Britannia dancer interviewed in the programme says: 'Bacup's got no steam trains, it's got no canals, it's got nothing else, but it has got the Britannia Coco-nut dancers' (*Still Folk Dancing … After All These Years,* 2010). England's locally specific dance traditions then, whether claiming a long history or not, rely on and reinforce a sense of the distinctiveness, the uniqueness, of places and local cultures in England.

Some tunes and dances are still practiced in their original locations, with a sense of spatial and historical continuity. This is particularly the case when they are related to and performed in the context of local customs and events. Those featured in the *Still Folk Dancing* programme include some of the most celebrated examples of these. Whilst very many local customs and traditions, such as those featured in *Still Folk Dancing,* do exist, the local practice of local traditions is, however, by no means always found within the cultures of English folk music and dance. Although linked to specific regions, Cotswold morris, border morris and rapper sword dance, for example, are all practiced by dance sides across the country and beyond. The significance of folk festivals within the cultures of English folk makes a particular contribution to the contemporary dissemination and circulation of traditional music and dance, acting as a focus for people who come together from across England and beyond. Agent and programmer Alan Bearman comments that:

> most young people learn their traditional tunes now by sitting in sessions in festivals at four o'clock in the morning, picking up tunes from people from all over the country … so they're not forging a genuine regional style of playing. (Alan Bearman, interview, 2008)

At Towersey Village Festival in 2008, the border morris side the Witchmen gave a dance demonstration and talk in which they spoke about their history as a dance side whose main existence is not through local activity but via festivals across the country. In the words of the presenter:

> We decided to do Festivals rather than pub nights and got more people from far away, but we lost our local identity. So we dance locally at Christmas and at the World Conker Championships, and all these chaps travel from all over England to practice, Suffolk to Halifax. They make every Sunday. (*Ibid.*)

So the Witchmen still like to maintain the idea of a local point of reference, despite the facts that their main forum for presentation is countrywide festivals rather than local events, and that they draw their membership from across the country. And many professional performers, who perform on national (and occasionally international) circuits, still maintain an identity related to a specific locality. Tunes circulate nationally and are contained within 'English' collections, but it is still important to be reminded of their local provenance. Cotswold morris, border morris, rapper sword, longsword, all maintain their associations with specific places even as they are performed by dancers located throughout the country. The historical association of traditional music and dance with specific places is valued, acknowledged and often highlighted, even as the nature of a mediated contemporary culture and a professionalising and festival-based folk culture means that its performance is often unfixed from those places.

The regions and locations that constitute this patchwork England do not necessarily coincide with England's existing regional political boundaries, although they often correspond roughly to them. Sometimes they refer to older designations, such as the use of the term 'Northumbrian' to designate a (broadly) northeastern musical culture and repertory. Often they refer to sub-regional units such as villages (the Bacup Britannia Coco-nut Dancers, for example), areas (Cotswold morris, North West morris, for example), or borderlands (the border morris of the English and Welsh border regions, for example). It might thus be seen as a bottom-up manifestation of sentiments of local belonging rather than a top-down imposition of regional categorisation.

Within this picture of England as a patchwork of distinctive locations, some places are also characterised as more precariously English than others. To go back to *Still Folk Dancing*: when in Cornwall, Rachel Unthank comments: 'for us it feels, well it does feel foreign. It feels like coming abroad'. This expression of 'feeling foreign' captures something about the two regions in question here, the programme's current location of Cornwall and Unthank's own region of the North East, the two regions of England that are, arguably, politically and geographically the most distant from the centre of government in London and whose status, culturally and politically, in relation to England has been contested and repeatedly debated.

'We're a long way from England,' says the folklorist Merv Davey interviewed at the Golowan festival for the same television programme, arguing that for a long time Cornwall was closer, in transport terms, to Brittany and Ireland than it was to London. He goes on: 'The Cornish identity arose about the same time in Cornwall as the very first Englishness of people like Cecil Sharp in England and the two were almost parallel. In 1904, which I think was about the same date as Cecil Sharp's book came out, Cornwall was admitted to the league of Celtic nations and that's the point that our modern Cornish identity can be pinned to' (*Still Folk Dancing ... After All These Years*, 2010). A Cornish sense of being 'a long way from England' is articulated through identification with the notion of the 'Celtic nation', and an identification with the 'Celtic nations' of Ireland and Brittany. This sentiment captures the extent to which folk arts have been and are a vehicle for a sense of local belonging that might be at odds with institutionally sanctioned boundaries and borders.

It is perhaps appropriate that the programme's presenters, who are offered as the outsiders discovering these various folk dance traditions of England on behalf of the viewer, are from the North East of England, a region whose folk arts are often characterised in a way that sets them apart from those considered English. The title of Kathryn Tickell's album *Debateable Lands* (2008) makes explicit reference to this description of the disputed border lands between Scotland and England. The term 'debatable lands' had been used since the sixteenth century to refer to this disputed territory, before being popularised by Sir Walter Scott in the romantic period (see Lamont and Rossington, 2007). As discussed in 4.2, within the cultures of English folk, the North East tends to be seen as a distinctive borderline region that is, in some respects, separate from England (see also Keegan-Phipps, 2007: 28). This is reinforced by the fact that it is the only region of England that has its own instrument – the Northumbrian smallpipes – and repertories associated with it. The use of the term 'Northumbrian' underlines this separateness. The ambiguously 'English/ Not English' nature of the Northumbrian musical identity is underlined in the status of North East tunes within the *Hardcore English* publication, for example. When explaining his reasons why the 'mighty treasury of Northumbrian music is not adequately represented' in *Hardcore English,* the author notes that 'there do appear, though, quite a number of Northumbrian tunes ... that have particularly embedded themselves into the English repertoire of musicians all around the country' (Callaghan, 2007: 10). In other words, within an 'English' collection it is those tunes from the Northumbrian repertory which have currency *outside Northumbria* that are represented, implying that Northumbria is both part of and in some way separate from England.

As was noted in Chapter 1, then, the term 'English', in its common-sense usage within the cultures of the English folk arts, is usually used to designate folk arts excluding not only the musics designated as Celtic (primarily the Irish and Scottish), but also the regional music and dance of 'Northumbria', which is seen as a distinctive traditional music culture in its own right, with its own repertory. This distinction (Northumbrian/English) tends to be made by those who inhabit the cultures of folk music and dance within England. It should also be noted, however, that when talk about Northumbrian music, for example, circulates more widely – at a national level via the media, or outside the country, it is often categorised more broadly as 'English'. The Northumbrian-identified singer Rachel Unthank, for example, when interviewed in the Irish newspaper the *Galway Advertiser,* speaks of her 'English' identity (Andrews, 2001). The London-based Thrales rapper sword dance group refer, in a notice publicising a workshop, to 'English rapper sword dancing and its Northern industrial roots' (Thrales Rapper, 2011). Of particular note here is the Demon Barber Roadshow's coining of the new term 'English clog' to designate its on-stage presentation of a range of regional clog dance styles.

6.4 Strange England

There is a discourse that presents the English folk arts through notions of 'strangeness'. The construction of a 'strange England' has been prominent, for example, in the work of a number of visual artists who have drawn on or been inspired by rural folk traditions. In 'An English Journey – Reimagined', Iain Sinclair was inspired by J. B. Priestley's 'An English Journey', and by English folk traditions such as the Whittlesea Straw Bear Festival, to undertake a travelling series of performances with a group of writers, musicians and artists, including the folk singer Shirley Collins. In what the *Daily Telegraph* describes as a journey 'into the weird heart of the UK', Sinclair 'will be hoping to tease out the weirdness locked within 21st-century England' (Burrows, 2010)

A language of 'strangeness' and 'otherness' can similarly be seen in an article by the journalist A. A. Gill, writing in the *Sunday Times Magazine* about the Bacup Britannia Coco-nut Dancers:

> It's not pretty and it's not clever. It is, simply, awe-inspiringly, astonishingly other. Morris men from southern troupes come and watch in slack-jawed silence. Nothing in the civilized world is quite as elementally bizarre and awkwardly compelling as the coco-nutters of Bacup. What are they for? What were they thinking of? Why do they do these strange, misbegotten, dark little incantations? … there's all the usual guff about harvest and spring and fecundity, but that doesn't begin to describe the strangeness of this troupe from the nether folk world. (Gill, 2009)

Gill's article implies that there may be a north–south dimension in this: it is morris men from 'southern troupes' who watch in silence as the (more northern – at least in relation to Cotswold morris) Bacup dancers perform, but this exoticising is applied elsewhere to southern dancers too. A series of photographs of Bedfordshire morris dancers by the artist Faye Claridge is entitled 'Only a Stranger Can Bring Good Luck, Only a Known Man Can Hang'. These 'strangers' are composed in stylised and formally constructed portraits, where the morris dancers are formally posed, in full costume, within a theatrically staged paradise-like setting of artificial plants and flowers (see the front cover of this book for an example from the series). As the exhibition title suggests, it is the 'strangeness' of the morris dancers that attracts the artist, and that strangeness is highlighted by her mode of staging and construction of the photographs. As an accompanying text puts it, 'Usually dismissed as harmless fun, these portraits show Morris dancing as a far stranger social phenomenon that deserves closer attention' (Artlounge, 2010).[5]

This exoticising discourse is one that most often originates from outside of the folk world. It is a discourse sometimes used by journalists, for example, or by fine artists, when they 'discover', report on, or represent English folk traditions. It can also be seen in the discourses of tourism. The National Tourist Board website 'Visit England', for example, refers to the 'whacky customs' and 'weird, wonderful and freaky traditions' of England (Enjoy England, 2011). However, there are also a few examples of participants within the folk culture who use this kind of discourse to characterise their own folk practice. Morris Offspring, for example, adopt a slightly tongue-in-cheek use of the phrase as a marketing tool on their website:

> Morris Offspring's dancers perform an unparalleled display of passionate and fiery dance from the exotic shores of England. (Morris Offspring, 2007)

In some cases it is a discourse more fundamental to the practice, as in the case of the border morris side the Witchmen who, as is often common with border morris sides, frequently invoke paganism. This discourse of a strange England amplifies the notions of local distinctiveness that were discussed above. Distinctiveness is so extreme in these local places, we might say, that it becomes characterised as bizarre or exotic.

An exoticising of England and English folk traditions can also be seen in the reframing of English folk music as world music. The discourse of 'English folk music as world music' appears to have entered into public circulation in April 1997 with the publication of an issue of *Folk Roots* magazine with the headline reading 'England: last undiscovered exotic outpost of World Music'. *Folk Roots* (now *fRoots*) is a world music magazine produced in England; the lead article, by music journalist Colin Irwin, 'celebrates a culture every bit as exotic as the most distant of World Music destinations' (Irwin, 1997, p. 36), and argues that *Folk Roots* has brought its readers exotic music from all over the globe, but has ignored the exotic within its own culture – England. Emphasising the bizarre and the eccentric within English traditions, the cover features images of the Bacup Britannia Coco-nut Dancers, men with blacked-up faces, white-hooped skirts and feathers (see 7.4.1). The article itself features an image of the antler-wearing Abbots Bromley Horn Dancers, 'the single most bizarre curio in a nation full of them' (Irwin, 1997, p. 37). Here, then, the orientalist gaze of world music (see e.g. Taylor, 1997; Feld 2000) is turned inwards, onto England itself. This has some parallels in the attention, since the 1980s, that young Japanese people have given to their own indigenous musical traditions, an attention that Mitsui terms 'domestic exoticism' (Mitsui 1998). The recent framing of English music as world music, and its attendant exoticising of English folk, might be seen in relation to England attempting to occupy a place in the 'world' (signified by 'world music') in all its relativity, not as a colonising or otherwise dominant force, but as just another nation, potentially as exotic as any foreign other.

6.5 Urban and cosmopolitan England

There is also a strand within the iconography surrounding the contemporary folk arts that directly associates folk with the realm of the urban. We have, for example, already discussed in Chapter 3 the significance of references to (implicitly urbanised) popular culture – both historical and contemporary. Many of the visual representations surrounding the resurgence more directly evoke the urban settings in which much contemporary folk music is practiced than the imaginations of the rural that may underpin it. The musicians of Faustus, for example, are pictured against an abstract evocation of a concrete urban land-scape (*Faustus*, 2008). The cover artwork for Spiers and Boden's album *Vagabond* (2008) pictures the fiddle player Boden as a busker in an urban street, visually presenting the folk musician as contemporary urban outsider on an album whose songs speak of a variety of outsiders from beggars to pirates. The first album by the Imagined Village reconfigures a traditional blue and white pattern redolent of a Delft tile, whose pastoral conventions are, on closer scrutiny, subverted. Nature, in the form of trees and open green space, is a city park with skyscrapers and an aeroplane in the background, and in the foreground a policeman examining a burned-out car.[6] This image blurs the boundaries of the categories of city and country, as well as those of the traditional and the contemporary. Similarly, the artwork of David Owen revisits the iconography of folk not only by refracting it through the prism of popular culture (see 3.6; 3.8) but also often by situating it in the context of the urban. The 5000 Morris Dancers event, for example, included performances and a street art campaign across central London. References to the urban are sometimes made in contexts that acknowledge and dismiss the ruralist fantasies that have underpinned the folk arts as practised in urban contexts. For example, a founder of the border morris side Wolfshead, Philip Kane, is reported in the press as saying: 'A lot of sides try to maintain a feeling for a rural tradition that just isn't there any more' ... 'Our style is quite urban. That's why people respond to it' (Moreton, 2008).

Some representations of the urban are, as discussed in 3.6, referencing historical urban popular cultures. Others are directly evocative of what Bryant terms 'Cosmopolitan England' (2006). This is a concept of an England that is contemporary, outward looking, culturally and ethnically diverse, characterised by hybridity and cultural exchange. It is evoked, for example, in those projects where English folk is hybridised with forms associated with other cultural traditions – the step dance and street dance of the Demon Barber Roadshow, for example (see 3.5), the Anglo-Turk musical identity of Dogan Mehmet (7.2.5), or the hybrid and multi-ethnic Englishness of the Imagined Village (7.3). A Cosmopolitan England is also invoked through a movement towards the celebration of cultural diversity within the realm of English folk culture. A key event in this regard was a concert, *Nowt as Queer as Folk* (2010), held at Cecil Sharp House, the headquarters of the EFDSS in the country's metropolitan centre, London. The concert was billed as

> a point of reflection and celebration of all the gay, lesbian, bisexual and transgender artists performing today who have found voice through British traditional song and songwriting and the road journeyed to reach this point. (EFDSS and The Magpie's Nest, 2010)[7]

The mood of this concert was a celebratory one, and many of the comments made by the performers indicated that they saw it as a watershed moment, and particularly resonant in that it took place in Cecil Sharp House, historically a key institutional base for the English folk movement. One performer quipped that this was a building where, in the past, 'you could have been thrown out for playing the wrong tune to the wrong dance', thus underlining the extent to which this occasion was perceived as marking a shift in the culture of English folk, as represented by one of its key institutions, and a move towards tolerance and diversity. The concert represented – at a symbolic level, if not necessarily quantitatively – an expansion of the range of identities associated with folk, and a spirit of openness and tolerance that is generally assumed by the ideal of

Cosmopolitan England. The issues raised by such a contemporary cosmopolitan construction of England are worked through more in the register of identity than that of place, and so will be addressed in more detail in Chapter 7.

6.6 Authentic England

'I think,' says Rachel Unthank, 'that people, some people, are into things that feel a bit more handcrafted just now. People are knitting again because they like the idea of making their own clothes; they go to farmers' markets because they like to know where their food is from; and they want to know a bit where their music comes from as well.' Rachel, the elder of the singing sisters who lead the Unthanks, is trying to explain the current revival of interest in English folk music. And pointedly, unlike some of the acoustic bands that are picking up prizes and hail vaguely from west London, there is no doubting where the Unthanks fell to earth. (Adams, 2011)

In this press interview, Rachel Unthank draws a connection between the appeal of the English folk arts and some wider practices in contemporary circulation, practices that value local rootedness, and hand craftedness. Many contemporary television food programmes, for example, celebrate local ingredients, local dishes, and home cooking skills. In *Jamie's Great Britain*, for example, the celebrity chef Jamie Oliver visits Yorkshire, the East Midlands, Essex, East London, Bristol and Somerset, South Wales and the Scottish borders in an exploration of the regional variety of British food, relating it to its local traditions and culture (*Jamie's Great Britain*, 2011). A key figure in the popular cultural circulation of such discourses has been the television presenter Kirstie Allsopp. *Kirstie's Handmade Britain*, for example, celebrates craft skills such as baking, cushion making and dressmaking, with the presenter visiting a series of rural county shows. In Episode 6 she visits the Chagford show in Devon and is shown trying her hand at some morris dancing, an act that demonstrates how closely the idea of folk connects with this celebration of the handcrafted, the rural and the locally distinctive (*Kirstie's Handmade Britain*, 2011).

Contemporary English folk's privileging of the authentic and the locally distinctive echoes the discourse circulated in Paul Kingsnorth's book *Real England* (2008), discussed in Chapter 5.

Kingsnorth lays the blame for what he sees as the homogenisation and control of England primarily at the door of globalisation and consumption:

We live in the age of the ascendant global market – the driver, we are told, of all that is good, modern, progressive; creator of wealth, destroyer of want. but we have encountered a flaw in the program. We are discovering that a global market requires a global identity; that not just goods, but landscapes and cultures must be branded and made safe for the universal act of consumption. (*Ibid*: 8)

The positioning of folk as an authentic response to the 'conveyor belt' (i.e. standardised) style of commercial music is explicitly invoked in the marketing of the *My Music* series of television programmes (2008). The series' executive producer Michael Proudfoot is quoted in the press as saying:

> The revival of this wonderful genre is a reaction against the synthetic, profit-driven, conveyor-belt style that so typifies commercial music today. (Rajan, 2008)

At the same time, we have argued in Chapters 1 and 2 that folk is more integrated into the mainstream music business than it ever was. Proudfoot captures that contradiction:

> Here we have four young artists who have circumnavigated the demands of the music industry, who have refused to compromise on their music for commercial purposes. Ironically, that's why they're now having such commercial success. (*Ibid.*)

6.7 On rural idyll nostalgia

Matless cautions against a 'tendency to lump all cultural expressions of ruralism together as representing a simple, nostalgic and conservative longing for a 'rural idyll' (1998: 16). In his analysis of landscape and Englishness, he points to the complexity of ruralist material: 'even that which seems most obviously nostalgic and conservative, turns out to have a complexity, either through exhibiting non-nostalgic/conservative traits, or because neither nostalgia nor conservatism are simple phenomena' (*Ibid.*: 17). The complexity of the relationship between rurality and nostalgia in contemporary popular culture can be seen, for example, in the cases of the television programmes *Countryfile* (BBC1), and *Springwatch* (BBC2). *Countryfile* is primarily concerned with informing about and celebrating all things rural, but goes to considerable lengths to discuss the rural landscape in terms of contemporary matters such as modern agricultural practices. *Springwatch,* meanwhile, situates its live presenters in the field in a way that evokes the rural idyll, but is centred around shots of the presenters – sporting the top of the range in hi-tech binoculars and outdoor clothing – discussing the latest developments in filming and research technology, and the implications of these for investigating animal behaviours, migratory patterns, etc. Though they remain indexically linked, the bonds between rurality, nostalgia and conservatism are problematised or clouded here.

As Jones (2005) has pointed out, ideas of rurality and rural idyll still resonate through British culture. The popularity of television programmes such as those mentioned above (and others like BBC2's *Escape to the Country* or *Edwardian Farm*) attest to this. Jones argues that it may be easy to dismiss these as shallow, nostalgic or consumption-led ideas, but that they speak of deeply embedded emotions and desires and should be taken seriously. It is in this spirit that we approach contemporary English folk with the aim of taking seriously its ruralist tendencies and its potential for nostalgia and, at the same time, being alert to their complexities.

For example, a direct voicing of nostalgia for a lost rural can be found in the opening track on the first album by the Imagined Village. This features what one reviewer describes as 'a nostalgic lament for the lost English countryside from John Copper, a member of the revered family of Sussex singers who have been performing traditional folk songs for six generations' (White, 2007). John Copper's spoken words begin with reminiscences about his grandfather, Jimmy Copper, who worked on the chalk Downs, and whose ashes were sprinkled on his favourite spot, a boundary stone where he would sit and eat his lunch, looking down through the valley to the sea. John speaks of going with his father to visit that place: 'You have to have a good imagination now to imagine it like it was when Jim was young though' (Imagined Village, 2007: ''Ouses, 'ouses, 'ouses'). He then goes on to quote his grandfather's words, spoken in a 1951 BBC recording:

> He said, 'I still do like to walk up on those old hills where I was a shepherd boy. But they've changed today. They're all different now', he said [...] There was a grace and a beauty in these chalk hills round here in them days. But now you look down there and all you see is 'ouses 'ouses 'ouses'. (*Ibid.*)

This is unashamedly nostalgic, and it is a complex offering of nostalgia. The sentiments that are being quoted speak directly of nostalgia for a lost rural: the replacement of rural beauty with ''ouses, 'ouses, 'ouses'. The words are emotionally resonant, the words of an ageing man remembering his dead father and his youth. They speak powerfully of a material connection with that lost past, through the generations of the family; the Copper family are renowned for their oral tradition of family singing, in which songs have been passed down through the generations, and so their presence stands for ties with the land, which guides the listener comfortably towards a nostalgic appreciation for Jimmy Copper's rural England. In performance, accompanied by rural imagery on a large screen and intensified by its musical treatment (in which singer Sheila Chandra sings mournful, soaring vocables over a steadily building backing of pedal bass and strings), this nostalgic expression of memory and loss is vividly tied to place. However, the nostalgic sentiment, whilst emotionally tangible, is at the same time somewhat removed. This Imagined Village track incorporates the recorded voice of a man quoting his grandfather's lament for the lost rural landscape of his youth. The sentiment is made in a way that is clearly a quotation, and its nostalgia might be seen as both heartfelt and somewhat distanced. The listener is faced with a band quoting a man, quoting his grandfather – mediated by a radio programme – about a lost rural England. Thus, attribution of the ruralist expression is ambiguous, and the sympathies of its publisher (the Imagined Village) are only to be inferred.[8]

6.8 Conclusion

The texts and practices of contemporary English folk do certainly mobilise associations with an idea of a pre-industrial rural England, associations that are built into the definitions of folk that were consolidated in the late nineteenth and early twentieth centuries. But they do not circulate ideas of rural idyll, Old England, or Merrie England in any uncomplicated way: sometimes their engagements with the rural seem both heartfelt and nostalgic, but they are often also distanced, knowing, ironic or overtly performative. Sometimes they actively work to recover historical associations with urbanised or industrialised popular culture, as we saw in 3.6, and to assert a more contemporary and/or urbanised vision of England. Moreover, these various associations can coexist in the output of the same artists, and even in the same text.

The picture of England that is circulated around contemporary English folk is a heterogeneous one, in terms of its associations with the ideas of the rural and the urban and its investments in the idea of the distinctiveness of local cultures, a distinctiveness that finds its apotheosis in local traditions that verge on the bizarre and arcane. If we are to pull any dominant strands out of this heterogeneous picture of England, then the first would be that heterogeneity itself. Within the realm of the folk arts it is this very variety that characterises England; there are multiple Englands constructed here. Within this construction of multiple Englands, however, there are two main tendencies. One is the pull towards the idea of rootedness, where the folk arts speak of connectedness – with the past, with place, with tradition – with communities, and with a particular notion of an authentic, historically rooted England. The other is the pull of the notion of a cosmopolitan England that is diverse, outwardly facing and with a contemporary orientation.

In 'A Place Called England', with which we began this chapter, Maggie Holland speaks of 'trying to find where I belong', and it is to that sense of belonging that we turn in the next chapter, which examines the constructions of English identities that are associated with the folk resurgence.

Notes

1 Hutchings already had a connection with the *Lark Rise* texts, having worked on the music for the National Theatre adaptation of the novel in 1980, and released the album *Lark Rise to Candleford* with the Albion Band (1981), to which 'Return to Lark Rise' makes reference. The nostalgia that infuses this latest *Lark Rise to Candleford* is perhaps twofold, then, encompassing not only the rural idyll evoked by the novel and television adaptation but also the venerated history of Hutchings and the Albion Band as key players in the second revival period.

2 *Lark Rise to Candleford* attracted average audiences of over 6.4 million viewers (BBC Press Office, 2009).

3 A good reproduction of the album artwork for Fruits of the Earth can be seen at http://goo.gl/6O8CJ. Various other images of Causley can be seen on his Myspace page, www.myspace.com/jimcausley.

4 On the Abbots Bromley Horn Dance, see Buckland (2001).

5 Examples of Faye Claridge's work can be seen at Claridge (2012).

6 The cover image from the Imagined Village album can be viewed on the group's website, http://goo.gl/q2OgC .

7 Notwithstanding the reference to 'British' traditional song and songwriting on this leaflet, the majority of artists on the bill were both English and closely associated with the English folk resurgence.

8 The imaginations of England that are associated with the Imagined Village are particularly complex, and although we will make some preliminary references to the band in this chapter, this key player in the resurgence will be examined in more detail in Chapter 7.

7

Englishness

'I think English people struggle with their own identity,' says Rachel [Unthank]. 'Celebrating being English could be seen as being colonial or right-wing which is the opposite of what folk music is all about. Folk music is about working men and women and their lives and troubles. These traditions, dances, and songs just happen to be English but they are something English people can say are our own and are a way of saying "I am proud to be English".' (Andrews, 2011)

The newspaper article from which this extract is taken, profiling the folk band The Unthanks, intimates that the performance of English folk might, for some individuals, be an explicit – even a proud – expression of an English identity, and it also points towards a perceived struggle around the assertion of Englishness, and its contested politics. These issues are at the heart of this chapter. Identifying the dominant constructions of Englishness to be found in and around the English folk arts, the chapter will also examine their politics, considering issues such as how they are positioned in relation to English nationalism, multiculturalism and whiteness.

7.1 English nationalism

We have used the idea of performing Englishness to refer to an understanding of national identity as something that is enacted, by individuals and groups. As Pfister puts it, 'It is by "doing being" English or Italian that Englishness or *Italianità* is constructed and performed' (Pfister and Hertel, 2008: 10). As a consequence, national identities are constantly in flux, being made, contested and remade. Before going on to examine the versions of Englishness that are made and remade in and around English folk, it will be useful to consider the issue of present day English nationalism.

Nationalism, which is both ideology and social movement, is a complex concept, and a full discussion of it is beyond the scope of this book (for such a discussion, see, for example, Smith 2010). Grosby offers a general definition: '[d]istinctive of nationalism is the belief that the nation is the only goal worthy of pursuit – an assertion that often leads to the belief that the nation demands unquestioned and uncompromising loyalty' (2005: 5). In 'Is there an English nationalism?' (2011), Richard English has examined the extent to which the resurgence of Englishness since the 1990s can be seen as nationalism or as what he views as a different phenomenon, that of English national identity. Kenny *et al.* refer to the latter as 'cultural nationalism' (2008: 6). English identifies three dimensions to the concept of nationalism, viewing its definition as lying in 'a particular interweaving of the politics of community, struggle and power' (2011: 2). The idea of national community is manifest, for example, in notions of shared culture and history, attachments to territory and to people. This is sometimes taken further with ideas of common descent through blood or, more recently, DNA. This tends to have an ethical dimension, in which the insider group is 'characterised by superior moral claims, values, purposes and obligations', or even considered to be exclusive, defining not only who is within the national community but also who is outside or excluded from it (*Ibid.*). Nationalism also involves struggle: 'collective mobilisation, activity, movement towards change, and a programmatic striving for goals' (*Ibid.*: 3). Such goals include things like 'sovereign independence, secession from a larger political unit, the survival or rebirth of national culture or the realisation of economic advantage for the national group' (*Ibid.*). Such struggle might be pursued through a variety of means from violence to electoral process or 'through the embedding of national ideas in repeated rituals and routines, and in the emblems built into national life and place' (*Ibid.*). Finally, nationalism is about power, usually in the form of the idea of the nation possessing full sovereignty over itself.

Using this understanding of nationalism, English argues that elements of an English nationalism do exist in contemporary England, but that primarily what has been resurfacing since the 1990s is an English cultural sensibility or sense of English national identity rather than nationalism. It is regarding the elements of struggle and power that English finds little that qualifies as nationalism: 'there simply is not the kind of significant, organised political struggle by English nationalists that the UK has seen in Ireland, in Scotland or in Wales (let alone in other settings of nationalist energy around the world)' (*Ibid.*: 5). English plays down the significance of the English Defence League (EDL), with its right-wing defence of what it views as English culture, describing its scale and impact as 'tiny' (*Ibid.*). Similarly, he argues, the Campaign for an English Parliament has, despite its energy, failed to achieve its desired momentum. He also points out that many with sympathies for English distinctiveness engage with parties such as the *United Kingdom* Independence Party (UKIP) and *British* National Party (BNP), arguing that this illustrates the lack of any serious political outlet for an English nationalism. It is worth noting, however, that the BNP did, in the first decade of the twenty-first century, begin to pursue a cultural strategy focusing explicitly on Englishness, 'forging a connection', as Michael Kenny points out, 'between the deeply felt sense of socio-economic marginalisation prevalent in some communities and the more overt espousal of pro-English, as opposed to pro-British nationalism' (Kenny, 2010). For Kenny, 'this is the brand of English nationalism that many liberal commentators and politicians, including the current prime minister, rightly see as a toxic antithesis to the civic and inclusive patriotism which they want to see grounded upon a broader sense of Britishness' (*Ibid.*).

Whilst English and Kenny place differing emphases on the importance of the emergence of the BNP's espousal of English nationalism, it is also important to acknowledge that political nationalism and cultural nationalism, whilst having different emphases, are entwined (Kenny *et al.*, 2008). Moreover, and significantly for the present analysis, the spectre of far-right English nationalism (particularly that of the BNP) has in the early twenty-first century become a key touchstone in opposition to which English folk has at times defined itself and its politics. The numerical size or political effectiveness of nationalist organisations like the EDL or the BNP may be 'tiny', but their symbolic value has been significant for the many within the English folk scene who have wished to declare their hostility to such politics.

The potential to essentialise an indigenous identity through the differentiation of national traditions means that the folk arts have the potential to successfully support and reinforce nationalist sentiment. This possibility has been exploited to varying extents by every far-right regime in European history, most notably in Franco's Spain, Salazar's Portugal and Nazi Germany (see Castelo-Branco and Toscano, 1988; Perez, 2000; Steinweis, 1993). Although much has been written about Nazi mobilisations of classical music to instil nationalist sentiment, Steinweis has indicated that in the period 1934–35 the number of folk performances overseen by the regime's cultural agency, Kraft durch Freude, was more than double the number of classical concerts (1993: 76). The concept of folk, with its ability to invoke a sense of a timeless, authentic purity, is therefore most likely to consolidate a sense of racial superiority. It is hardly surprising, then, that the BNP should have turned towards the folk arts in its attempts to stir up English nationalist sentiments, and this is something to be discussed later in this chapter (7.4.2).

Whilst the brands of nationalism discussed above issue from the right of the political spectrum, there has also been an emerging debate on the political left since the turn of the twenty-first century, with some commentators urging the adoption of 'radical' or 'progressive' forms of English patriotism. (See Aughey, 2007: 101–20 for a fuller discussion of this English radical patriotism and its relationship to its historical antecedents.) Of particular significance for this book is the presence here of the voice of the singer Billy Bragg. Through song lyrics, journalism, his book *The Progressive Patriot* (2006) and his participation in the Imagined Village, Bragg has been a contributor to public debate about Englishness, arguing that English patriotism should be reclaimed by the political left from the hands of the right. Such a discourse of 'radical Englishness' is one that (mostly implicitly) runs through the resurgence, and we will return to it in due course.

7.2 Constructions of Englishness

This most recent folk resurgence has been characterised by its regular engagement with public discourse around Englishness. A key marker of the emergence of public talk about Englishness in English folk circles was the release of Eliza Carthy's album *Anglicana,* whose liner notes declare: 'This album is an expression of Englishness as I feel it' (Carthy, 2002). Carthy has also spoken about Englishness in press interviews at around the time of the release of *Anglicana* and in the intervening years, avowing in one interview: 'I think that Englishness has become a bit of a talking point, and I'm looking to say something positive about the English' (Turner, 2004). In the same interview, Carthy says: 'I wanted to make an all-English album, because I think that English music needs a media-visible performer, and I want to be that person' (*Ibid.*). Eliza Carthy was not the only folk artist to enter into this wider discourse about Englishness at this time. For example, Jim Moray's *Sweet England*, another high-profile album that was, like *Anglicana*, nominated for the Mercury Music Prize in 2003, was also accompanied by press interviews in which Moray spoke about his Englishness.

Perhaps the most high-profile and prolific discourse on Englishness has circulated around the activities of the Imagined Village, a band that will be examined in more detail later in this chapter (7.3). For the band's founder Simon Emmerson, the very emergence of the project was born out of that debate,

> The whole project came out of a debate and a discussion. I just felt we had to participate in that discussion as musicians and I wanted to engage in the debate, as did Tim Weedon from Trans Global [Underground], as did Johnny Kalsi. I just thought it was about time that we stood up as musicians and just got stuck in, because every week I'd turn on the radio – Radio 4 – and there'd be a discussion about English identity. (Simon Emmerson, interview, 2008)

The Imagined Village made it a mission to generate debate about the nature of English identity, and many of their performances have been preceded by a question-and-answer session with the audience on the topic of English identity. Their website also offers itself as a forum for debate and has published articles and interviews on the topic, by Simon Emmerson, Chris Wood and others. The inclusion in the band of the singer Billy Bragg, who was already known for his participation in public debates on Englishness, highlights the intention and the profile of the band's participation in public debate.

Whilst engagement with English folk music or dance is not always openly or primarily articulated as a direct manifestation of a desire to express one's English identity, it is significant that a growing number of English folk participants do talk about having actively sought out English folk music or dance, or about their folk activity as an expression of their English identity or search for their English 'roots'.

7.2.1 Englishness as historically rooted

Looking towards musical and dance traditions that are rooted in the past is one of the defining characteristics of folk. The notion of Englishness as a historically rooted identity is mobilised, for example, when England is characterised, as we have seen in 6.2, through visual and musical references to an idyllic rural landscape. The historical element of this construction is often non-specific ('people have done this for hundreds of years'). But it has also become increasingly specific to the period of the first folk revival (approximately 1890–1930), with an increasing amount of activity invested in celebrating the achievements of that revival's leading figures. For example, the Mary Neal Project has told and celebrated 'the story of social reformer, suffragette and radical arts practitioner Mary Neal CBE for the first time' (Mary Neal Project, 2012). Comprising an archive, projects, events and an educational programme, the project sets out to inspire practitioners to consider the following questions:

> How are English indigenous song and dance traditions inherited, and to whom do they now belong? [and] How do these traditions connect to a continuum of participatory arts practice today? (*Ibid.*)

Thus an exploration of the rootedness of 'today's' arts practice in 'indigenous' traditions is encouraged. In 2011, the EFDSS held a series of events to celebrate the centenary of its foundation by Cecil Sharp. The following year, the Society received £585,400 of Heritage Lottery funding for a project, The Full English, 'to archive, conserve and digitise materials from six archives containing some of the country's most important folk music collections', creating 'the world's biggest online portal of English folk music and dance' alongside a learning and participation project (EFDSS, 2012). There has, as noted in 4.5, been a general return to the source materials collected by Sharp and his contemporaries, and the Full English project will afford even easier access to such materials.

Finally, the reference to 'English indigenous song and dance traditions' on the Mary Neal project's website indicates the allegiance of this notion of historically rooted identity to a discourse on Englishness as an 'indigenous' identity. We will be offering some further reflections on the significance of this in 7.3.

7.2.2 Englishness within multicultural Britain

Many participants in the English folk arts speak of their English identities with explicit reference to the context of a Britain that is multicultural. One such version of Englishness offers it as a discrete, distinct and bounded identity within Britishness, which is understood in turn as a mosaic of diverse cultural identities. This position is clearly expressed by Jim Moray in a newspaper interview, where he speaks of his life as taking place in a contemporary urban multicultural context:

> Where I live in Birmingham is a predominantly Asian area. It's quite run down, and it's where all the student houses are. And, just as there's a large British-Asian community, I feel with the music I'm playing I'm part of a kind of British-English community. It's like your nationality is British, but the sub-context of that is being English ... If the country has lost its sense of Englishness, then effectively I feel like a second-generation English person. Just like the guy that lives next door is a second-generation Asian guy. So, just as he goes and practices his tabla every night to get in touch with the culture behind the surface of contemporary life, I go and sing these songs out. (McCormick, 2003)

This construction of Englishness reconciles the historically rooted concept of Englishness with contemporary multiculturalism. It does not does not ask for (implicitly historically rooted) Englishness to be privileged over other cultural identities, as does for example the nationalist discourse of the BNP, but assumes or asks for equivalence with other cultural identities within Britain.

In the same newspaper interview the author introduces Moray as follows:

> On a day when the Mobo awards celebrate ethnic diversity in the UK music scene, I would like to draw readers' attention to a young man who could be just about the whitest individual in British pop. (*Ibid.*)

Whilst Moray was speaking of his Englishness as a cultural identity, expressed through the musical cultures that he inhabits, his framing here as 'the whitest individual in British pop' within the context of a wider celebration of ethnic diversity in the UK slides the discourse into the realm of ethnicity. In doing so, it captures the essentialising tendency within this construction of Englishness. If it is Britishness that is multicultural and multi-ethnic, then Englishness exists alongside those other British cultural identities as, implicitly, white.

7.2.3 Englishness as internally variegated

> The point about Englishness is it's so diverse. The point about morris dancing is it's so diverse. You get these different styles from everywhere, different teams, lots of colour, lots of different things, lots of different music. (Laurel Swift, interview, 2008)

As noted in 5.3, a dominant construction of England within folk culture is as a patchwork of distinctive localities. In line with this, the sense of belonging that is articulated by many folk practitioners is focused on regional or local affiliations over and above, or in combination with, Englishness. Speculating in the context of the debate about the inclusion of morris dancing in the Olympic opening ceremony, Swift criticises the tendency for institutionalised versions of Englishness to present an inauthentic, monolithic version of English folk dance and, by implication, English identity. She speculates:

> And if they had it in the Olympics ... you'd have 500 people in the same kit doing exactly the same thing and it would be so over-rehearsed and so perfected you might as well just get a bunch of dancers and teach them how to do morris

dancing. And they can do a little bit of Cotswold, little bit of North West. You know, they can do a little bit of everything, but is it genuine? (*Ibid.*)

As we have seen in 5.3, the explicit celebration of regional and local identities is particularly the case in the discourse of artists such as Seth Lakeman and Jim Causley, who make clear their strong identification with their home region of the South West. As Causley puts it:

I'm very attached to where I'm from and I'm really proud of the region that I'm from. I love coming from there. And I'm very lucky that we have a very strong tradition still where I'm from, where some areas of the country don't. (Jim Causley, interview, 2008).

Notably, where specific regional identities are foregrounded, this is often done in terms of rurality and agricultural history, demonstrating strong links between this construction and the historically rooted identity construction discussed above.

An exception to this, and a band that has a particularly strong local identity, is Mawkin, which both relishes and markets the identity of 'Essex boy'. For Dave Delarre: 'I'm an Essex boy … And there's a strong Essex identity, and it's like, your cheeky Cockney chappy, basically, if you're a bloke, or … you can fall in to the blonde kind of Essex girl stereotype.' (Dave Delarre, interview, 2008). He goes on to talk further about the Essex boy/girl stereotypes as laughable, but still providing a sense of identity:

And although we laugh at them, and we think they're really funny, it's still an identity, and we still like it … All my friends, you know, they don't mind being known as Essex girls, because it gives them something to actually be known as. (*Ibid.*)

Mawkin have pursued a strategy of becoming known as an Essex band, and developing a local audience:

We have done loads of local activities to make us known as an Essex band, and stuff like that … We put on a folk festival, I put on my own festival – a step dance festival for a load of old people in Suffolk [*laughs*]. But we've also done loads of local gigs and things like that. But it's brilliant – whenever we do an Essex gig, we can pretty much guarantee we'll sell it out. (*Ibid.*)

In Delarre's account, the sense of local identity encouraged by Mawkin sometimes over-rides their folk identity:

And the people who turn up are not folkies … Like we're playing at the High Barn in a couple of weeks, and I can pretty much guarantee anyone who turns up there, probably about five per cent of them will be folkies and the other ninety five per cent will just be Essex people – you know, people who've stumbled across us somehow, and thought it's cool, and it's Essex, and just turn up. It's weird, we do seem to have our Essex following but who aren't folkies. (*Ibid.*)

Delarre argues that a reason for people 'resorting to' regional over national identities is because of the Americanised nature of the national identity and culture:

> I think the whole resorting to your regional identity instead of the national is mainly because the national one is just rubbish [*Laughs*]. Cos if you have to resort to the national identity, you have to resort to the national media, and national genre of music and things like that, and it's rubbish anyway. I mean, it's not even English, is it? Let's be honest. We're eating American food most of the time, and we're listening to American music most of the time, and we're watching American programmes most of the time. So there is no English culture … But there is a regional culture, I think – or there probably were more regional cultures, but they all died out, and they're kind of coming back a bit. (*Ibid.*)

The notion that English national culture is absent, Americanised or mediated, resonates with the 'Real England' discourse discussed in 6.6. There is an interesting tension around Mawkin in this regard, because they also embrace many aspects of mediated popular culture – marketing themselves as a 'folk boy band', for example.

The literature on folk movements in other nations over the course of the twentieth century demonstrates the significant role often played by regionalist discourse in the consolidation of a national identity (as in Ireland and Portugal: see Castelo-Branco and Toscano, 1988; Smith and Ó Súilleabháin, 1997). Where nations' authorities have sought to consolidate and encourage the celebration of a national identity, this has often been done through an emphasis on the comparison (through competition, for example) of local versions of a particular form of tradition. A particularly clear example of this would be the propagation of *Ranchos Folkloricos* in Salazar's Portugal, in which troupes were encouraged to represent localities, became standardised in format, and competed against each other (*Ibid.*). Such activities are effective since they highlight not simply the localities but also the shared cultural capital across a nation: the scenario is similar to the celebration of a national sport, even though the performance of such a sport ostensibly requires regional or local teams to enact their differences (through different clothing, styles of playing, etc.). However, the processes involved in this case are quite different, not least of all because they appear to be 'bottom-up' expressions of belonging rather than 'top-down' institutionalised constructions of regionalism. In other words, the discourse has seemed to develop out of the assertions of local identity from individual artists and groups – assertions that have been subject to positive reception and response from the media and the broader English folk culture.

7.2.4 Englishness as lost or beleaguered

It is striking how often references to English cultural traditions are couched in a language of loss. This is palpable, for example, in journalist A. A. Gill's elegiac account of the Abbots Bromley Horn Dance:

> Down a winding cobbled street from the church trips the Abbots Bromley Horn Dance, the most evocative and strangely dramatic of all morris dances, performed

for perhaps hundreds of years, conceivably for thousands. They are led by a single fiddler, dressed in a rag coat, playing a tune that is childlike and simple, but also full of sadness and an ethereal, mordant power, like the soundtrack of a dream. Behind him come men carrying antlered fallow deer heads in front of their faces. Behind them, a man-woman, a hunter and a hobbyhorse. They dance in silence, slowly. The hunt turns and turns, casting patterns in the moonlight. You feel its mossy, shadowed meaning beyond understanding. A ghost dance, a silently keening sadness. The things we misplace always bear a heavier loss than the things we choose to grasp with white knuckles. And in the darkness, quite unexpectedly, I feel tears of mourning on my cheek. (Gill, 2009)

Not all talk of loss is quite so nostalgically expressed. Sometimes the idea of loss is more implied, as in the invocation of the metaphor of English cultural traditions as buried treasure. For example, the EAC's website (see 3.7.1) has as its strapline a line from a song written by Chris Wood: 'The gold that you are searching for is in your own backyard' (English Acoustic Collective, no date). The same website profiles a quote from Kazuo Ishiguro, speaking at the 2003 BBC Folk Awards in London:

The way I see it is like this ... There is this kind of treasure chest you have sitting in front of you, and if you were American or perhaps Irish you might have opened it by now, but because you live here it probably hasn't occurred to you to do so yet. Well, I would urge you to open that thing up and delve inside it, because I believe you'll find there a sublime vision of life in the British Isles at it has been lived over the last few centuries; and it's the kind of vision that you can't readily get from the works of say, Dickens or Shakespeare or Elgar or Sir Christopher Wren. If you don't open that treasure box I think you are going to miss a certain dimension, a whole dimension of cultural life in this country so I urge you to do it. (*Ibid.*)[1]

The idea that the English have been blind to, or need to search for, their own folk traditions presents the performance of English folk within a narrative of discovery. Typically within this narrative the subject is looking to discover their cultural or individual roots, and their discovery of their personal identity is tied up with the discovery, or rediscovery, of English folk traditions. We saw this narrative, for example, in the film *Way of the Morris* (discussed in 6.2), and it is called up also by Colin Irwin's book *In Search of Albion*, which is subtitled 'From Cornwall to Cumbria: A ride through England's hidden soul' (Irwin, 2005).

The trope of journeying around and discovery of England is not restricted to the discourses about English folk. It is evoked in the titles of a wide range of popular books, including those that do not reference folk *per se* (e.g. Bragg, 2006; Crystal, 2007; Hemming, 2009; Irwin, 2005; Wood, 1999). Neither is it new. Examining a burgeoning literature featuring journeys around England that flowered between the 1920s and the second world war (and including J. B. Priestley's *English Journey* (1934) and H. Morton's *In Search of England* (1927), Simon Featherstone notes that the notion of England as a 'lost or neglected place in need of discovery relates both to nationalism and to the revivalism of Sharp and Neal' (Featherstone, 2009: 67).

Various reasons are given (or implied) for the lost or hidden nature of English cultural traditions. Consider this account by musician and dancer Laurel Swift, speaking of teaching North West morris, longsword and border morris in a Worcester primary school:

> I say 'Where does it [morris dancing] come from?' and they start off and they say 'Ireland' and I say 'Close'. They say 'Scotland' and I say 'Close', and they say 'France' and I say 'Still quite close', and they say 'Spain', and then they say 'America', and they go the whole way round the world, and usually you have to say 'Where do we live?' before they get it. Sometimes somebody will go 'England'. And they all go 'Really? Wow!' (Laurel Swift, interview, 2008)

In this discourse, these English urban schoolchildren are simply ignorant of or estranged from English folk dance traditions. The idea that the English are ignorant of their 'own' cultural traditions has circulated widely in discourses within the resurgence. It is echoed here, for example, by Eliza Carthy, who connects this ignorance with English 'identity trouble':

> It's a fact that as a race the English are ignorant about our roots, and that's a major hole in the national psyche. As a people the English are floundering; we have trouble establishing our identity and recognising our culture. (Turner, 2004)

As in the quote with which we began this chapter, the English, who are perceived to be ignorant of their own folk traditions, are often contrasted with other cultural groups within Britain, which are considered to be more closely connected with theirs. Jim Causley, for example, commented in interview:

> I heard Jim Moray being interviewed on Late Junction [by] Fiona Talkington, and she said to him, 'Why do you sing English traditional music?' and it made me think actually when I heard her say that, because I thought, 'Would you say that to an Irish person?' Imagine interviewing an Irish person and saying 'Why do you sing Irish traditional music?' You just wouldn't, would you? (Jim Causley, interview, 2008)

A sense of the estrangement of the English from their folk traditions is closely related to the propensity for the ridiculing of English folk arts within the wider culture and particularly the media. Noting the 'invisibility of English roots music', for example, Simon Emmerson notes 'the fact that it's marginalised and pushed to the side and treated as this kind of weird, aberrant sort of eccentric world' (Interview, 2008). Indeed, for some, English cultural traditions or English identity are not passively lost or forgotten, but have been actively suppressed, marginalised, 'pushed to the side', thus constructing Englishness as a somewhat beleaguered identity.

A number of reasons are proposed (or implied) for this sense of English identity as lost or beleaguered. Dave Delarre, for example, speaks of the English 'resorting back' to their English identity as a consequence of multiculturalism:

> I think sociologists have studied things like that where, if you a get a mix of loads of different people, such as ... the English people in Spain, they become even more English because they're removed from their culture ... So they stick up

their English St George flags, and they're proud of being, you know ... So if you're living in a multicultural society where there's so much different things going on – there's so many different cultures and identities – the easiest thing to do is to resort back to your cultural identity, so you become more English. If you're from Devon ... you become more Devonish. (Dave Delarre, interview, 2008)

For some, the perceived institutional endorsement of multiculturalism is argued to have promoted the cultures of other groups within Britain over and above those of the English. For example, the following quote from the Archbishop of York, speaking before his enthronement in November 2005, is profiled on the EAC's website:

What is it to be English? It is a very serious question. The English are somehow embarrassed about some of the good things they have done. Multiculturalism has seemed to imply, wrongly for me, 'Let other cultures be allowed to express themselves but do not let the majority culture at all tell us its glories, its struggles, its joys, its pains'. A failure to rediscover English culture would fuel greater political extremism. (English Acoustic Collective, no date)

For Jim Causley, it is the perceived governmental promotion of multiculturalism that represses 'this country's culture':

[It] almost feels like the government's repressing this country's culture and it doesn't want us even to know about it. It's really weird. Like with the whole music licensing laws and all sorts, and I read an article about a chap in London who ... had a pub and he wanted to apply for a late licence to hold a St George's Day event, and have music and all sorts, and he was denied this licence for whatever reason. And so just to test it he applied for a late licence to celebrate the Chinese New Year, and he was given it straightaway, just because it was celebrating multiculturalism. Which, you know, I think is a great thing to celebrate that and not exclude anyone, but I feel that to appreciate other cultures you've got to understand your own first. (Jim Causley, interview, 2008)

The notion that Englishness is beleaguered in the context of the 'promotion' of a multicultural society is a common thread in the nationalist discourse issuing from the extreme political right. Many of our research participants were at pains, however, to distinguish their own position from that one. Laurel Swift, for example, argues that the promotion of English folk arts risks being misinterpreted as racist.

One of the schools I used to teach in ... they had Turkish Club after school. Now about fifty per cent of the kids in the school if not more were Turkish. Okay, so it wasn't like Turkish is a minority group that needs supporting. And at Turkish Club they did Turkish dancing once a year, but they mainly played football and socialised. And I was just like, if I started English Club at school and we learned English songs and we did mummers' plays and we did English dance and maybe learned to play the fiddle, it would be up in arms for being racist. No way would that be acceptable, even though ten to twenty per cent of the kids in the school were English. And that's quite a minority group, you know ... The Turkish kids have Turkish dancing. They have their own language, their own food, and ...

> Asian kids similarly. They have this identity and … a lot of the Chinese kids at
> school would go to Chinese school on Saturdays, and they're learning millions of
> languages and everything else, and they have Chinese New Year, and they have
> these strong identities, and the English kids have got what everybody else has got
> but nothing extra. (Laurel Swift, interview, 2008)

This account paints a picture of a school context within which the English are numerically a minority culture, and in which the cultural identity of the English children is something of a void in comparison with others.

Such discourses often depict Englishness as actively suppressed, unsupported or unrecognised by comparison with the 'strong identities' of other cultural groups within Britain. Here we can begin to see the clear parallels with the statements of indigeneity noted in 7.2.1. As was discussed earlier, the concept of indigenousness is normally characterised by a political subordination. Here indigenousness, whilst not spoken or written, is being expanded to encompass what is perceived to be a form of cultural subordination. Along these lines, the programme notes for the Morris Offspring/EAC performance *On English Ground* contain a quote from the ethnomusicologist Alan Lomax's 'Appeal for Cultural Equity': 'All cultures need their fair share of the airtime' (Lomax, quoted in Morris Offspring and English Acoustic Collective, 2005: no page). The selection of the quote tells a good deal about the framing of this particular discourse. Whilst many audience members will be vaguely aware of the work of Lomax in the field of folk music scholarship, they are unlikely to be aware of this relatively obscure text. However, rather than lending scholarly weight to the suggestion that Englishness is beleaguered (which such a general remark cannot), reference to this scholarly piece may be seen as an apparently authoritative statement that such a suggestion is worthy of consideration, and an indication of its seriousness. In fact, the choice of text is a significant one: Lomax is – to English folk artists and audiences – indexical of the socialist American folk movement of the 1960s; his 'appeal for cultural equity' was a commentary on what he considered the globalisation of Western cultural media and an outspoken attack on 'pollution of the symbolic environment' to the detriment of non-Western, subaltern societies and cultures (Lomax, 1977: 125). His discourse was an anti-capitalist one, and his invocation in the pages of the programme for the *On English Ground* tour is therefore two-fold. On the one hand, a plea originally made on behalf of marginalised music cultures is mobilised in support of English folk culture, whilst possible associations with far-right nationalist sentiment are deflected through the largely unspoken identification of American-led globalisation (and not immigration) as the culprit. Revisiting the lyrics from the title song of the tour illustrates this:

> We hear the songs of Africa
> We hear the Celtic bard
> but the gold that we are searching for
> is in our own back yard
>   (Chris Wood)[2]

The musical cultures identified here as predominating England (and overbearing English folk culture) are notably cultures which are not closely associated with broader, contentious debates around physical immigration to England (which, as mentioned in Chapter 5, are generally those of the Indian Subcontinent, the Middle East and Eastern Europe). The song appears to refer to a globalised World Music industry, with the 'Celtic bard' symbolising the globalised consumption of traditional music as an economic export. The 'Celtic Bard' comment is particularly resonant for English folk enthusiasts, who are now aware of the saturation of England's folk scene with Irish and Scottish acts in the twenty or so years leading up to the English folk resurgence. Besides the inclinations of the World Music market, one could also argue that the 'songs of Africa' line might reference African influences on perceivedly globalised contemporary popular culture.

It is worth clarifying that the 'appeal' emanating from the *On English Ground* tour is a bid for English traditional culture to share an equal platform with other traditions present in England, rather than dominate them. It is expressed as a desire for English cultural traditions to be afforded the respect and visibility that are perceived to be given to other cultural groups within multicultural Britain. Those who believe this recognise that belief to be politically controversial, and open to misconstrual as potentially racist. This is a considerable concern to English folk artists and audiences, the vast majority of whom are supporters of a tolerant, inclusive, multicultural society, as are those cited above. Whilst the candid comments of Delarre, Causley and Swift were made in interview, this is not a view that is regularly expressed directly or publicly by folk artists and audiences. The discourses circulated by the *On English Ground* tour are unusually explicit in this regard. Where the position is rehearsed publicly, it commonly takes the indirect form of comparative discussion, which questions 'our' own denigration of 'our' cultural heritage by citing those cultural groups within Britain that celebrate theirs. A clear example of this can be found in Steve Knightley's lyrics to the Show of Hands' song 'Roots':

> The Indians, Asians, Afro-Celts
> It's in their blood, below their belt
> They're playing and dancing all night long
> So what have they got right that we've got wrong?
> (Show of Hands, 2006)

Elsewhere, the comparison is extended by involving the support of the English authorities or media in the celebration of the others' cultural heritage over and above English traditions. A belief that cultural policy makers have, to some extent, played a role in institutionalising the denigration of English folk is privately held by a significant proportion of folk artists and activists. This can be seen in the citation of Lomax by the *On English Ground* tour, where an accusatory finger is being implicitly directed at the English media, who must be complicit in the alleged limiting of the air time for English music and dance traditions. In either version of the Englishness-as-beleaguered discourse, the possibility of appearing overtly nationalistic is avoided, then, because the threat to English traditional culture is identified – albeit often implicitly – as being the English themselves.

The final explanation given by our research participants is one that connects the 'hidden' nature of English folk traditions with a sense of shame about asserting one's Englishness. For Jim Moray, for example:

> Folk music in this country seems to be hidden away. It's somehow shameful to assert your Englishness and sing about it and celebrate it. Irish music and Scottish music and even Welsh music don't have this problem. (McCormick, 2003)

Rachel Unthank, quoted at the head of this chapter, suggested that 'celebrating being English could be seen as being colonial or right wing' (Andrews, 2011). Similarly, Simon Emmerson invokes 'post colonial guilt' (interview, 2008) in considering the blind spot that the English seem to have to their own identity.

7.2.5 Englishness as a 'melting pot'

We have already noted some of the ways in which an English identity is constructed in relation to the notion of contemporary multicultural British culture. A variant on this offers a view of Englishness as an identity that is, in itself, pluralistic, and to be shared, celebrated and shaped by people of multiple ethnic backgrounds and cultural genealogies. In this construction, acknowledgement is given to the influence of global markets and migrations within contemporary England, aligning it with the idea of a 'Cosmopolitan England' discussed in 5.5 (Bryant, 2006: 192).

This is not an exclusively contemporary construction of England, however. Consider the sleeve notes for the CD *Looking for a New England 2: The Other Traditions*:

> England is a multicultural musical hub and always has been. How could it not be? Wave upon wave of refugees and émigrés have made England their home since … well since forever. And they've always brought their music with them – along with their food, language and culture – which has mixed with what was already here. Add in the stuff English travellers bring back from foreign parts (Moorish dancing anyone?) and you've got the mother of all melting pots. (Renton, 2010)

It is not only contemporary England that is characterised here as culturally diverse. In fact, this piece cites the folk arts as a prime example of how England has historically been shaped by multiple cultures. The influences of incoming cultures are celebrated: 'fusion, schmoozian, this is a natural development, always has been – how do you think our tradition got all those polkas, waltzes and squeezeboxes?' (*Ibid.*) Laurel Swift speaks of Englishness in a similar way:

> I never think of it as Englishness versus multiculturalist. I inherently see that Englishness is multicultural because England has looted, stolen and welcomed everything from everywhere for years. I mean, morris dancing possibly came from the Spanish courts via Moorish pirates – like English national dance comes from Spain … St George was born in the Lebanon wasn't he? … To be English is

to be multicultural. I'm fairly sure human life didn't evolve here. People travelled here, you know. (Laurel Swift, interview, 2008)

For Roger Watson:

A thousand years ago … we had Viking music, Saxon music, Norman music and some Celtic music going on in the same space. Now we call it English, because somebody decided that rather than stick a sword in somebody else, they were going to have a jam session with them! Okay, naïve, but still, as far as I can see, the basic situation. So if we've managed to blend that, and if we've absorbed all the other immigrations that we've had in those thousand years, we now have, living amongst us, populations of people who've come here to stay. And, as far as I'm concerned, their influence on our music is vital to its forward progression. (Roger Watson, interview, 2008)

Steve Heap talks about the 'jumbling up' inherent in English culture and identity, in terms of both national and regional migrations:

If you go to the North East … look at all the connections they have with Scandinavia, and Scotland, and the Scottish with the Danes, and so on. And quite a lot of the tunes and the names and the words in Northumberland are from Scandinavian words, Scotland, Shetland and so on … And in the West Country, there are enormous links with northern France. And in that part of northern France, there is a great deal of African movement, so it's very likely that a good deal of what you might hear from the tin mining traditions of Cornwall, and the fishing industry of Cornwall – in shore fishing – have got French links, and in turn African links and so on … I know from spending a lot of time in Lancashire, obviously, when I was growing up … it never occurred to me that a lot of the so-called Lancashire dialect and traditions came from anywhere other than Lancashire, but in fact they can easily be traced to lots of other areas, not unlike the Cornish tin miners, who went from Cornwall to Lancashire to work the mines [and] teach people up there how to mine. They'd been tin mining, and we had coal, so they went to teach them how to do it. […] And it's obvious that when communities travel like that they take with them their folk cultures, so they all get jumbled up together. (Steve Heap, interview, 2008)

These accounts are significant, because they indicate that a historically rooted version of Englishness does not necessarily posit it as a pure or essentialised identity, but can accommodate – or even emphasise – the idea of Englishness as plural or hybrid. Some professional folk artists have made it their business to explore or assert an English identity that explicitly offers itself as multicultural or hybrid. A prime example is the Imagined Village, who will be examined in detail in 7.3; another is the musician Dogan Mehmet, whose identity is described on his website as follows:

Brighton born and bred, Dogan Mehmet is a second generation Turkish Cypriot, with both sides of his family from the island. A fluent Turkish speaker, Dogan's heritage forms a big part of his musical identity, alongside his love for Southern English traditional music. He is singer first but also a multi-instrumentalist, playing Violin, Guitar, Melodeon, Tenor Guitar, Cajon and other Percussion as well as a having good knowledge of traditional Turkish instruments. (Dogan Mehmet, no date)

Mehmet presents a hybrid, Anglo-Turk musical identity that one reviewer calls 'a roaring fanfare for multicultural Britain' (*Ibid*).[3]

This discourse of Englishness as an inherently plural or multicultural identity has proliferated around the resurgence, and it has often been invoked as a rejoinder to those who might assume that to perform English folk is to invoke an essentialised English identity that is somehow pure or fixed. At the same time, however, apart from the examples that have been given here (which we would argue have great symbolic significance), there are relatively few professional performers associated with English folk who are explicitly presenting such versions of Englishness. Moreover, observation indicates that the participatory folk culture in England, as evident in festivals, folk clubs, sessions and traditional dance sides, is overwhelmingly white, and whilst this observation can only be a crude indicator of its cultural and ethnic mix, which may well include those who identify as Irish, Scottish, Welsh or European, the cultural mix seen on stage in the Imagined Village, for example, is not necessarily reflected in the audience for English folk or the participatory culture of festivals, clubs or sessions.

The constructions of Englishness that have been discussed in this chapter do not exist in isolation from each other, but merge and overlap. We move now to a case study that demonstrates the intersection of some of these constructs of Englishness, as well as exemplifying many of the processes examined throughout this book. This is the Imagined Village, a band that has been a key and high-profile player within the English folk resurgence.

7.3 The Imagined Village: the roots and routes of Englishness

Launched in 2007 at the WOMAD (World of Music, Arts and Dance) world music festival, the Imagined Village is the brainchild of world music producer and musician Simon Emmerson. Emmerson's professional musical background began in popular music during the 1980s, when he played with the jazz/soul group Working Week. However, his most significant work has been as a producer and performer in the world music genre: in 1992 he produced Manu Dibango's acid jazz album *Polysonik*, and in 1996 he was nominated for a Grammy Award for his production of Baaba Maal's album *Firin' in Fouta*; in the early 1990s he formed the globally successful fusion act Afro Celt Sound System, which has sold over 1.2 million albums and received two Grammy Award nominations (Afro Celt Sound System, 2012). Clear parallels can be drawn between the *modus operandi* of that group (the fusion of African and Celtic traditional musics) and those of the Imagined Village.

The Imagined Village started out as a fluid 'project' (although it has taken on the form of a self-contained band since 2010). Its output has included two albums and live touring performances since 2007, designed to:

recast age-old traditions in the shape of the twenty-first century. A daring mix of ancient and modern, The Imagined Village fuses fiddles and squeezebox with dub beats and sitars. (The Imagined Village, 2007)

As this statement suggests, the band has drawn on a large pool of musicians and performers, all of whom explicitly identify themselves as English, and who fall into three generic categories: English folk musicians; world music performers; and those most readily associated with Western pop music.

Negotiating the concept of Englishness is an activity very much foregrounded by the band. As noted earlier, it has actively worked to stimulate debate about the nature of English identity. Notably, the Imagined Village doesn't attempt to present a monolithic or even a coherent version of Englishness – in fact the point is regularly made that the constituent members of the group do not necessarily agree on the topic. It can be inferred, however, that the members do universally consider English national identity as something that is open to discussion, and that is not fixed but in the process of being negotiated. The debate around Englishness is acknowledged as a political one, too. The Imagined Village doesn't speak as a unified front on this but one of the dominant voices, around the time of the launch of the band and its first album, was that of musician Billy Bragg, who, as noted earlier, is associated with English radical patriotism.

In 1997 *Folk Roots* magazine characterised English traditional culture as 'undiscovered' by the world music industry (*Folk Roots*, 1997). In the following decade and a half it became, however, well and truly discovered by the genre: it was possible to see, for example, the booking of some English folk acts in world music contexts such as the WOMAD festivals, and some English folk acts began to describe themselves in this way. For example, the band Bellowhead had the descriptor 'English World Music' attached to their website in 2007. In contradistinction to the conventional positioning of English folk music, the world music genre can be generally regarded as a more commercially orientated cultural realm – an integral facet of the wider mainstream music industry (see for instance: Taylor, 1997; Frith, 2000; Feld, 2005). The 'English music as world music' discourse is closely tied, then, to the developments examined in Chapters 2 and 3. The Imagined Village is the act perhaps most closely associated with this alignment of English folk with world music, and is unique in that it is arguably born directly out of this discourse. We will focus our discussion here on the band's initial project, launched at WOMAD 2007, and its first album (*The Imagined Village*, 2007) and associated touring.

The project constituted a collaboration of musicians more readily associated with pop music and world music, alongside those connected to English folk music. It is important to acknowledge that these musical categories are fluid and in some instances ambiguous, but they are useful for understanding both the musical and discursive activities of the group. English folk music was represented here by a number of artists. The involvement of father-and-daughter team Martin and Eliza Carthy was particularly central; the Waterson-Carthy family (of which they are the most visible members) is often referred to as the 'Royal Family' of English folk music, and very closely associated with the second period of revival

(1950–70s); Martin's introduction of Paul Simon to the song 'Scarborough Fair' has taken on legendary status as a narrative within an unofficial canon of folk histories, whilst Eliza is also well known for her combination of folk and popular music styles in earlier albums (such as *Red Rice*, 1998). They were joined by Chris Wood (fiddler, singer, guitarist and outspoken discussant of English traditional music and culture), whose other work has been considered more closely in 3.7.1. Also involved were two ceilidh bands, the Gloworms and the Tiger Moths, representing the younger and older generations, respectively. Finally, English folk music was represented in the project by the Young Coppers, who are presented as the seventh generation of a family of traditional singers. Here, they were offered as the embodiment of a direct link with pre-industrial rural England: singers from earlier generations of the Copper family have played important roles in the revival movements of both the early- and mid-twentieth century. The Young Coppers are, however, the first to acknowledge that they are not renowned for their singing abilities *per se* – rather, they present themselves simply as ordinary people who enjoy singing. Clearly, then, they were involved in the Imagined Village project primarily because of who they are and what they represent.

World music performers included the Dhol Foundation front-man and prolific percussionist, Johnny Kalsi; the singer Sheila Chandra, as well as performance poet Benjamin Zephaniah. The members of Transglobal Underground were involved in producing sequencing for the project, whilst their sitar player, Sheema Mukherjee, took a particularly prominent role in the band's music and live performances. Pop musicians involved include the popular Brit-Pop artist Paul Weller (although he only sang lead vocals on one track of the album and never appeared live with the group) and the kit-drummer Andy Gangadeen, formerly a drummer for Lisa Stansfield and the Spice Girls. Finally, a central figure to the Imagined Village's live performances was the singer-songwriter and left-wing activist Billy Bragg, whose outspoken political orientations have enabled his bridging of the divide between the English folk music culture and pop music.

The group produces music that consciously combines English folk music with elements of other musical traditions and what Frith has referred to as the 'universal pop aesthetic' (Frith, 1989: 2). The boundaries between the musical content of these categories are, of course, highly problematic, and so the audible signatures of such labels are often ambiguous. Taylor (1997) has shown, for instance, how Frith's universal pop aesthetic has become a common feature of the World Beat phenomenon (hence its 'universality'). Nonetheless, it is important to draw a distinction between those musical elements of the Imagined Village's output that signal contemporary pop characteristics and those which indicate a source of 'traditional' material separate from English folk, primarily because of the nature of the latter category and the way in which it is represented. On the group's eponymous debut album, the English folk element is represented first by the songs themselves, second, by the regular appearance of the fiddle, played by both Eliza Carthy and Chris Wood, and third, by the nature of the vocals, which are (on the majority of the tracks) unmistakably those of the English folk singers listed above, clearly identifiable as 'folk' voices through a nasal, 'closed' or 'head-voice' quality coupled with the articulation of regional accents (e.g. Chris Wood's Kent-inflected voice). The universal pop aesthetic is here manifested through sampled and sequenced beats, along with synthesised ambient backing tracks and an ever-present drum- and bass-based rhythm section. It can also be recognised in the emphasis on equally phrased and repetitive harmonic movement, similar to that identified in the arrangements of Lakeman (3.2) and numerous ceilidh bands (3.4). Finally, the world music element of the Imagined Village's sound comes in the form of a rather specific musical (and cultural) other – Indian music. Mukherjee's sitar, Chandra's vocals and Kalsi's dohl and tabla are frequently heard features that hint at the exotic and foreign (to English folk, if not to contemporary *England*).

Excepting the clearly Afro-Caribbean accented vocals provided by Benjamin Zephaniah for the track 'Tam Lin', Indian music is the most clearly identifiable musical other represented in this project. And it is often foregrounded as strongly as the English folk element: the song 'Cold, Hailey, Rainy Night' (awarded Best Traditional Track in the 2008 BBC Radio 2 Folk Awards), opens with Mukherjee strumming the sympathetic strings (chikari) of the sitar, before a shruti box (a drone instrument of North Indian classical music) sounds and the sitar and dohl combine in a 20-bar introduction comprising a simple octave-based riff and three drum strikes repeated every second bar. Only in the twenty-first bar does the full rhythm section enter, and the sitar gives an exposition of the song's melody. Since the introduction contains remarkably little musical material, it is safe to assume that its purpose is the introduction of a generic soundscape, and that soundscape is overwhelmingly Indian. When performing the song live on *Later With Jools Holland* (2008), the significance of the Indian aspect of the music was also made visually striking – Kalsi began the performance positioned well upstage of the rest of the band, in a white frock-coat reminiscent of Punjab traditional dress, and danced as he played the introduction to the song. The camera moved between capturing his movements and close-up shots of Mukherjee's fingerwork on the sitar.

The semiotic impacts of some of the instruments used are more ambiguous: for instance, the acoustic guitar that Martin Carthy contributes to the project (and has always played throughout his career) could be reasonably associated with either English folk music – particularly in its second revival form – or Frith's universal pop aesthetic. Simon Emmerson's instrument in the project – a cittern – is particularly interesting in this respect, since it is clearly associated with European folk musics generally, and is visibly alien to Anglo-American pop music, but is strummed throughout the album in much the same way as an acoustic rhythm guitar, and (thanks to its double courses of strings) achieves a sound similar to that of a twelve-string guitar. As in the other examples discussed in this chapter, then, generic boundaries are permeable and under constant renegotiation. However, it is important to acknowledge that the singularity and foregrounded distinctiveness of Indian music indicates that its role extends beyond simply enabling facilitation of a generic World Beat aesthetic.

The dominant construction of Englishness embodied in this combination

of soundscapes is the inherently multicultural Englishness discussed earlier
(7.2.5) – a melting-pot English identity, apparently illustrated through the
group's musical hybridity. This is a construction of Englishness that has been
energetically proposed by band frontman Billy Bragg in many contexts, including
the Imagined Village's pre-concert question-and-answer sessions. At WOMAD
2007, for example, he spoke of 'the fact that Anglo-Saxon has a hyphen in it',
explaining: 'it's the only racial type in the world that has a hyphen in it; that
little hyphen has been there ever since our country was founded' (The Imagined
Village: workshop, 2007). The hyphen represents, as Aughey points out, 'the
virtue of the "mongrel" quality of Englishness' (2007: 110). The Imagined Village
presents, visually and aurally, a strikingly plural, inclusive, multi-ethnic and
multicultural version of Englishness. It is at the same time, however, invested in
the historically rooted construct of Englishness discussed earlier.

This comes partly through the notion of 'roots' that is embedded in the concept
of world music. Emmerson accounts for the genesis of the project in terms of a
search for English musical roots:

> I just started thinking about doing something that was kind of rooted in my own
> culture, and Baaba Maal had always said to me, 'You shouldn't. You don't have to
> become a West African *sufi* mystic to discover your own roots. You should look
> under your own feet. You should look at the earth under your own feet.' (Simon
> Emmerson, interview, 2008)

This also evokes the construction of Englishness as a lost identity, examined
earlier. The invocation of rootedness in both history and place is clearly signalled
in the presence of the Young Coppers within the project. Tacit construction of
an authentic English folk song and music is at the heart of their involvement,
as are close ties with both the land and the rural past. Similarly, the song texts
performed by the band are generally those that have played significant roles in
the first and second English folk revival periods. The 'authentic' Englishness that
is constructed here is iconographically linked to the rural and the historical, and
unambiguously white. At first glance, then, this construction of Englishness is
in some way at odds with the band's over-riding concept of an inclusive, multi-
ethnic vision of Englishness.

The Imagined Village project was a ground-breaking intervention into English
folk and its representations of Englishness, with its overt attempts to negotiate
new imaginations of Englishness, through discussion as well as through its
musical and ancillary outputs. The project also illustrates some of the difficulties and contradictions inherent in this reimagining of Englishness. It might be
argued, for example, that alongside its discourse (and intentions) of inclusiveness,
the discourse of authentic, implicitly white, Englishness plays an important role
in the band's output. Chandra sings her version of 'The Blacksmith', employing
Indian ornamentation, but the audience is not furnished with a clearly labelled
'English' interpretation of an Indian traditional song or musical text. Likewise,
Zephaniah performs his rewrite of Tam Lin, but we don't hear an 'English'
version of an Afro-Caribbean traditional story. The Englishness is inherent in

the *text*, rather than stylistic, and therefore highlights an Englishness bound up in historical texts, in a way that potentially disturbs the multicultural English identity discursively supported by the group. It could be noted also that the pre-show talks, and written discussions, are almost exclusively populated or authored by the white middle-class, middle-aged, male members of the group. It might also be argued that within the presentation and content of the project's written, visual and musical material, the world music element (predominantly Asian – specifically Indian) takes on the role of the exotic other, albeit a subsidiary one.

In fact, a very visually and aurally striking dichotomy of the English and the other is made subordinate – through intertextual references, iconography and discourse – to a focus on intertemporal exchange between the ancient and the modern. A return to the project's mission statement illustrates how any controversial 'them/us' dualism is significantly diluted by the inclusion of a politically safer 'then/now':

> [The Imagined Village] recast age-old traditions in the shape of the twenty-first century. A daring mix of ancient and modern, The Imagined Village fuses fiddles and squeezebox with dub beats and sitars. (The Imagined Village, 2009)

This contemporisation discourse draws from an ossified song canon and revivalist personnel to present English folk music as something that needs to be 'brought up to date'. But, crucially, this updating process has been played out through a conflation of modernity with multiculturalism. Images and sounds of the exotic East, therefore become associated with the contemporary. We even see a situation where a version of 'Scarborough Fair' unlikely to predate the eighteenth century is 'updated' through the application of a sitar (an instrument with its own, extremely long history). This turns the norms of world music as a concept on its head – non-Western music may play the role of exotic other to a Western audience, or a focus of identification amongst its 'glocal', domestic audience, as a resistance to Anglo-American globalisation. But in both cases, the Western pop musical element (Frith's universal pop aesthetic) has generally represented modernity (good or bad), whilst the non-Western elements stand for a traditional, historical music and culture. Here, through referencing multiculturalism, the role of the non-Western other is reversed.

In considering the nostalgic opening track "Ouses 'Ouses 'Ouses' (2007), which was discussed in 6.7, a reviewer of the band's first album comments that '[t]his theme of a disappearing rural idyll seems a little incongruous on a record that is supposed to celebrate the vibrancy of England in the 21st century' (White, 2007). White is picking up on a perceived incongruity between a notion of historically rooted Englishness and that of a cosmopolitan, plural, open, contemporary construct of Englishness. This has echoes in some theoretical discussions of identity. The concepts of roots and routes have been employed by a number of scholars as a way of understanding the construction of identities (see, for example, Gilroy, 1993; Hall, 2008; Ni Laoire and Fielding, 2006). Roots allegedly represent origins, are seen as 'timeless, traditional, authentic and natural, associated with a sense of place and often with "the land" itself' (Ni Laoire and Fielding, 2006: 108–

9). Routes refer to 'the very different pathways which different cultures, peoples, traditions, languages and religions have taken to the present' (Hall, 2008). This characterisation of roots and routes aptly describes the approach to Englishness that is taken by The Imagined Village, which is invested in both the rootedness and routedness of Englishness. It brings together the idea of an English identity rooted in history and place with that of a contemporary cosmopolitan English identity that acknowledges movement and diversity. Whilst theorists such as Hall and Gilroy argue that it is necessary to place an emphasis on the routes of identity, The Imagined Village, in imagining its 'new England' does not separate the roots from the routes, but celebrates both. This is both its strength and the source of its contradictions.

7.4 Controversies and political engagements

7.4.1 'Blacking up'

A practice undertaken within the context of certain dance traditions is that of blackening the face. See, for example, Buckland's discussion of the Britannia Coco-nut Dancers of Bacup, Derbyshire, whose blackened faces are part of an outlandish and unique costume that includes 'decorated clogs with bells; long white socks;; black velvet knee-breeches; a white skirt decorated with red horizontal bands; a white hat adorned with red or blue braid, pom-poms, and feather' (1990: 1). The Coco-nut Dancers have performed this practice at least since their dances were recorded by first revival collectors in the 1920s, although it claims much earlier origins (*Ibid.*). Blacking up also takes place as part of the Guizing tradition in Padstow, Cornwall, which Davey argues can be traced back to the 1800s, 'with some justification for speculation about much earlier roots' (2006:11). More recently adopted practitioners of blacking up include many border morris and molly sides, where the blackening of faces was revived since the 1960s and 1970s as part of the revival and reinvention of these traditions. The origins of this practice in its different manifestations are unclear, but there is a range of explanations in circulation. One is the disguise function – many dancers now consider the practice to have developed in order to facilitate anonymous (and illegal) begging – whilst another invokes links with minstrelsy in the nineteenth century (see Buckland, 1990 for a fuller discussion). It should be said, however, that the great majority of practitioners roundly reject any imitation or mimicry of black people as contributing in any way to the development of the activity.

Nonetheless, this practice of white men and women 'blacking up' as part of folk traditions has, for obvious reasons, been the focus of some controversy in both England and America (see Greenhill, 2002, on the Canadian context). Two to three years prior to our fieldwork period for this book, there was some public controversy relating to the Padstow case (see Davey, 2006, and Schofield, 2005, for discussions of this). The so-called 'Padstow Debate' (Davey, 2006) related to the tradition known then as 'Darkie Day'. Played out in the press and the House of Commons, accusations of racism led to the attendance of the police at the

2004 Boxing Day event, where they took video footage for submission to the Crown Prosecution Service, which subsequently decided not to proceed with a prosecution (*Ibid.*). Taking police advice, and 'in recognition of meaning and negative connotations of the term 'Darkie' in modern English usage compared to Cornish dialect' (*Ibid*: 9), the word 'darkie' was eventually replaced with 'mummer' in the event's title. The 'Padstow Debate' articulated two positions. The criticisms, articulated most publicly by MPs Diane Abbott and the late Bernie Grant, accused the event of racism. The defence of the practice, outlined by Davey (2006), argues that an interpretation of blacking up as offensive is based on a misunderstanding of the tradition. From the perspective of this book, the interesting point is perhaps that since the 'Padstow Debate', there has been very little discernible public controversy about this issue. Whilst many border morris dancers have now adopted coloured face paint in order to avoid controversy, many more continue to black up, but public controversy over the practice has seemingly subsided.

7.4.2 Folk Against Fascism

The period between, roughly, 2006 and 2012, saw a development in which English folk participants were drawn to engage quite explicitly with challenges concerning the politics of Englishness. The catalyst was the BNP's strategy of championing English folk and the celebration of English folk traditions as a way of gaining support for its nationalist agenda. This strategy is described in its Activists' and Organisers' handbook:

> We've had some major successes, for example, with local groups set up to encourage the celebration of St. George's Day. Fun activities for children and families which are linked to our Christian heritage – such as Pace-Egging in many northern towns – are particularly suitable candidates for revival as popular awareness of the growing power of Islam increases interest in and support for our own religious and cultural traditions (BNP, no date: 9).

Later in the handbook, supporters are urged: 'Why not do some research to see if there's a lost local tradition that you can inspire a team of enthusiasts to revive?' (*Ibid*: 18). The personal taste of the BNP leader Nick Griffin for folk music generally, and some English folk artists in particular, came to light when he wrote in a blog:

> Radio Two has a slot with Kate Rusby ... As usual, her set mixes her own material with traditional songs delivered in her unmistakable southern Yorkshire accent. It's a welcome contrast to the multi-cult junk played incessantly on Radio One – not so much entertainment as an instrument of torture (Griffin: 2007 cited in Lucas, 2010).

In May 2006 the band Bellowhead discovered that the owner of a Bellowhead fan club site on MySpace's social networking platform was a BNP member. The site was closed down and a new one was opened, adorned with a 'Love Music Hate Racism' logo. Later, John Spiers and Jon Boden (the central members of

Bellowhead), found that tracks they had recorded some years earlier (and for which they had signed away the rights) had been packaged into a compilation album that was on sale on the BNP's partner website Excalibur. Speaking of these incidents, Jon Boden speaks of his discomfort at the realisation that the audience for his music may misinterpret its sentiments as nationalist:

> It made me uncomfortable actually thinking that there might be people in the audience to a Bellowhead gig that are misinterpreting the fact that we're doing English material for the fact that we might be nationalist – even with a small 'n' […] I'm not even nationalist with a small 'n'. (Jon Boden, interview, 2008)

Boden's solution was to respond by attaching an anti-Nazi league sticker to his fiddle.

> That sort of solved it in a way – it's a silly, minor little thing, sticking a sticker on your fiddle, but I just thought, well, if there's anyone in the audience who is under any illusions, then they'll see that and then they won't come again, you know, and good riddance. (*Ibid.*)

Boden's quiet attempt to control the meaning of his English folk music was a forerunner of the formation of the campaign Folk Against Fascism (FAF) that was officially launched at a concert on Friday, 7 August 2009 at Sidmouth Folk Week. FAF had a very singular purpose:

> Folk Against Fascism has been created to take a stand against the BNP's targeting of folk music, a stand against the appropriation of our culture. […] The BNP's Activists and Organisers Handbook encourages its members to get involved in the folk scene; Folk Against Fascism aims to make such infiltration impossible. (Folk Against Fascism, 2009)

FAF was started as a grassroots campaign, rather than a membership organisation, and within a short time its logos, badges and T-shirts were prominent at folk events. Its website gives a summary of the kinds of activities that it engaged in since 2009:

> there have been numerous events across the country, from ceilidhs and morris danceouts to gigs and concerts – all organised by people who wanted to spread the word and take a stand. Many festivals and bands support FAF – too many to list here, but you can see them on our website – and have held their own FAF concerts and tours. Supporters have sold our merchandise, displayed our banners, loaned us their venues, worn our t-shirts on stage (including at the BBC Folk Awards), put the FAF logo on their CDs, and even made limited edition products for us to sell … They also organised loads of events for FAF Week, which lasted from St George's Day to May Day 2010. The week's biggest event was the FAF Village Fête at the SouthBank Centre in London on 2 May – an afternoon of traditional fête games, WI cake stalls, maypole, ceilidhs, morris dancing and music, followed by an incredible concert on the night featuring some of the

top bands on the folk scene. We also produced our first (of three) compilation albums, which features music from a wide array of new and established artists and styles (each of whom have donated a track because they believe in what FAF stands for). (Folk Against Fascism, 2012)

Significantly, just as Boden's response was to intervene in the realm of representation, so the FAF campaign has placed a central emphasis on images – badges, logos, T-shirts, and so on. The FAF logo, a drawing of a guitar carrying the slogan 'Folk Against Fascism', references iconography from the second folk revival period – the guitar carried by Woody Guthrie, and emblazoned with the slogan 'this machine kills fascists'.

Whilst the FAF intervention is made in response to the activities of a political organisation, its own political position is deliberately ambiguous:

> FAF is neither left-of-centre nor right of-centre. It is simply a coalition of people who care passionately about British folk culture and don't want to see it turned into something it's not: a marketing tool for extremist politics. (Folk Against Fascism, 2012)

It has essentially been a reactive campaign, rather than a proactively political one. Jon Boden, for example, blogging on the FAF website in 2009, published the following statement:

> I do think it's important for those of us with left wing views to detach our politics from our folk music. Politics should only become an issue when political groups attempt to annexe traditional folk music/song/dance/custom to their own political agenda and attempt to restrict participation on the basis of background, politics, colour, etc. This is currently the case with the BNP, and resisting that attempt is where Folk Against Fascism comes in. (Boden, 2009)

In 2012, the team of volunteer organisers of the FAF website scaled back their activities. An email sent to supporters explained:

> The threat from the BNP to traditional English music and culture seems, like many of the BNP's dreams and schemes, to have imploded in a noxious cloud of scandal, infighting and financial ruin. We should all feel proud to have played even a tiny part in helping to drive the nail in the coffin of their political ambitions … If the threat returns, we won't be far away, ready to resurface and pick up Woody's guitar if and when we need to. (FAF, Pers. Comm.)

This move highlights the fundamentally reactive character of the campaign's politics. It also underlines its diffuse, bottom-up disposition as a grassroots campaign, rather than a stable organisation:

> We intend to leave the web resources up for you to use and promote your own events – FAF isn't just the four of us, or an administrative headquarters, it's all of you. (*Ibid.*)

7.5 Conclusion

The phenomenon of Folk Against Fascism highlights a key aspect of the twenty-first-century folk resurgence – that it is primarily described by its participants as an expression of cultural identity rather than a political act. The cultural identity in question is still to be negotiated, and the negotiations have so far yielded a variety of Englishnesses, which have their own implicit politics. In whichever form it takes, the identity – as with all identities – is necessarily collective and exclusive. That is to say, it is invariably constructed through articulations of insiders and outsiders. In those expressions that couch Englishness in terms of history and locality, the boundaries between insider and outsider are – albeit implicitly – drawn around a notion of native belonging and ownership: the outsider in this narrative does not share the English cultural history, and originates (in the very loosest sense) from somewhere other than England. Those expressions that portray Englishness as a discrete and equal but forgotten piece in the British cultural jigsaw expand on the characterisation of the outsider, by presenting them as a figure with his or her own – more celebrated, 'successful' or 'acceptable' – traditional culture. As we shall discuss further in 8.3, these constructions suggest a significant shift towards the expression of an idea of English indigeneity.

The construction of English identity as inherently multicultural or multi-ethnic, such as that found in the work of The Imagined Village, appears to contradict the characterisation of Englishness as exclusive. It is difficult to identify an outsider in this narrative. There is a tacit assumption that one would need to be resident in England in order to claim Englishness, but beyond that, it would seem that the identity is available to all, and that availability is its distinctive quality. We have shown how close analysis of The Imagined Village's output indicates the difficulties and contradictions inherent in the musical reification of such an identity, but the project's over-riding discourse is indubitably centred on a principle of inclusion across historical, local, ethnic and cultural boundaries. So we conclude that the 'melting-pot' construction is not only a celebration of a particular identity but also a celebration of the *idea* of identity. This version is set not against a threat of other, more celebrated, 'successful' or 'acceptable' cultures, but rather against a threat of a more general failure to identify, to belong and to commune. And herein lies the 'outsider' – those who might profit from, or otherwise pursue, a homogenised Britain, Europe or world. The outsider in this narrative is global capitalism writ large.

Notes

1   Although the reference here is to the British Isles, it is England that is implied in the references to Dickens, Shakespeare, Elgar and Sir Christopher Wren.
2   The imagery here comes from the traditional story 'The Pedlar of Swaffam'.
3   Mehmet's emergence onto the national performance stage occurred just after the end of our main period of research fieldwork, and so has been less fully explored here than it perhaps justifies.

8

Conclusion

The contemporary English folk resurgence has been a challenging subject on which to write for a number of reasons. For one thing, the field is amorphous and in no small part a construct of the authors. Whilst we stand by the suggestion that some such field of activity exists and is recognised by its participants, we must acknowledge that its boundaries are, at various points and in various ways, permeable and have been somewhat arbitrarily set here for the purposes of maintaining focus and achievability. It might be argued, for instance, that more could be done to integrate the multiple contributions of nu-folk artists to the broader debates discussed in this book, or the perspectives of more grassroots participants within this field. Emphases might otherwise have been assigned in such a way as to privilege aspects necessarily summarised here, such as experiential ethnographic description. Such ethnographies would add much to a largely unexplored area of research. There is presently a relative lack of ethnographic documentation on the subject of the contemporary English folk arts, and we hope that this book has demonstrated the fertility of the field as an area for further research. We look forward to discovering the varied interpretations that differing approaches will no doubt generate.

We hope, also, that the book demonstrates the benefits of a dual disciplinary approach. The two disciplines brought together in the researching and writing of this volume – ethnomusicology and British cultural studies – are both to a large extent interdisciplinary in themselves, but the combination of approaches has allowed for a movement beyond the respective conventional comfort zones of each. Although some key exponents of contemporary ethnomusicology have pushed to improve the scope of the discipline, discussion of music cultures in the contemporary, globalising West is still relatively sparse; and whilst there has been a resounding push in recent years for greater contextualisation of case studies within the global political landscape, this is something still considered rather secondary to many in the field. On the other hand, ethnographies of music cultures within cultural studies remain unlikely to engage with the music (the common denominator of any such culture in question) at the same analytical level as they do with, for example, discourse or iconography. In many ways, this book has been a project in relating the most detailed minutiae of the foreground (e.g. a non-tonic pedal note, a group's choice of bass instrument, a decision to dance Cotswold morris without handkerchieves) to the widest possible vista of the background.

Through this breadth of coverage, we are able to draw some general conclusions that not only speak to the specific field of the post-revival English folk arts but also suggest a new emphasis for future research on Englishness. We will now conclude by providing a discussion of these main themes.

8.1 Folk, politics and reconciliation

Of the various artistic and contextual elements of the English folk resurgence discussed in this book, the feature that has generated the greatest public discussion and debate has been the appropriation and mobilisation of folk music by the BNP. The far-right's involvements with contemporary English folk not only resulted in the development of the Folk Against Fascism campaign (as discussed in 7.4.2) but has also drawn considerable attention to the topic of folk by cultural commentators who might not otherwise have been directly interested. A good deal of debate has been generated about the subject in the national broadcast media – something in which the authors of this book have had some small involvement. Although the attentions of the BNP have been quite unwelcome and deeply concerning to most English folk artists, a net result of subsequent clashes between the folk world and the far-right has been a rise in the profile of the English folk arts as important beyond the boundaries of their own artistic substance. The frequently expressed desire, within the folk scene, for folk to be 'taken seriously' has been partially met through this conflict, albeit for reasons quite undesirable to the majority of the English folk community.

The interests of the BNP in folk music came as a considerable surprise to many, within and without the English folk culture. In discussion with informants, at industry conferences and during informal conversations with musicians, dancers and activists, it became evident that historical relationships between the concept of folk and a right-of-centre political stance were often quite unknown. Media reports of the scenario also often implied that the event was an entertainingly bizarre and unforeseen turn of events. This is perhaps not surprising, since associations of folk music with post-war socialism persist in the living memory of the English folk community and are diametrically opposed to the nationalist ideologies of the BNP.

The episode has brought into stark relief the duality of the folk arts as a genre able to satisfy the cultural requirements of two different ends of the political spectrum. On the one hand, it has an enduring ability to instil a sense of timeless, authentic purity, in ways that speak directly to exclusive, nationalist discourses. On the other hand, it has helped to crystallise the idea of the 'common man' in the Marxist sense, a deployment of the folk arts that has been evident in Soviet Russia, in counter-cultural America and in the UK during the mid-twentieth century. Whilst we recognise that this is an exceptionally simplistic portrayal of a very complex set of political and ideological interactions, it is nonetheless helpful as a conceptual representation of folk's political meanings in contemporary England. What appears to be particularly interesting about the cultural moment discussed in this book is the way in which both political deployments have been attempted simultaneously. Folk Against Fascism's clashes with the far-right characterise a distinctive cultural moment in which folk moves from being a weapon of either extreme of the political spectrum to being the battleground itself.

The notion of the folk as indexical of leftist agendas has been relatively implicit – or dormant – during the 1990s, and has only really received reinforcement in recent years in direct protest at the efforts of the BNP. That is not to say, however, that the re-engagement with politics has been purely reactive: the activities of artists like Billy Bragg and the Imagined Village were gathering pace before the full emergence of the BNP's interests, and would no doubt have received similar levels of attention with or without the conflicts with the far-right. This is because there was an accepted need to accompany the increasingly explicit assertions of English identity emanating from the folk community with a disclaimer – an approach that defended against the possible misinterpretations of commentators outside of the folk establishment. In other words, radical explorations of Englishness within the folk scene have been primarily engaged in justifying the celebration of English cultural identity for the relatively liberal English majority – justification that would have been necessary with or without active engagement from the BNP.

The resurgence has shed light on the accents and emphases of a cultural memory. Whilst the folk community has continued to celebrate and com-memorate the activities of the first revival period, particularly in terms of the considerable collections of tunes, songs and dances made by Sharp and his contemporaries, few have actively engaged in remembering the essentialising, nationalist ideologies on which such activities were so often based. The passing of time and a second revival period have led to a subtle forgetting of these political implications of the late nineteenth- and early twentieth-century movement in a way that enables a coming together of first-revival materials, second-revival attitudes to participation and inclusivity, and contemporary approaches to the reworking of tradition. In this way, the resurgence may be understood not only in terms of the particular political context of contemporary England but also as a partially self-contained reconciliation of the two earlier revivals. This reconciliation was shown in specific relation to the growth of a 'folk industry' in Chapter 2, but can be located throughout the many activities of the resurgence. Most recent at the time of writing has been the announcement of a grant (nearly £600,000) from the Heritage Lottery Fund to enable the EFDSS to digitise large amounts of materials including original manuscripts, transcriptions and notes made by key figures of first revival period, including Sharp himself (see 7.2.1). The Full English project was announced on the EFDSS website thus:

NATIONAL PROJECT TO WIDEN THE REACH OF FOLK MUSIC
AND DANCE GIVEN GO AHEAD

The English Folk Dance and Song Society (EFDSS) has secured a grant […] to archive, conserve and digitise materials from six archives containing some of the country's most important folk music collections and allow free public access to 58,400 digitised collection items through a new web portal.

Katy Spicer, Chief Executive of EFDSS, said: […] 'We are very grateful to the Heritage Lottery Fund for the funding which will safeguard the future of these important collections and bring folk music to a generation that may otherwise never had heard of it.' (English Folk Dance and Song Society, 2012)

While Spicer's last comment would appear to chime absolutely with the concerns of a hundred years earlier, the publication of these – in many cases *unedited* – materials on the internet represents an ultimate act of democratisation. It is a significant 'handing back' of the materials to the general public, something more likely to have pleased Lloyd than Sharp, and the action is likely to encourage a yet broader range of stylistic interpretations from the new participants it recruits.

8.2 Reviewing revivals and resurgence

The resurgence of interest in – and profile of – English folk music and dance in contemporary England is an important illustration of the need for scholars in ethnomusicology, cultural studies and cognate disciplines to look beyond conventional theories and unpublished wisdom pertaining to folk revivals. We explained in Chapter 1 our reasons for choosing to label the cultural moment a 'resurgence' rather than a 'revival'; principal among those was our need to acknowledge that the recent popularisation of the English folk arts has not been the result of any one dominant underlying ideology or explicit motivating factor. In fact, the politically multifaceted history of English folk music prevents against that kind of a movement from gaining much ground in contemporary England. The two revival movements of the early- and mid-twentieth century broadly stemmed from differing motivations: speaking very simplistically, the first was primarily concerned with the redefinition of *England* through seeking a 'pure' strain of English music, whilst the second was principally concerned with the unification of a working-class community (i.e. the *folk*) through engagement with a historically rooted vernacular culture. By contrast, current events in the English folk arts are not so obviously accompanied by explicit concerns beyond a desire to be heard and seen. No clearly expressed reasoning underpins the resurgence, but the political climate (along with the temporal proximity to the second revival period) means that constructions of Englishness and 'authentic' vernacularity originating from the earlier eras demand acknowledgement.

The heritage of the English folk artist includes not just songs, tunes and dances, but also a combination of often contradictory discourses to which their contemporary performance must speak. Though most participants are keen to distance themselves from the explicit and driving politics of the preceding revivals, all are drawn into simultaneous negotiations of Englishness and 'folkishness', through (for instance) the foregrounding of historical musical and choreographical texts or via the celebration of 'authentic', participatory forms of communal expression and creativity. And it is from this mediatory condition that the extraordinarily varied characteristics of the current English folk resurgence stem. Participants' positions on, for example, nationalist or socialist ideologies can be rejecting, responding, indifferent or allegiant, and tacitly embedded or explicitly rehearsed in almost infinitely diverse ways; the vast range of textual and stylistic responses that make up contemporary English folk music and dance is – to some extent – the result of this condition.

Alongside the myriad meanings to be found within the texts of the resurgence, we have also identified a considerable array of interconnected modes for the circulation of such meanings. For instance, one particularly significant feature of the current resurgence has been the expanding nature of media involvement. The profiling of folk within broadcast media and the texts and discourse made available through vernacular circulations (e.g. amateur websites, blogs, social media, etc.) have played a significant role in shaping the resurgence. Meanwhile, the involvement of mediating systems and technologies in the folk resurgence can be expanded to include the now extensive machinery of marketing, public relations, management and agency, as discussed in Chapter 2. In the name of maximising participation and awareness, some quarters of the English folk world have wholeheartedly adopted the trappings of the professionalised pop industry. Activists and other participants have therefore been required to downplay or not acknowledge much of the anticapitalist ideology which underpinned the second revival. Meanwhile, the very concept of 'folk' is being complicated by the pop industry's own engagements with folk as a label to denote a variety of acoustic-based singer-songwriters. The two worlds collide and interconnect at points such as the BBC Radio 2 Folk Awards and various mainstream festivals, and the moments of interconnection are – for the most part – lauded as desirable acknowledgement (folk being 'taken seriously') by those from a more 'traditional' folk background.

We have, however, demonstrated that a reading of the mainstreaming aspects of the resurgence as, in any simplistic way, an incorporation of folk into a dominant culture would inappropriately gloss the complexities of the contemporary English folk world. The idea of participation remains a central element in discourse emanating from the resurgence, regularly rehearsed as a distinctive quality of the folk scene, and celebrated in forms such as sessions, singarounds, ceilidhs and amateur morris dancing. It could be argued that the participatory ideal has become an aesthetic that pervades – to varying extents – all regions of the English folk context. Furthermore, it may be suggested that the presence of this participation, in one form or another, is perhaps one important character of the English folk arts that gives a boundary to this seemingly undefinable culture and identity.[1] But the aesthetic is itself amorphous and porous, without clear sources of direction or core–periphery relationships. The English folk resurgence is, then, a 'headless' movement, without any clearly acknowledged leaders, decision makers or 'folk police' (although influence across the scene is far from equally distributed amongst all artists, activists, professionals and institutions). This headless movement has produced a nexus of approaches

– a huge range of stylistic, formal, and discursive manifestations and responses. As we have seen in Chapter 3, English folk has been presented in diverse musical and artistic terms, ranging from contemporary electronica to Vaudeville – and these various presentations are displayed side-by-side at the centre of the English folk scene, often with no distinguishing labels beyond 'English folk' to separate them. Within this environment, homogeneity is actively avoided, and anti-conformity predominates – fuelled by the implied unifying rationale of participation-as-aesthetic (i.e. that 'doing English folk' – in whatever form – *is* 'English folk'). This highlights the need to consider this resurgence as very different from the revival as it has been previously conceived by Livingston (1999) and others.

We have shown that the ethos of folk music and dance in contemporary England remains, for many involved, oppositional to the idea of mainstream culture, but that folk's relationship with that discourse of resistance is complex and often contradictory. Some elements of the folk resurgence, such as quasi-social-realist or historically referent song texts, 'traditional' approaches and even the folk label itself are sometimes deployed as an explicitly countering response to the perceived artifice of a pop-music dominated mainstream. Much of the resurgence, however, revolves around a mainstreaming approach that seems actively to orient folk in parallel and close proximity to popular culture. Whilst the multiple approaches have in-built – and generally unspoken – 'traditionalness' ratings, they are not clearly segregated by venues or audiences. The acoustic concert band Crucible, for instance, rates highly on a traditionalness scale, but shares festival stages, fan bases and personnel with the metalcore ceilidh band Glorystrokes; many of their audience are likely to be ironically head-banging in the evening ceilidh after a hard day of traditional morris dancing. If the term 'folk' is, then, encapsulating such a wide range of sounds, images and activities, then attention to its affective qualities must be directed away from 'what' and 'how' to the more fascinating question of 'why?'. Specifically, why should such a quickly increasing number of people desire such a quickly increasing number of sights and sounds to *be* 'folk'? The term has been sufficiently robust to withstand stylistic diversification whilst quietly supporting statements of ideology and national identity that underpin much discourse of the cultural moment in contemporary England.

8.3 Englishness as an indigeneity

It is tempting to conclude by placing an emphasis on those strands within the folk resurgence that overtly celebrate more progressive, hybrid or multi-ethnic visions of Englishness, and we have done this in Chapters 6 and 7. We must acknowledge, however, that some of the output of the resurgence also appears to be related to the construction of an Englishness that invokes the concept of indigeneity or indigenousness. This may be an uncomfortable acknowledgement, but we need to take this aspect of the movement seriously and think about its significance. It therefore seems appropriate to relate our research on the English context generally, and English folk music specifically, to the burgeoning literature on the study of indigeneity.

No clear definition of the term seems to predominate, but the concept is of great importance within a number of disciplines, including the fields of cultural geography, international legal theory and anthropology. The approach taken by legal theorists stems from a pragmatic enterprise to establish the indigeneity (or indigenousness) of a group or individual for legal purposes (see, for instance, Waldron, 2003), whilst that adopted by athropologists originates with a desire to understand the meaning of indigenousness as it relates to the lives of those who identify themselves – or are identified by others – as being indigenous (e.g. Shaw, Herman and Dobbs, 2006). The two approaches are, of course, at opposite ends of a spectrum, along which midway junctures such as the matter of individual and group self-determinism can be plotted (e.g. Bennett, 2005; Canessa, 2007).

Many discussions of indigeneity – spanning the range of approaches – look to its etymological synonymity with terms such as 'nativity' and 'aboriginality'. Waldron (2003) opens his discussion of indigeneity's literal meaning with a perusal of the Oxford English Dictionary definitions of aboriginality ('[t]he quality of being aboriginal; existence in or possession of a land at the earliest stage of its history') and indigenous ('[b]orn or produced naturally in a land or region; native or belonging naturally to (the soil, region, etc.)'; Oxford English Dictionary, cited in *Ibid*.: 55). Certainly, these definitions appear to suggest a strong relationship between the concept of indigeneity and some of the key discourses circulated in the contemporary English folk resurgence. However, working usage of the term across disciplines is more specifically directed at labelling those groups throughout the world who share a very particular role within a colonial or postcolonial narrative. Shaw, Herman and Dobbs tentatively suggest that indigenous peoples are 'generally groups with ancestral and often spiritual ties to particular land, and whose ancestors held that land prior to colonisation by outside powers, and whose nations remain submerged within the states created by those powers' (2006: 268). The comments of Shaw *et al.*, and the subjects explored in the other articles that populate the journal issue to which their own acts as introduction, are indicative of a largely unacknowledged consensus, amongst cultural geographers, cultural anthropologists (including ethnomusicologists) and others, that the 'indigenous people/s' are those who are distinct from a ruling group of sometime interlopers. Specifically, indigeneity is a term commonly used to label the social, cultural or legal situations of those who have – or whose ancestors have – been suppressed, displaced or otherwise disenfranchised through the processes of European colonisation in the Americas, Africa and Australasia.

Within Western cultural academic discourse, the quality of being indigenous is generally reserved for – and assigned to – those who are in positions of minority (or, at least, political subordination) within colonised 'settler societies' (*Ibid*.). Historically speaking, this is perhaps unsurprising: within the colonial narrative, the experience of the coloniser is likely to have been assumed, since the Western coloniser was the primary generator of academically sanctioned knowledge. In recent years, much revision of the concept has affected a move away from an orientalist, homogenising representation of the world's 'indigenous peoples', and towards a qualitative epistemology that seeks to understand the plights, triumphs and politics of indigenousness in terms of specific, postcolonial and postmodern texts and contexts. Shaw *et al.* attempt to rescind an orientalist approach to the classification, stating categorically that '[b]ifurcating "indigenous" from "Western" is misleading and problematic' (2006: 269). Nonetheless, the tale of a British colleague's 'playful' claim of indigeneity is relegated to an aside in a footnote, arguably indicating the stubbornness of ingrained assumptions about the term's meanings (274). It could reasonably be argued that a truly revisionist use of the word indigeneity is one that does not preclude any particular population or set of populations, but rather relates to any people's sense of nativity and construction of a collective and exclusive identity on the basis of prior occupancy (or 'we were here first'; see Bennett, 2005).

In the case of contemporary England, expressions of Englishness often tend to meet these criteria precisely. Some of the broad discourses discussed thus far point to: a historically rooted sense of belonging; ownership of – or at least a strong identification with – a 'homeland'; and a consolidation of a cultural identity (along such lines of belonging and ownership) in conscious distinction from immigrant peoples and externally originating forces. When English people seek to affirm their Englishness in terms of their historically grounded relationship with the place called England, they are – it would appear – asserting indigeneity. This is not to say, of course, that contemporary expressions of indigeneity by Western European populations should be regarded as of the same order as those of (for instance) native Americans. Clearly, the experiences, goals, concerns, etc., of (to take another example) people who assert a need to identify themselves as indigenous Frenchmen and women are not likely to be the same as those of people asserting their Cheyenne identity in North America. However, if we are to subscribe to the anti-orientalist approach of Shaw *et al.*, then that goes without saying, since the cultural, social and political situation of the Cheyenne is specific to that population, and not to be generalised to any other 'indigenous' groups.

For now, then, the term indigenous continues to be the reserve of those studying peoples who are experiencing new opportunities to assert postcolonial, post-oppressed identities that distinguish them from historical invaders. It is, of course, essential that such work continues, and that such groups be given voice and recognition within academic cultural scholarship. The subject is a particularly popular one at present, with such a concept of indigeneity providing the materials for conferences, projects and publications across the cultural disciplines.[2] The contemporary expressions of Englishness, however, would appear to disrupt some current assumptions about what constitutes indigeneity. One might argue that this demonstrates a parallel need to understand expressions of indigenousness within Western European nations – a context that presents a very different narrative from that associated with indigeneity elsewhere in the West (e.g. the Americas).

A key difference between the English population and those populations more commonly accepted as indigenous is that the English remain essentially dominant within the political environs of their home state. Merlan (2009) identifies 'relational definitions' as key among definitions of indigeneity, and quotes Maybury-Lewis' assertion that 'indigenous peoples are defined as much by their relations with the state as by any intrinsic characteristics that they may possess' (quoted in Merlan, 2009: 305). In conventional deployment of the term indigeneity, those relations are likely to be characterised by a lack of governmental representation or political potency (although, again, much is assumed). Here, the case for Englishness-as-indigeneity appears to fail (or break with the norm), since the English – however defined – are the politically dominant group in their native land by most empirical and anecdotal measures. It seems fairly unquestionable that those who in one way or another self-identify as 'native English' make up the considerable majority of the electorate, although exact figures are hard to come by, since the census data for England and Wales place English identity within a generic 'White, British' category (Office for National Statistics, 2012). At the time of writing, both the elected Prime Minister and the monarchical head of state are widely accepted as being English.[3] The majority of the MPs who represent the constituencies of England are white, English men, including the leaders of the main opposition parties.

It is difficult, then, to regard the political disenfranchisement of 'the English' in clear and factual terms of state representation or legislation on a scale generally expected of 'indigenous' peoples globally. However, the discourses surrounding Englishness in contemporary England would certainly indicate that concerns over appropriate levels of English representation within UK politics are significant. A typical voicing of these concerns came in the *Times* article by William Rees-Mogg, which we cited in Chapter 5 as an exposition of the 'West Lothian Question': 'The people of the UK's biggest, richest country won't accept second-class status much longer' (Rees-Mogg, 2005). His complaint appears to be made on behalf of 'the people of England', who are, of course, not the same as 'the English'. But the argument is illustrative of a common, more directly Anglo-centric narrative that depicts the English as a comparatively silent majority, suffering from increasing under-representation at various political and cultural levels.

This particular debate indicates two things. Firstly, it suggests that the significance and nature of relations between population and state are not absolute or something to be empirically evaluated, but rather located in the perceptions of those asserting indigeneity. Secondly, the Rees-Mogg example works as a stark reminder that indigeneity has in large part to do with responses to perceived outsiders. In the case of the issues inherent in UK devolution, the 'other' is the increasingly autonomous Welsh or Scots person, whose encroachment into England itself is effectively figurative and political, rather than a physical invasion. Meanwhile, other debates point to alternative outsiders. The concern in some vocal quarters regarding the potential loss of English electoral power through further consolidation of the European Parliament would seem to chime very closely with Stavenhagen's comment that 'indigenousness, independently of biological or cultural continuity, frequently is the outcome of governmental policies imposed from above and from outside' (quoted in Muehlebach, 2003: 244).

Despite the various similarities between the characterisation of indigeneity throughout academic literature and contemporary debates about Englishness, it is important to acknowledge that the term 'indigenous' is rarely used in relation to those debates. Words like indigeneity, indigenous, native, aboriginal, etc., have started to appear in places (see 7.2.1), but are rare in public discourse, and were largely absent in our interviews during the research for this book. Whilst the concepts are most relevant to the ways in which English cultural identity is being couched, they go largely unreferenced, arguably due to the significant connotations that they share. However academic discourse may evaluate or portray indigenousness, in common parlance these terms imply biological and racial claims to ownership of the homeland that are too aggressively exclusive for most English people. In short, they are the language of an approach that is unpalatably fascist (in the literal sense), and therefore recognisable to most commentators (and the public) as too closely associated with the discourses of regimes such as Nazi Germany and Franco's Spain. These associations are made concrete by the fact that this form of language is indeed invoked in the discourse of the far-right parties in England. The BNP makes the following declarations on its website:

> Given current demographic trends, we, the indigenous British people, will become an ethnic minority in our own country well within sixty years – and most likely sooner [...] Non-indigenous births will soon account for more than half of all the babies born in Britain [...] At least twenty percent of the currently resident population were either born overseas or are descendants of foreign-born parents [...] To ensure that [...] the British people retain their homeland and identity, we call for an immediate halt to all further immigration [...] We will abolish the 'positive discrimination' schemes that have made white Britons second-class citizens. (British National Party, 2010)

The use of 'indigenous' or related term in such contexts, alongside references to homelands and birth-rights, renders it objectionable to the majority of the people in England to whom the discourse is directed. The mention of 'white Britons' indicates the thinly veiled racial motivations of the organisation, and their failures in the 2010 general election suggest that such views remain unpopular.[4] Certainly, these views are widely considered to be socially unacceptable, hence the paucity of references to indigeneity in the discourses circulated within more mainstream English society. That is especially the case for the English folk music scene where, as we have already discussed, predominating political allegiances are left-of-centre. However, the folk scene represents a peculiar political arena, in that this left-wing-inclined culture continues to celebrate the first period of revival that took place at the beginning of the twentieth century, during which protagonists like Cecil Sharp expressed, quite explicitly, a strong belief in the concept of an indigenous Englishness, at least in the literal senses of 'aboriginal' and 'native'.

The forty-first conference of the International Council for Traditional Music, held in St Johns, Newfoundland, in July 2011, included as a conference theme 'indigenous modernities'. The majority of papers presented under this title met with the common usage of the term indigeneity, but a notable anomaly was the session devoted to expressions of Englishness in English music. The panel, which included a presentation by one of this book's authors, was not prearranged, but its coming together was serendipitous in that it highlighted a need to reassess the concept of indigeneity. Specifically, the English subject may perhaps indicate a new sub-category of post-coloniser indigeneity. There is activity in Western Europe and Scandinavia to support the notion that expressions of indigeneity are growing. For instance, far-right activists are gaining in voice and profile across Europe. The BNP has dwindled significantly in stature since its defeat in the UK's 2010 general election, but its place as the highest-profile representative body of the far-right in England has been taken by the English Defence League – a street protest group bearing disturbing similarities to the militant, neo-Nazi National Front of the 1970s and 1980s. The EDL positions itself as specifically anti-Islamic and its predominating discourse is a demonstration against 'Islamic Extremism' and 'Islamism' in English culture (English Defence League, 2012a). Central to their protest is a celebration of links with similar organisations throughout Europe, commonly uniting or affiliating under a number of titles, such as Stop Islamisation of Europe (SIOE) and Stop the Islamisation of Nations, among others. SIOE has particular ties with Denmark, Norway and the Netherlands, but claims to have 'branches' across the European continent (SIOE, 2012). This, then, appears to be one aspect of the developing landscape of a new concept of indigeneity within postcolonial Western Europe, and such organisations specifically draw a relationship with ideas of traditional culture. Like the BNP, for instance, the EDL makes reference in its mission statement to 'Promoting the Traditions and Culture of England' (English Defence League, 2012b). Perhaps further case studies such as that outlined in this book might begin to shed more light on some of the nuances within the cultural expression of indigeneity. We can observe, for example, that to perform English folk is, for many, to assert an 'indigenous Englishness' that is inherently diverse and inclusive, and that this runs counter to these alternative cultural understandings of the folk arts as reinforcing 'traditional' (exclusive, even racist) conceptions of what it means to be English. Of course, the flavour of discourses present in such a field of study is likely to be most unpalatable for the majority of cultural academics (the ideologies promoted by far-right groups have made exceptionally uncomfortable reading for the authors of this book), but a failure to engage with the topic will not make it go away.

Notes

1 For other examples of this, see Turino (2008: 33–6).
2 See for example the five-year project, funded by the European Research Council, and entitled 'Indigeneity in the Contemporary World: Politics, Performance, Belonging'

(Indigeneity in the Contemporary World: Politics, Performance, Belonging, 2009).

3 Of course, the royal family's multicultural European heritage is relatively well known to their public. Nonetheless, their residence is in England for most of the year, and the Queen speaks the 'Queen's English'. These are among numerous facts that contribute to the strength of the Royals' link with England – a link that is far stronger than they might have with any other nation, within the UK or without.

4 That said, we should acknowledge that it would be wrong to cite a lack of support for their immigration policies as the clear, single cause of the BNP's failures.

References

Adams, T. (2011). 'The Unthanks: "We're miserable buggers and not afraid of it"'. *The Observer,* 27 February. http://goo.gl/OBe01 (accessed 27 April 2012).

Afro Celt Sound System (2012). http://goo.gl/63s0Y (accessed 19 August 2012).

Anderson, B. (2006). *Imagined Communities* (2nd edn). London: Verso.

Andrews, K. (2011). 'The Unthanks: it's a family affair'. *Galway Advertiser,* 7 April. http://goo.gl/D0QaA (accessed 18/04/2011).

Artlounge (2010). 'Faye Claridge at Three White Walls'. Internet location formerly at www.artlounge.com/news_printable.php?uid=126 (accessed 23 February 2010).

Arts Council England (2010). http://goo.gl/2BZJi (accessed 20 April 2012).

Association of Festival Organisers (2003). *A Report into the Impact of Folk Festivals on Cultural Tourism.* Matlock: The Association of Festival Organisers.

Aughey, A. (2007). *The Politics of Englishness.* Manchester: Manchester University Press.

Balzano, W., Mulhall, A., and Sullivan, M. (eds) (2007). *Irish Postmodernisms and Popular Culture.* Basingstoke: Palgrave Macmillan.

Banes, S. (1987). *Terpsichore in Sneakers: Post-Modern Dance.* Middletown, CT: Wesleyan University Press.

Barber, D., and Walker, B. (2011). 'Time Gentlemen Please'. *Animated,* Winter, pp. 6–9.

BBC (2008). *Proms Folk Day – Sunday 20 July.* http://goo.gl/tcYfH (accessed 22 July 2008).

BBC (2010). *Still Folk Dancing … After All These Years.* www.bbc.co.uk/programmes/b00wgrtr (accessed 20 December 2010).

BBC News Scotland (2011). *Answer Sought to the West Lothian Question.* 8 September. http://goo.gl/3BDPi (accessed 20 November 2011).

BBC Press Office (2009). *BBC One Confirms Third Series of Lark Rise to Candleford.* http://goo.gl/y8T6y (accessed 3 March 2009).

BBC Radio 2 (2012). *It's Got Bells On.* www.bbc.co.uk/programmes/b017xbtj (accessed 20 December 2012).

Bearman, C. J. (2002). 'Cecil Sharp in Somerset: some reflections on the work of David Harker'. *Folklore,* vol. 113, no. 1, pp 11–34.

Bennett, M. (2005). '"Indigeneity" as self-determinism'. *Indigenous Law Journal,* vol. 4, pp. 71–115.

Biddle, I., and Knights, V. (eds) (2007). *Music, National Identity and the Politics of Location.* Aldershot: Ashgate.

Blacking, J. (1981). 'Making artistic popular music: the goal of true folk'. *Popular Music,* no. 1, pp. 9–14.

Blaukopf, K. (1992). *Musical Life in a Changing Society,* trans. David Marinelli. Portland,

OR: Amadeus Press.

Boden, J. (2009). *Folk against fascism.* www.folkagainstfascism.com (accessed 30 October 2009).

Bohlman, P. V. (1988). *The Study of Folk Music in the Modern World.* Indianapolis, IN: Indiana University Press.

Booth, G. D., and Kuhn, T. (1990). 'Economic and transmission factors as essential elements in the definition of folk, art and pop music'. *The Musical Quarterly,* vol. 74, no. 3, 441–38.

Born, G. and Hesmondhalgh, D. (eds) (2000). *Western Music and its Others: Difference, Representation and Appropriation in Music.* Berkeley, CA: University of California Press.

Bowen, G., Bowen, L., Shepherd R., and Shepherd, R. (1998). *Tunes, Songs and Dances from the 1798 Manuscript of Joshua Jackson North Yorkshire Cornmiller and Musician.* Ilkley: Yorkshire Dales Workshops.

Boyes, G. (1993). *The Imagined Village: Culture, Ideology and the English Folk Revival.* Manchester: Manchester University Press.

Bradtke, E. (2001). 'Molly dancing: a study of discontinuity and change', in Boyes, G. (ed.), *Step Change: New Views on Traditional Dance.* London: Francis Boutle, pp. 61–86.

Brady, S., and Walsh, F. (eds) (2009). *Crossroads: Performance Studies and Irish Culture.* Basingstoke: Palgrave Macmillan.

Bragg, B. (2006). *The Progressive Patriot: a Search for Belonging.* London: Bantam Press. Reprint, London: Black Swan (2007).

Bragg, B. (2007). Pre-show workshop discussion at WOMAD Charlton Park. Audio MP3. http://imaginedvillage.com/audiovideo (accessed 24 September 2009).

British National Party (2010). *Immigration: Open Your Eyes.* www.bnp.org.uk/policies/immigration (accessed 12 April 2012).

British National Party (no date). *Activists' and Organisers' Handbook,* BNP Education and Training www.bnp.org.uk/PDF/activists.pdf (accessed 12 April 2012).

Brocken, M. (2003). *The British Folk Revival 1944-2002.* Aldershot: Ashgate Publishing.

Bryant, C. G. A. (2006). *The Nations of Britain.* Oxford: Oxford University Press.

Buckland, T. J. (2001a). 'Dance, authenticity and cultural memory: the politics of embodiment'. *Yearbook for Traditional Music,* vol. 33, pp. 1–16.

Buckland, T. J. (2001b). 'In a word we are unique': ownership and control in an English dance custom', in Boyes, G. (ed.), *Step Change: New Views on Traditional Dance.* London: Francis Boutle, pp. 49–60.

Buckland, T. J. (1990). 'Black faces, garlands and coconuts: exotic dancers on street and stage'. *Dance Research Journal,* vol. 22, no. 2, pp. 1–12.

Bunce, M. (1994). *The Countryside Ideal: Anglo-American Images of Landscape.* London: Routledge.

Burns, R. (2012). *Transforming Folk: Innovation and Tradition in English Folk-Rock Music.* Manchester: Manchester University Press.

Burrows, T. (2010). 'An English journey – reimagined'. *The Telegraph,* 26 January. http://goo.gl/uCf5k (accessed 23 February 2010).

Butler, J. (1990). *Gender Trouble: Feminism and the Subversion of Identity.* New York: Routledge.

Butler, J. (1993). *Bodies that Matter. On the Discursive Limits of Sex.* London: Routledge.

Callaghan, B. (2007). *Hardcore English.* London: English Folk Dance and Song Society.

Campbell, P. (1996). *Analysing Performance.* Manchester: Manchester University Press.

Canessa, A. (2007). 'Who is indigenous? Self-identification, indigeneity, and claims to justice in contemporary Bolivia'. *Urban Anthropology,* vol. 36, no. 3, pp. 195–237.

Castelo-Branco, S. E-S., and Toscano, M. M. (1988). '"In search of a lost world": an overview of documentation and research on the traditional music of Portugal'. *Yearbook for Traditional Music*, vol. 20, pp. 158–92 .

Chan, T. W. and Goldthorpe, J. H. (2007). 'Social stratification and cultural consumption: music in England'. *European Sociological Review*, vol. 23, no. 1, pp. 1–19.

Claridge, F. (2012). www.fayeclaridge.co.uk (accessed 15 January 2012).

Collins, J. (ed.) (2002). *High-Pop: Making Culture Into Popular Entertainment*. Oxford: Blackwell.

Colls, R. (2002). *Identity of England*. Oxford: Oxford University Press.

Come Clog Dancing: Treasures of English Folk Dance (2011). Television programme, BBC4, 14 August.

Connell, J. and Gibson, C. (2003). *Sound Tracks: Popular Music, Identity and Place*. London: Routledge.

Corrsin, S. D. (2001). 'English sword dancing and the European context', in Boyes, G. (ed.), *Step Change: New Views on Traditional Dance*. London: Francis Boutle, pp. 19–48.

Crystal, D. (2007). *By Hook or by Crook: A Journey in Search of English*. London: Harper Press.

Davey, M. R. (2006). 'Guizing: ancient traditions and modern sensitivities'. *Cornish Studies*, no. 14. pp. 229–44.

Dimitriadis, G. (2009). *Performing Identity/Performing Culture: Hip Hop as Text, Pedagogy and Lived Practice*. New York: Peter Lang Publishing, Inc.

Doc Rowe Archive and Collection (2010). www.docrowe.org.uk (accessed 1 April 2012).

Dodd, R., and Colls, R. (eds) (1987). *Englishness: Politics and Culture, 1880–1920*. Australia: Croom Helm.

Dogan Mehmet (no date). www.doganmehmet.com/about (accessed 16 April 2012).

Drury, I. (2008). 'Victory: metric martyrs finally win the right to sell their fruit and veg in pounds and ounces', *Mail Online*, 18 October. http://goo.gl/PlbAL (accessed 18 November 2011).

Edensor, T. (2002). *National Identity, Popular Culture and Everyday Life*. Oxford: Berg.

English Acoustic Collective (no date). http://goo.gl/HUQR6 (accessed 2 April 2008), and www.englishacousticcollective.org.uk (accessed 16 June 2011).

English Acoustic Collective (2007). http://goo.gl/wjyvy (2 April 2008).

English Defence League (2012a). http://englishdefenceleague.org (accessed 4 April 2012).

English Defence League (2012b). http://englishdefenceleague.org/about-us (accessed 4 April 2012).

English Folk Dance and Song Society (2012). *The Full English: Heritage Lottery Fund Announcement: National Project to Widen the Reach of Folk Music & Dance Given Go Ahead*. www.efdss.org/news/newsId/259 (accessed 16 April 2012).

English Folk Dance and Song Society, and The Magpie's Nest (2010). *Nowt as Queer as Folk: Monday 3 May Cecil Sharp House*. London: English Folk Dance and Song Society.

English, R. (2011). *Is There an English Nationalism?* London: Institute for Public Policy Research. http://goo.gl/HU24C (accessed 12 April 2012).

Enjoy England (2010). www.visitengland.com/Traditional-entertainment (accessed 25 September 2011).

Ethno (2012). www.ethno-world.org/about (accessed 19 April 2012).

Featherstone, S. (2009). *Englishness: Twentieth-Century Popular Culture and the Forming of English Identity*. Edinburgh: Edinburgh University Press.

Feld, S. (2000). 'The poetics and politics of pygmy pop', in Born, G., and Hesmondhalgh, D. (eds.), *Western Music and Its Others: Difference, Representation and Appropriation in*

Music. London: University of California Press, pp. 245–79.

Feld, S. (2005). 'From schizophonia to schismogenesis: on the discourses and commodification practices of "world music" and "world beat"', in Feld, S., and Keil, C. (eds), *Music Grooves*. Tucson, AZ: Fenestra Books.

Fink, R. (1998). 'Elvis everywhere: musicology and popular music at the twilight of the canon'. *American Music*, vol. 16, no. 2, pp. 135–79.

Finnegan, R. (1989). *The Hidden Musicians; Music-Making in an English Town*. Cambridge: Cambridge University Press.

Foley, C. (2001). 'Perceptions of Irish step dance: national, global, and local'. *Dance Research Journal*, vol. 33, no. 1, pp. 34–45.

Folk Against Fascism (2009). *About Folk Against Fascism*, www.folkagainstfascism.com/about.html (accessed 30 October 2009).

Folk Against Fascism (2012). www.folkagainstfascism.com (accessed 29 August 2012).

FolkArts England (2007). *FAE Training Days; Folk Industry Focus Days; The Association of Festival Organisers Conference (Programme)*. Matlock: FolkArts England.

FolkArts England (2008). *The Folk Industry and AFO Conference 2008*. Matlock: FolkArts England.

FolkArts England (2009). *Folk Industry and The Association of Festival Organisers Conference 2009: The Big Agenda*. Matlock: FolkArts England.

Francmanis, J. (2002). 'National music to national redeemer: the consolidation of a 'folksong' construct in Edwardian England', *Popular Music,* vol. 21, no. 1, pp. 1–25.

Frith, S. (2000). 'The discourse of world music', in Born, G., and Hesmondhalgh, D. (eds), *Western Music and its Others*. London: University of California Press, pp. 305–22.

Frith, S. (ed.) (1989). *World Music, Politics and Social Change*. Manchester: Manchester University.

Gade, R., and Jerslev, A. (2005). *Performative Realism: Interdisciplinary Studies in Art and Media*. Copenhagen: Museum Tusculanum Press.

Gade, S. (2005). 'Playing the media keyboard', in Gade, R., and Jerslev, A., *Performative Realism: Interdisciplinary Studies in Art and Media*. Copenhagen: Museum Tusculanum Press.

Gammon, V. (1980). 'Folk song collecting in Sussex and Surrey, 1843–1914'. *History Workshop*, vol. 10, pp. 61–89.

Gammon, V., and Laughran, A. (1982). *A Sussex Tunebook*. London: English Folk Dance and Song Society.

Gill, A. A. (2009). 'A. A. Gill meets the morris dancers'. *The Sunday Times,* 9 August. (accessed online 1 April 2010).

Gilroy, P. (1993). *The Black Atlantic*. London: Verso.

Glendinning, L. (2009). 'Musicians demand BNP stop selling their songs'. *The Guardian*, 28 May. http://goo.gl/TXPOc (accessed 12 April 2012).

Glennie, A. (2011). *Are the Eurosceptics Winning?* London: Institute for Public Policy Research. http://goo.gl/ZB5d8 (accessed 20 November 2011).

Goertzen, C. (1997) *Fiddling for Norway: Revival and Identity*. Chicago, IL: University of Chicago Press.

Greenhill, P. (2002). 'Folk and academic racism: concepts from morris and folklore'. *Journal of American Folklore,* vol. 115, no. 456, pp. 226–46.

Grosby, S. (2005). *Nationalism: A Very Short Introduction*. Oxford: Oxford University Press.

Hall, D. (2011). 'Time Gentlemen Please featuring the Demon Barber Roadshow, Theatre Royal Brighton, New Road', *The Argus*, 12 September. http://goo.gl/z7bMf (accessed 5 January 2012).

Hall, S. (2008). 'Cultural diversity', in *Routes '08*. Amsterdam: European Cultural Foundation. http://goo.gl/4AZ9X (accessed 28 April 2012).

Halnon, K. B. (2005). 'Alienation incorporated: "f*** the mainstream music" in the mainstream'. *Current Sociology*, vol. 53, no. 3, pp. 441–64.

Harker, D. (1985). *Fakesong: The Manufacture of British 'Folksong' 1700 to the Present Day*. Milton Keynes: Open University Press.

Hast, D. E., and Scott, S. (2004). *Music in Ireland; Experiencing Music, Expressing Culture*. Oxford: Oxford University Press.

Hellier-Tinoco, R. (2011). *Embodying Mexico: Tourism, Nationalism and Performance*. Oxford: Oxford University Press.

Hemming, H. (2009). *In Search of the English Eccentric*. London: John Murray.

Hield, F. (2010). *English Folk Singing and the Construction of Community*. Unpublished PhD thesis, University of Sheffield.

Hill, J. (2009). 'The influence of conservatory folk music programmes: the Sibelius Academy in comparative context'. *Ethnomusicology Forum*, vol. 18, no. 2, pp. 205–39.

Hobsbawm, E., and Ranger, T. (eds) (1983). *The Invention of Tradition*. Cambridge, Cambridge University Press.

Hound, R. (2009). 'Round 12: who's the greater debater? No argument...'. *Dave*, 17 November. http://uktv.co.uk/dave/blogpost/aid/631911 (accessed 16 April 2012).

Hughes, D. W. (2008). *Traditional Folk Song in Modern Japan: Sources, Sentiment and Society*. Folkestone: Global Oriental.

Hutera, D. (2011). 'Time Gentlemen Please! Churchill Bromley'. *The Times*, 13 September. http://goo.gl/DoXcv (accessed 11 January 2013).

Icons: a Portrait of England (2009). www.icons.org.uk/introduction (accessed 10 June 2009).

Indigeneity in the Contemporary World: Politics, Performance, Belonging (2009). www.indigeneity.net (accessed 2 October 2010).

Imagined Village, The (2007). http://goo.gl/vGKko (accessed 20 December 2012).

Ingold, T. (1993) 'The temporality of landscape'. *World Archaeology*, vol. 25, pp. 152–74.

Irwin, C. (1997). 'This is England: Colin Irwin celebrates a culture every bit as exotic as the most distant of world music destinations'. *Folk Roots*, no. 166, pp. 36–41.

Irwin, C. (2005). *In Search of Albion*. London: André Deutsch (paperback edn, 2006).

Jacobson, M. S. (ed.) (2008). 'Accordion Culture', issue of *The World of Music*, vol. 50, no. 3.

Jamie's Great Britain (2011). Television programme, Channel 4, 25 October.

Jones, O. (2005). 'Dwelling – the heart of discourses of rural neo-idyll?'. Paper presented at Dwelling and Rural Geography Session, Royal Geographical Society–Institute of British Geographers Annual Conference, London, 30 August – 2 September 2005.

Judge, R. (1993). 'Merrie England and the morris 1881–1910'. *Folklore*, vol. 104, no. 1/2, pp. 124–43.

Karpeles, M. (1967). *Cecil Sharp; His Life and Work*. London: Routledge and Kegan Paul.

Keegan-Phipps, S. (2003). *'Folk Music' and the Pub Session in Durham*. Unpublished MA thesis, Durham University.

Keegan-Phipps, S. (2007). 'Déjà vu? Folk music, education, and institutionalization in contemporary England'. *Yearbook for Traditional Music*, vol. 39, pp. 84–107.

Keegan-Phipps, S. (2008). *Teaching Folk: The Educational Institutionalization of Folk Music in Contemporary England*. Unpublished PhD thesis, Newcastle University.

Keegan-Phipps, S. (2009). 'Folk for art's sake: English folk music in the mainstream milieu'. *Radical Musicology*, vol. 4. www.radical-musicology.org.uk.

Kenny, M. (2010). 'Englishness: the forbidden identity'. *The Guardian*, 11 February.

http://goo.gl/WnJtW (accessed 12 April 2012)

Kenny, M., and Lodge, G. (2009). 'More than one English question', in Perryman, M. (ed.), *Breaking Up Britain*. London: Lawrence & Wishart, pp. 222–39.

Kenny, M., English, R., and Hayton, R. (2008). *Beyond the Constitution? Englishness in a Post-devolved Britain*. London: Institute for Public Policy Research. http://goo.gl/JKLrP (accessed 19 August 2011).

Kingsnorth, P. (2008). *Real England: The Battle against the Bland*. London: Portobello Books Ltd.

Kirstie's Handmade Britain (2011). Television programme, Channel 4, 23 November.

Koch, C. (2010). 'Osama Van Halen and the 50 cent dictator'. *The Guardian*, 16 January http://goo.gl/6I3Dr (accessed 15 April 2012).

Kumar, K. (2003). *The Making of English National Identity*. Cambridge: Cambridge University Press.

Lamont, C., and Rossington, M. (eds) (2007). *Romanticism's Debatable Lands*. Basingstoke: Palgrave Macmillan.

Lark Rise Band, The (2012). https://sites.google.com/site/thelarkriseband (accessed 26 April 2012).

Lark Rise to Candleford (13 January 2008 – 13 February 2011). Television series, BBC1.

Later with Jools Holland (2003). Television programme, BBB2, 3 May.

Later with Jools Holland (2006). Television programme, BBC2, 6 December.

Later with Jools Holland (2008). Television programme, BBC2, 15 February.

Lewis, R. (2005). *The Magic Spring: My Year Learning to be English*. London: Atlantic Books.

Life in the UK.net (2012). 'Polish Score Top Marks in Britishness Test'. http://goo.gl/3o0Vv (accessed 21 April 2012)

Livingston, T. E. (1999). 'Music revivals: towards a general theory'. *Ethnomusicology*, vol. 43, no. 1, pp. 66–85.

Lloyd, A. L. (1967). *Folk Song in England*. London: Paladin.

Locke, R. (1994). 'Paradoxes of the woman music patron in America'. *The Musical Quarterly*, vol. 78, no. 4, pp. 798–825.

Lomax, A. (1977). 'Appeal for cultural equity'. *Journal of Communication*, vol. 27, no. 2, pp. 125–38.

Lucas, C. (2010). 'The imagined folk of England'. *New Territories in Critical Whiteness Conference*. Conference presentation, University of Leeds, 18–20 August.

Lupton, H., and the English Acoustic Collective (2007). *Christmas Champions*. Performance at The Sage Gateshead, 10 December.

Macdonald, M. (2003). *Exploring Media Discourse*. London: Arnold.

MacKinnon, N. (1993). *The British Folk Scene: Musical Performance and Social Identity*. Buckingham: Open University Press.

Macnagten, P. and Urry, J. (1998). *Contested Natures*. London: Sage.

Magpie's Nest, The (2012). www.themagpiesnest.co.uk (accessed 24 April 2012).

Mary Neal Project, The (2012). 'Mary Neal … An Undertold Story'. www.maryneal.org/about (accessed 16 April 2012).

Matless, D. (1998). *Landscape and Englishness*. London: Reaktion Books Ltd.

McCormick, N. (2003). 'The reinvention of folk music'. *The Telegraph*, 25 September. http://goo.gl/QfRLR (accessed 15 April 2012).

McNulty, B. (2010). 'Thoroughly modern morris dancing'. *The Telegraph*, 1 September. http://goo.gl/4dg2a (accessed 11 November 2011).

Medhurst, A. (2007). *A National Joke: Popular Comedy and English Cultural Identities*. London: Routledge.

Merlan, F. (2009). 'Indigeneity: global and local'. *Current Anthropology*, vol. 50, no. 3, pp. 303–33.

Methera (2008a). 'Gig book'. www.methera.co.uk/reviewsgigbook.html (accessed 2 August 2008).

Methera (2008b). MySpace. www.myspace.com/methera (accessed 2 April 2008).

Methera (2008c). Sleeve notes: *Methera* (self-published CD, AN001).

Mitsui, T. (1998). 'Domestic exoticism: a recent trend in Japanese popular music'. *Perfect Beat*, vol. 4, no. 4, pp. 1–12.

Moreton, C. (2008). 'Hey nonny no, no, no: Goths and pagans are reinventing morris dancing: why the newcomers are putting the fear of God into the traditionalists'. *The Independent*, 11 May. http://goo.gl/K7qLZ (accessed 17 April 2012).

Morgan, M., and Leggett, S. (eds) (1996). *Mainstream(s) and Margins: Cutural Politics in the 90s*. Westport, CT: Greenwood Press.

Morley, D., and Robins, K. (eds) (2001). *British Cultural Studies*. Oxford: Oxford University Press.

Morris Offspring (2007). www.englishacousticcollective.org.uk/morrisoffspring/ (accessed 27/4/2012).

Morris Offspring and The English Acoustic Collective (2005). Programme for *On English Ground*.

Morris Offspring and The English Acoustic Collective (2006). *On English Ground*. Performance at The Sage Gateshead, 30 March.

Morris: A Life With Bells On (2009). Film directed by Lucy Ackhurst. Safecracker pictures.

Muehlebach, A. (2003). 'What self in self-determination? Notes from the frontiers of transnational indigenous activism'. *Identities: Global Studies in Culture and Power*, vol. 10, no. 2, pp. 241–68.

Music Room, The (no date). 'Hohner Pokerwork D/G melodeon'. http://goo.gl/X2Fuj (accessed 27 April 2012).

My Music (6 April 2008 – 4 May 2008). Television series, Channel 5.

Negra, D. (ed.) (2006). *The Irish in Us: Irishness, Performativity and Popular Culture*. Durham, NC: Duke University Press.

Nercessian, A. (2007). *Defining Music; An Ethnomusicological and Philosophical Approach*. London: Edwin Mellen Press.

Nest Collective, The (2012). http://thenestcollective.co.uk/about/the-nest (accessed 24 April 2012).

Nettl, B. 'Folk music', in Randel, D. M. (ed.) (1986), *The New Harvard Dictionary of Music* London: Harvard University Press, pp. 315–19.

Nettl, B. (1965). *Folk and Traditional Music of the Western Continents*. Englewood Cliffs, NJ: Prentice Hall.

Newcastle University (2008a). 'Mr. Alistair Anderson; Lecturer'. Staff profile at School of Arts and Cultures. www.ncl.ac.uk/sacs/staff (accessed 22 April 2008).

Newcastle University (2008b). 'Ms. Kathryn Tickell; Lecturer'. Staff profile at School of Arts and Cultures. www.ncl.ac.uk/sacs/staff/profile/kathryn.tickell (accessed 22 April 2008).

Ni Laoire, C., and Fielding, S. (2006). 'Rooted and routed masculinities among the rural youth of Northern Cork and Upper Swaledale', in Campbell, H., Bell, M., and Finney, M., *Country Boys: Masculinity and Rural Life*. Pennsylvania: The Pennsylvania State University Press, pp. 105–20.

Nowt as Queer as Folk (2010). Performance at Cecil Sharp House, London, 3 May.

Office for National Statistics (2012). *Ethnicity and Identity*. http://goo.gl/6M2BK (accessed 27 April 2012).

Parkinson, J. (2005). ' Morris dancing for the Olympics?' *BBC News.* http://goo.gl/bSksB (accessed 07 September 2011).

Paxman, J. (1998). *The English: A Portrait of a People.* London: Penguin.

Pegg, C. (2001). 'Folk music', in Sadie, S. (ed.), *The New Grove Dictionary of Music and Musicians.* London: Macmillan. Vol. 9, pp. 63–7.

Perez, J. (2000). 'Spain, §II, 6: traditional and popular music; contemporary developments', in Sadie, S. (ed.), *The New Grove Dictionary of Music and Musicians.* London: Macmillan. Vol. 24, pp. 151–2.

Perryman, M. (ed.) (2008). *Imagined Nation: England after Britain.* London: Lawrence and Wishart.

Pfister, M., and Hertel, R. (2008). *Performing National Identity: Anglo-Italian Cultural Transactions.* Amsterdam: Rodopi.

Pillai P. (1996). 'Notes on centres and margins', in Morgan, M., and Leggett, S. (eds), *Mainstream(s) and Margins: Cultural Politics in the 90s.* Westport, CT: Greenwood Press.

Pine, J., and Gilmore, J. (1999). *The Experience Economy.* Boston, MA: Harvard Business School Press.

Popular Music (2000). Vol. 19, no. 1 (issue devoted to place).

Port Isaac's Fisherman's Friends (2012). www.portisaacsfishermansfriends.com (accessed 8 January 2012).

Proper Distribution (2010) 'Proper Access', *Proper Distribution.* http://goo.gl/2QU0e (accessed 3 December 2010).

Radcliffe, C. (2001). 'The ladies' clog dancing contest of 1989', in Boyes, G. (ed.), *Step Change: New Views on Traditional Dance.* London: Francis Boutle.

Rajan, A. (2008). 'Channel Five to showcase new talents from folk scene' *The Independent,* 8 February. http://goo.gl/LchLE (accessed 15 June 2009).

Rapport, N. (ed.) (2002). *British Subjects: An Anthropology of Britain.* Oxford: Berg.

Rees-Mogg, W. (2005). 'The battle for England', *The Times,* 9 May: p. 20.

Renton, J. (2010). *fRoots: Looking For a New England 2.* http://goo.gl/5uZUy (accessed 16 April 2012).

Reuss, R. A., and Reuss, J. C. (2000). *American Folk Music and Left-wing Politics – 1927– 1957.* Lanham, MD: Scarecrow Press.

Russell, I. (2004). 'Sacred and secular: identity, style, and performance in two singing traditions from the Pennines', *The World of Music,* vol. 46, no. 1, pp. 11–40.

Schechner, R. (2002). *Performance Studies: An Introduction.* New York: Routledge.

Schofield, D. (2004). *The First Week In August: Fifty years of the Sidmouth Festival.* Sidmouth: Sidmouth International Festival.

Schofield, D. (2005). 'A black and white issue?'. *English Dance and Song,* vol. 67, no. 2, p. 12.

Scutt, R., and Bonnet, A. (1996). 'In search of England: popular representations of English-ness and the English countryside'. *Centre for Rural Economy Working Paper Series,* no. 22. Newcastle upon Tyne: University of Newcastle.

Seattle, M. (ed.) (2008). *The Great Northern Tune Book: William Vickers' Collection of Dance Tunes AD 1770.* London and Morpeth: English Folk Dance and Song Society in associa-tion with the Northumbrian Pipers' Society.

Sharp, C. J. (1907). *English Folk Song, Some Conclusions.* London: Mercury Books.

Shatwell, B., and Sartin, P. (eds) (2006). *Hampshire Dance Tunes.* Henfield: Hobgoblin Books.

Shaw, W. S., Herman, R. D. K., and Dobbs, G. R. (2006). 'Encountering indigeneity: Re-imagining and Decolonising Geography'. *Geografiska Annaler,* vol. 88B, no. 3, pp. 267–76.

Shaw, C., and Chase, M. (1989). *The Imagined Past: History and Nostalgia.* Manchester: Manchester University Press.

Shrewsbury Folk Festival (2008) *Shrewsbury Folk Festival Programme.* Bridgnorth: Shrewsbury Folk Festival.

Slater, N. (2007). *Eating for England: The Delights and Eccentricities of the British at Table.* London: Harper Perennial.

Slobin, M. (1993) *Subcultural Sounds: Micromusics of the West.* Hanover, PA: Wesleyan University Press.

Smith, A. D. (2010). *Nationalism* (2nd edn). Cambridge: Polity Press.

Smith, T., and Ó Súilleabháin, M. (1997). *Blas: the Local Accent of Irish Traditional Music.* Limerick: Irish World Music Centre, University of Limerick [and] Folk Music Society of Ireland.

Steamchicken (2011). www.steamchicken.co.uk/ceilidh.html (accessed 23 April 2011).

Steinweis, A. E. (1993). *Art, Ideology, and Economics in Nazi Germany: the Reich Chambers of Music, Theatre, and the Visual Arts.* Chapel Hill, NC: University of North Carolina Press.

Stevenson, L. (2004) '"Scotland the Real": The Representation of Traditional Music in Scottish Tourism'. PhD Thesis, University of Glasgow.

Still Folk Dancing … After All These Years (2010). Television programme, BBC4, 10 December.

Stock, J. (1999). 'Is ethnomusicology relevant to the study of British folk music? Some thoughts and key references'. *Music Traditions Internet Magazine.* www.mustrad.org.uk/articles/ethnomus.htm (accessed 30 October 2006).

Stock, J. P. (2004). 'Ordering performance, leading people: structuring an English folk music session'. *The World of Music,* vol. 46, no. 1, pp. 41–70.

Stokes, M. (1994). *Ethnicity, Identity and Music; the Musical Construction of Place.* Oxford: Berg.

Stop Islamisation of Europe (no date). sioeeu.wordpress.com (accessed 4 April 2012).

Storey, J. (1997). *An Introduction to Cultural Theory and Popular Culture* (2nd edn). Hemel Hempstead: Prentice Hall/Harvester Wheatsheaf.

Storey, J. (2002). '"Expecting rain": opera as popular culture?', in Collins, J. (ed.), *High-Pop: Making Culture Into Popular Entertainment.* Oxford: Blackwell, pp. 32–53.

Storey, J. (2003). *Inventing Popular Culture: From Folklore to Globalization.* Oxford: Blackwell.

Storey, J. (2010). 'Becoming British', in Higgins, M., Smith, C. and Storey, J. (eds), *The Cambridge Companion to Modern British Culture.* Cambridge: Cambridge University Press, pp. 12–25.

Sumner, P. D. (ed.) (1997). *Lincolnshire Collections Volume 1: The Joshua Gibbons Manuscript.* Grimsby: Breakfast Publications.

Sweers, B. (2005). *Electric Folk; The Changing Face of English Traditional Music.* Oxford: Oxford University Press.

Sweeting, A. (2002). 'Eliza Carthy: Anglicana', *The Guardian,* 1 November. http://goo.gl/NyjYP (accessed 19 August 2011).

Turner, J. (2004). *Albion Magazine Online.* http://goo.gl/JJ0vl (accessed 22 February 2012).

Taylor, T. D. (1997). *Global Pop: World Music, World Markets.* London: Routledge.

Telegraph View (2011). 'Testing Scotland's tuition fees'. *The Telegraph,* 29 August. http://goo.gl/rRYNs (accessed 18 November 2011).

Thomas, P. (2008). *Geographies of the Music Festival: Production, Consumption and Perfor-*

mance at Outdoor Music Festivals in the UK. PhD thesis, Newcastle University.

Thrales Rapper (2011). *Facebook*. http://goo.gl/e2sur (accessed 27 April 2012).

Time Gentlemen Please! (2011). www.tgpdanceshow.co.uk (accessed 1 November 2011).

Time Gentlemen Please! Promo 2010 (2010). [Video] www.thedemonbarbers.co.uk (accessed 5 January 2012).

Titchmarsh, A. (2007). *England, Our England*. London: Hodder and Stoughton.

Turino, T. (2008). *Music as Social Life: The Politics of Participation*. London: The University of Chicago Press.

Waldron, J. (2003). 'Indigeneity ? First peoples and last occupancy'. *New Zealand Journal of Public and International Law*, vol. 1, pp. 55–82.

Walters, S. (2011). 'Secret report warns migration meltdown in Britain', *Mail Online*. 8 September. http://goo.gl/V8TGl (accessed 18 November 2011).

Way of the Morris (2011). Film directed by Tim Plester and Rob Curry. Fifth Column films. www.wayofthemorris.com (accessed 21 December 2011).

Weber, W. (2003). *Music and the Middle Class: The Social Structure of Concert Life in London, Paris and Vienna Between 1830 and 1848*. Aldershot: Ashgate.

White, C. (2007). 'The Imagined Village', *BBC Music Reviews*. www.bbc.co.uk/music/reviews/dxgb (accessed 13 January 2012).

White, C. (2008). 'The Lark Rise Band: Lark Rise Revisited', *BBC Music Reviews*. www.bbc.co.uk/music/reviews/x3w6 (accessed 26 November 2010).

Whitehead, T. (2011). 11th Oct, 2011. 'Immigrants must pass test on British history, says David Cameron', *The Telegraph*. http://goo.gl/XRxER (accessed 18 November 2011).

Whiteley, S., Bennett, A., and Hawkins, S. (2004). *Music, Space and Place: Popular Music and Cultural Identity*. Aldershot: Ashgate.

Wiener, M. (2004). *English Culture and the Decline of the Industrial Spirit, 1850–1980* (2nd edn). Cambridge: Cambridge University Press.

Williams, R. (1973). *The Country and the City*. Chatto & Windus Ltd. Reprint, St Albans: Paladin (1975).

Williams, R. (1983). *Keywords: a Vocabulary of Culture and Society*. London: Fontana Press.

Wood, C. (2006). 'Not icons but jewels: music and loss in England', *Journal of Music in Ireland*. www.thejmi.com/article/413 (accessed 2 April 2008).

Wood, M. (1999). *In Search of England: Journeys into the English Past*. London: Viking.

Woolfe, G. (2007). *William Winter's Quantocks Tune Book*. Crowcombe, Somerset: Halsway Manor Society.

Wulff, H. (2003). 'The Irish body in motion: moral politics, national identity and dance', in Dyck, N. and Archetti, E. P. (eds), *Sport, Dance and Embodied Identities*. Oxford: Berg, pp. 179–96.

Wulff, H. (2005). 'Memories in motion: the Irish dancing body', *Body and Society*, vol. 11, no. 4, pp. 45–62.

Discography

Anderson, A. (1982). *Steel Skies* [LP]. Topic Records.

Askew Sisters (2007). *All in a Garden Green* [CD]. Wildgoose Records.

Bellowhead (2008). *Matachin* [CD]. Navigator Records.

Bellowhead, (2006). *Burlesque* [CD]. Westpark Music.

Carthy, E. (1998). *Red Rice* [CD]. Topic Records.

Carthy, E. (2002). *Anglicana* [CD]. Topic Records.

Carthy, E. (2005). *Rough Music* [CD]. Topic Records.

Causley, J. (2005). *Fruits of the Earth* [CD]. WildGoose Records.
Causley, J. (2007). *Lost Love Found* [CD]. WildGoose Records.
Demon Barbers (2008). *+24db* [Self-published CD].
Dibango, M. (1990). *Polysonik* [CD]. Bird Production.
English Acoustic Collective (2004). *Ghosts* [CD]. RUF records.
Faustus (2008). *Faustus* [CD]. Navigator Records.
Harbron, R. and Van Eyken, T. (2001). *One Sunday Afternoon* [CD]. Beautiful Jo.
Harvey, P. J. (2011). *Let England Shake* [CD]. Island Records.
Imagined Village (2007). *The Imagined Village* [CD]. Real World Records.
Lakeman, S. (2004). *Kitty Jay* [CD]. I Scream Music.
Lakeman, S. (2006). *Freedom Fields* [CD]. I Scream Music.
Lakeman, S. (2008). *Poor Man's Heaven* [CD]. Relentless Records.
Lark Rise Band (2008). *Lark Rise Revisited* [CD]. Talking Elephant.
Maal, B. (1994) *Firin' in Fouta* [CD]. Mango.
Mawkin:Causley (2008). *Cold Ruin* [CD]. Navigator Records.
Methera (2008). *Methera* [Self-published CD].
Moray, J. (2001). *I am Jim Moray* [Self-published CD].
Moray, J. (2003). *Sweet England* [CD]. Weatherbox.
Moray, J. (2004). *Sprig of Thyme* [CD]. Weatherbox.
Moray, J. (2008). *Low Culture* [CD]. NIAG Records.
Ornette Coleman Double Quartet (1960). *Free Jazz (a Collective Improvisation)* [LP]. Atlantic Records.
Newcastle University (2009). *Folk Degree Sampler 2009* [CD]. Newcastle University.
Show of Hands (2006). *Witness* [CD]. Hands On Music.
Spiers, J. and Boden, J. (2003). *Bellow* [CD]. Fellside Recordings.
Spiers, J. and Boden, J. (2005a). *Tunes* [CD]. Fellside Recordings.
Spiers, J. and Boden, J. (2005b). *Songs* [CD]. Fellside Recordings.
Spiers, J. and Boden, J. (2008). *Vagabond* [CD]. Navigator Records.
SpinnDrift. (2009). *SpinnDrift* [Self-published CD].
Tickell, K. (2008). *Debateable Lands* [CD]. Park Records.
Van Eyken, T. (200610). *Stiffs Lovers Holymen Thieves* [CD]. Topic Records.
Various Artists (2009). *Looking for a New England* [CD]. fROOTS and Arts Council England .
Various Artists (2010). *Looking for a New England 2: The Other Traditions* [CD]. fROOTS and Arts Council England.
Wood, C. (2005). *The Lark Descending* [CD]. RUF Records.
Wood, C. (2008)*Trespasser* [CD]. RUF Records.

Interviews

Askew, E., and Askew, H. (2008). Interview by Simon Keegan-Phipps, 12 March.
Barber, D. (2008). Interview by Simon Keegan-Phipps, 14 April.
Bearman, A. (2008). Interview by Simon Keegan-Phipps, 11 March.
Besford, T. (2008). Interview by Simon Keegan-Phipps and Trish Winter, 6 February.
Boden, J. (2008). Interview by Simon Keegan-Phipps and Trish Winter, 19 March.
Brenner, J. (2008). Interview by Simon Keegan-Phipps, 15 April.
Causley, J. (2008). Interview by Trish Winter, 14 March.
Coe, P., and Coe, S. (2008). Interview by Trish Winter, 9 March.
Delarre, D. (2008). Interview by Simon Keegan-Phipps, 12 March.

Emmerson, S. (2008). Interview by Simon Keegan-Phipps and Trish Winter, 27 February.

Heap, S. (2008). Interview by Simon Keegan-Phipps, 25 January.

Lee, S. (2008). Interview by Simon Keegan-Phipps and Trish Winter, 12 June.

Leverton, D. (2008). Interview by Trish Winter, 25 May.

Swift, L. (2008). Interview by Simon Keegan-Phipps, 11 March.

Van Eyken, T. (2008). Interview by Simon Keegan-Phipps and Trish Winter, 22 April.

Watson, R. (2008). Interview by Simon Keegan-Phipps, 4 March.

Wood, C. (2008). Interview by Simon Keegan-Phipps and Trish Winter, 31 January.

Index